INSTITUTIONAL INDIVIDUALISM

For Robert,
with gratitude and respect,
Michael

INSTITUTIONAL INDIVIDUALISM

Conversion, Exile, and Nostalgia in Puritan New England

Michael W. Kaufmann

Wesleyan University Press
Published by University Press of New England
Hanover and London

Wesleyan University Press

Published by University Press of New England, Hanover, NH 03755

Printed in the United States of America

5 4 3 2 1

CIP data appear at the end of the book

TO MY MOTHER AND FATHER

Contents

Acknowledgments

The dedication of this small book to my parents could never equal their great dedication to their family. I thank them and my brother Robert for all of their support in the years leading to this book and for so much else as well.

I owe special thanks to Daniel O'Hara, Donald Pease, and Susan Wells for their timely interventions at a critical moment. I would also like to thank a number of my colleagues in the Temple English Department for their advice and encouragement: Robert Caserio, Steven Cole, Shannon Miller, Alan Singer, and Lyn Tribble. Thanks also to Catherine Wiley for her help with preparing the book for publication.

An earlier version of this project was awarded Columbia University's Bancroft Dissertation Prize; I am very grateful to the faculty committee for such an honor. The libraries at Columbia University and Union Theological Seminary were ideal places for reading and research. I am especially indebted to Seth Kasten for his good cheer and assistance in accessing many important rare books. Temple University supported my work with a Summer Research Grant.

The staffs of Wesleyan University Press and the University Press of New England have been exceptionally helpful in seeing the book through acquisition, editing, and production.

This project began, in very different form, as a dissertation in the English Department of Columbia University. Many faculty members and fellow students there directly or indirectly shaped my work through the high standards they set for me and for themselves. I would especially like to thank Patricia Crain for her unwavering interest and support at every stage of this project, and Richard Bushman, Kathy Eden, and Wayne Proudfoot for their generous criticism of the dissertation. Two faculty members deserve special thanks. Robert Ferguson is an ideal model of scholarly rigor and professional integrity; I continue to learn from his example. Early on, Andrew Delbanco did the best thing a teacher could ever do for a student: he expected more from me than I expected from myself. Through these expectations and his own example, he has taught me that good work must combine rigorous reading, independent thinking, graceful writing, and—above all—deep commitment to questions that matter. For these lessons and much else, I thank him.

INSTITUTIONAL INDIVIDUALISM

Introduction

The Puritans migrated to New England to establish new relationships between individuals and institutions. The fate of these attempts to redefine both individuals and institutions has, in turn, been the focus of the best scholarship on American Puritanism. This scholarship accepts a general narrative according to which the Puritans rebelled against oppressive institutions in England; then some came to the New World only to establish institutions that were more patriarchal, more oppressive, and less tolerant. A few brave dissenters—most famously, Anne Hutchinson and Roger Williams—attempted to subvert these patriarchal institutions in the name of individual autonomy. This narrative has become so familiar, in fact, that it is often relegated to a subordinate clause. Scholars concede that "given the patriarchal nature of the Puritan church" or "given Hutchinson's desire for independence," and then proceed to argue about other issues: language, gender, toleration, and so on. Thanks to this narrative, however, the instability and excitement of dissent have been tamed into predictable axioms; individual motivations and contradictions have been generalized into a background called historical context. This book aims to reopen for examination concepts that have long been accepted, often uncritically, as historical "givens" in Puritan studies: individualism (and related ideas such as self, subjectivity, identity, autonomy, and independence) and institutionalism (and related ideas such as patriarchy, submission, oppression, and affiliation). This reexamination generates alternative models for imagining the relationships between institutions and individuals. Further, these explorations pay close attention to particulars—the particular relationships among figures such as John Cotton, Anne Hutchinson, and Roger Williams and the particular nuances and complexities of the religious language in which these relationships have been formed and recorded.

I

One widely accepted model for describing institutional relationships posits an ideal version of individuality based on absolute autonomy or, as one scholar puts it, "pure, unfettered subjectivity," a self completely independent of cultural and political limitations.[1] In this model, any compromise of autonomy results in representations of individuals as cultural constructs or ideological precipitates with little or no genuine agency in the face of oppressive, patriarchal institutions. Any middle ground seems to be elusive at best and illusory at worst; it is almost impossible to find even a fleeting moment of genuine freedom. The choice between extreme individualism and extreme institutionalization always remains circumscribed by ideological systems such as family, state, language, and religion. Another, related model opposes the margins and the center of a given society. Scholars who follow this model argue that Puritan culture can best be understood as a division between a large, dominant hegemony at the center and a small band of radical dissenters (identified by gender, race, or to a lesser extent, social status and religious beliefs). The center oppresses the margins, subtly or not, and the margins attempt to subvert the center, successfully or not. Even apparently voluntary forms of submission, such as joining a church, are actually just oppression or subversion in disguise.

When applied to the Puritans under consideration in this book, these models either fail to account for important facts or they result in logical contradictions.[2] If, for example, Puritan ministers marginalized female congregants, then why did Anne Hutchinson claim that she followed John Cotton to the New World? If the "center" constructs the idea of "individual autonomy" as a means of control and discipline, then why would a radically subversive Hutchinson desire to achieve such an autonomy? If dissenters are categorically silenced and disenfranchised, then why was Roger Williams essentially made governor of his own colony as punishment for his dissent? Perhaps such contradictions, as Sacvan Bercovitch has so persuasively argued in *The American Jeremiad*, lie at the very heart of Puritan ideology. Perhaps, however, they can be better explained by altering our operative assumptions about institutions and individuals.

The term *institutional individualism* offers one such redefinition. The intentionally anachronistic use of *individualism* with reference to the Puritans is meant to call attention to the etymological history of the word. *Individualism* as we now understand it to signify something like the autonomy of self-determination did not gain currency as a term until the nineteenth century. Before that time, *individual* meant an entity that could not be divided into distinct parts (from the Latin *in-dividere*, "not divisible"). So defined, the word stands as a synonym for *indivisible*. Around the middle of the seventeenth century—exactly the period covered in this book—the meaning shifted emphasis, slightly but significantly, to represent a unique entity that stands apart or distinct from the whole. An individual was still something that could itself not be divided into parts (as the older definition indicates), but it also represented something that had been divided or separated from a group: the individual person—itself not further divisible—stands separate from the mass of society.[3]

The adjective *institutional* suggests that individuality must always be defined and qualified by means of relation to some form of institution, whether it refers to actual organizations with clearly established administrative and linguistic structures and rules (church and state, for example) or, more generally and colloquially, to other societal practices such as the "institution of marriage" or the family. This qualification further suggests that for the Puritans, pure, unfettered autonomy did not represent a desirable ideal; in fact, it was a form of damnation. To exist without any institutional affiliation was to be abandoned to one's corrupt and degenerate self. Excommunication from the church and banishment from the colony (i.e., cutting off all institutional connections) were thought of as severe forms of punishment, not as moments of great liberation from oppression.

A sense of individual identity for the Puritans derived, then, from affiliation with, rather than separation from, institutions. This affiliation could take the form of actual membership and participation in church and state, and it was almost always mediated through particular rhetorical practices: speaking about one's spiritual conversion or interpreting a passage from Scripture in institutionally sanctioned ways. Submission, deference, and dependence represent the most common modes of association, but in their uniquely religious manifestations these modes were not perceived as a denial or weakening of self but rather as a development and strengthening of a desirable identity. That is, in the religious convictions of the time, an individual's sense of "self" depended on strong devotion and submission to the strongest and purest institutional authorities. In this context, criticism of powerful authorities (such as those offered by Hutchinson and Williams) was often intended to improve and strengthen these authorities, not to undermine or subvert them. Following the logic of affiliation, to strengthen these institutions was also to strengthen, not diminish, one's sense of self. Indeed, criticism often signals an individual's most loyal obedience to and dependence on institutional authority.

Through an exploration of the implications of institutional individualism, this book attempts to fill a gap left open by current scholarship in the fields of Puritan studies in particular and American studies in general. Students of early modern England—a period coincident with Puritan settlement in New England—have produced an impressive range of scholarship about the rise of the modern liberal subject and its relations to the family, church, state, and marketplace. Along similar lines, scholars of later periods of American history (notably the early republic and antebellum eras) have begun to articulate various kinds of "individualisms" and their relationships to democratic and capitalist ideologies. For the most part, however, the insights and implications garnered from these various fields have yet to be worked out by scholars of American Puritanism, who have, as suggested above, tended to rely on individualism as a historical given. The present book, then, looks across space—from seventeenth-century New England to seventeenth-century England, and forward in time, from the early colonies to nineteenth-century America. By so doing, however, I do not necessarily intend to argue for exceptionalism from England or to narrate a teleology from the Puritans to, say, Emerson. Instead, I simply wish to ask some of the same questions of the New England Puritans that have been so productively asked by scholars of early modern England and antebellum America.[4]

Much of the work on early modern England has relied on Lawrence Stone's magisterial *The Family, Sex and Marriage in England, 1500–1800*. This sweeping historical work narrates fundamental changes in family structure from medieval kinship and clan ties to the modern nuclear family. These changes in family structure accompany the emergence of what Stone calls "affective individualism"—a sense of identity based on introspection, autonomy, and self-expression—as well as "possessive individualism"—a sense of identity based on ego, envy, greed, and a desire to distinguish oneself from others.[5] The Protestant Reformation (with, for example, its emphasis on personal piety and holy matrimony) and the resultant English civil war (with its contributions to the demise of aristocracy and the rise of a middle class) are offered as both causes and effects of these major cultural changes. The period Stone analyzes also results in a paradox that is at the heart of institutional individualism: the rise of a modern sense of self led, however momentarily, to an *increased* desire for and dependence on patriarchal authority and not, as one might expect, to an immediate call for complete autonomy.[6]

That call for freedom from patriarchal authority did not come in America until the Revolutionary War, which is where American scholars such as Jay Fliegelman pick up Stone's narrative. Like many other scholars, Fliegelman uses the philosophy of John Locke to mark a divide between early modern and Enlightenment views of family, self, and society. Locke effectively argues for at least a partial decoupling of an analogy that compares the family to other forms of patriarchal authority, such as church and state. Whereas the family had previously been thought of as a "little monarchy," with the father as king and children as obedient subjects, the rise of affective individualism (as described by Stone) places new emphasis on the right to filial autonomy; once children become rational individuals, they gain freedom from parental control.[7] This shift in family relationship, argues Fliegelman, also underwrites the American Revolution. If an adult child can break free from parental control, so too can mature colonies gain independence from royal control.[8]

Where Fliegelman analyzes the emergence of the American ideal of individual freedom and rights, scholars such as Gillian Brown and Christopher Newfield examine the limitations of these ideals in the nineteenth century. Notably, these scholars offer important qualifications to the idea of a pure, unfettered individualism. Gillian Brown, for example, argues that "domestic individualism" combines concepts previously seen as mutually exclusive: male, public self-reliance on the one hand and female, private domesticity on the other. Her persuasive book delineates "the role of domestic ideology in updating and reshaping individualism within nineteenth-century American market society."[9]

Working in the same general period as Brown, Christopher Newfield describes the development of "corporate individualism," which in some ways approximates the model of institutional individualism in that it develops a sense of identity through submission to, rather than distinction from, corporate entities. For Newfield, Ralph Waldo Emerson marks a key moment in the question of American individualism: "His [Emerson's] answer propels a very significant shift in the history of U.S. liberalism from a democratic toward a corporate kind of liberalism. It does so by introducing submission at the center of an extravagant American freedom."[10] Unlike institutional individualism, which for the devout Puritan centralized and strengthened both personal and public authority, the diffusion of power demanded by corporate individualism ultimately weakened both personal autonomy and public sovereignty.[11] These different characterizations of submission—a gain of power in one case, a loss of power in another—result primarily from the different periods under consideration and the relative weight assigned to religion in each period. In the context of Emerson's relatively secular, avowedly democratic America of the mid-nineteenth century, submission could be seen, as indeed Newfield sees it, as a loss of political power. But in the context of the Puritans' relatively pious, avowedly undemocratic New England of the early seventeenth century, submission to the proper forms of religious authority could be seen as a fundamental necessity for salvation, a radical reconfiguration of individual authority.

I say "could be seen" because submission has been interpreted quite differently in several notable works of Puritan scholarship that have addressed the question of individualism. Most famously, in *The Puritan Origins of the American Self*, Sacvan Bercovitch argues that the Puritan call for pious self-denial is, in the end, political self-assertion in disguise. "We cannot help but feel that the Puritans' urge for self-denial," writes Bercovitch, "stems from the very subjectivism of their outlook, that their humility is coextensive with personal assertion."[12] Bercovitch expands on this dynamic in his study of Puritan dissent, *The American Jeremiad*. If attempts at self-denial always eventuate in self-assertion, then attempts to dissent in the name of this asserted self ultimately ratify the hegemonic authority to which they were initially opposed. The ideological power of modern individualism in all its forms exerts so great a force that even the most radical dissent or critique is absorbed into consensus.

Bercovitch's argument is itself so powerful that dissent from it indeed becomes difficult.[13] Nevertheless, the inescapable circularity of his account of the jeremiad (wherein dissent turns into consent) also raises an interesting problem of historical logic.[14] Although Bercovitch offers an explanation of the *origins* of the American self (the self further described, for example, by Brown and Newfield as liberal, autonomous, self-reliant, etc.), his explanation actually presupposes the existence of such a self. That is, if self-denial was only self-assertion in disguise, then some concept of modern, autonomous individualism must already be in place in order for it to be denied and for it to do the denying. Further, the modern self is the place from which dissent is authorized (e.g., Hutchinson's criticizing patriarchy in the name of her own autonomy) and the place to which dissent inevitably returns.[15] But if we are to believe scholars such as Fliegelman, Brown, and Newfield, this concept of self was not recognizably available in America until around the Revolution. In a sense, then, Bercovitch's arguments have it both ways: the Puritans originated the American self, and the American self originated the Puritans. By examining the historical development of individualism as it is reflected by particular moments of dissent, I hope to construct a textured logic for a premise that has long been accepted as an assertion.[16]

In the course of constructing this logic, I also aim to work out some tentative solutions to methodological problems that are acute in, if not unique to, the study of Puritanism. Many of these problems stem from the assumption that writing ideological or political criticism itself constitutes a form of political action or intervention. Of course, it is not surprising that the study of American culture has been politicized for so long since the motives for its origination were as much political (to delineate a distinct tradition of American letters) as aesthetic. But even as academics have grown skeptical of claims to "originality," "progress," and "enlightenment" as historical phenomena, such terms are still often applied to assess the presumed political value of our own work. That is, terms that have lost some explanatory power in historical politics (such as radical, subversive, conservative, reactionary, progressive) have been displaced into evaluations of academic politics.[17]

These displaced political evaluations, in turn, shape the stances we adopt toward our subjects of scholarly inquiry. Almost all Puritan scholarship (including the present book) makes value judgments by looking from the Puritans forward to the present (projection), from the present looking backward to the Puritans (retrojection), or some combination of the two.[18] Projection is the tendency to locate the origins of a tradition—good or bad—in Puritan New England and then to trace the legacy of this tradition through American history.[19] Projection thus assumes a continuity with the past that enables a narrative account of a paradigmatic experience (immigration, conversion), an ideology (liberalism, capitalism, sexism, racism), or even a genre (captivity narrative, jeremiad). Retrojection refers to a tendency to evaluate the past in terms of present political, aesthetic, or cultural standards. Such a stance does not necessarily posit a continuous tradition; often, in fact, it implies—or at least hopes for—a radical discontinuity between past and present attitudes toward, for example, women, Native Americans, religious toleration, the environment. While projection and retrojection look more or less in opposite directions, both tend to idealize the past and present.[20] Such idealization can manifest itself in a tone of sentimental nostalgia that hints that the past was better than the present, that "they" knew better than "we" do. Or it can manifest itself in an attitude of presumptuous self-righteousness that implies that the present *should* be better than the past, that we *should* know better than they did.

The limitations of political criticism become even more evident when it turns its attention to religion. The Puritans and other religious dissenters risked their lives because of their beliefs: they were persecuted and executed; they fought wars, went into exile, and uprooted their families to form better churches and godly communities. And yet many scholars write as if they understand the Puritans better than the Puritans understood themselves. For such critics, religious belief serves only as an ideological mask for the "real" reasons the Puritans migrated to the New World: materialism, capitalism, imperialism, genocide. To make such arguments, terms of religious self-understanding must be translated into some other analytical category.[21] Most famously, Max Weber and R. H. Tawney emphasize the economic implications of Calvinist doctrine.[22] More recently, Ann Kibbey attempts to "go beyond Weber" and "to be more skeptical than he was about the theological terms in which the Puritans saw themselves."[23] She stops just short of stating that religion was nothing more than a mask for prejudice and violence, but she does claim that "to a great extent prejudice and religious beliefs were indistinguishable."[24] Stephen Greenblatt sticks a bit closer to the goal of understanding a culture's self-interpretation, but the self-interpretation he finds reveals the "wrenching possibility that their [Catholics and Protestants] theological system was a fictional construction; that the whole, vast edifice of church and state rested on certain imaginary postulates."[25] If religion does not translate into economics, violence, or representational practice, it easily translates into political terms. Philip Gura, for example, sees an implicit connection between radical spiritism and radical politics. Similarly, Amy Schrager Lang suggests that the language of antinomianism could be "translated into the secular language of self and community."[26] These analytical translations seem to betray an anxiety that if we believe *that* the Puritans believed, then we come dangerously close to believing *what* the Puritans believed.[27]

The present study is committed to working out possible solutions and alternatives to these problems of ideological criticism through a careful engagement with Puritanism on its own terms.[28] To achieve an understanding of these terms, I have placed the New England Puritans in dialogue with key intellectual and cultural questions from early modern England as represented by both seventeenth-century contemporaries and twentieth-century scholars. Further, this dialogue includes not only English Puritans, such as Milton, but also other key figures, such as John Donne and Francis Bacon, and not only scholars of English Puritanism but also those of early modern culture in general. This somewhat larger field of inquiry provides points of reference and comparison for questions of individual identity, language, family, and patriarchal authority. While such questions clearly comprehend secular culture at large, I have attempted to trace how they shape and are shaped by the unique language of Puritan piety, a language that is related to yet distinct from the politics of court and council. Scholars of later periods of American culture provide additional inspiration and insight to the questions under consideration, but again I do not invoke them to suggest a narrative of the "rise of American individualism." Rather, awareness of these later periods helps to maintain a healthy respect for the difference, even the strangeness, of the past.

Of course, practitioners of a variety of disciplines—history, literature, anthropology—may agree with the spirit of this stance toward the past and yet may have significant disagreements about how best to realize it.[29] For all of the recent emphasis on interdisciplinary studies, it is still very much the case that different disciplines have their unique protocols for assembling and assessing evidence. Although the arguments in this book depend heavily on a sense of history, the fundamental method of accessing that history is literary analysis—very close attention to language and form, alertness to subtle shifts in tone, examination not only of what is written but of *how* it is written. Metaphors and analogies used to express familial relations or the experience of conversion receive such scrutiny because, as one scholar notes, "These analogies are not merely rhetorical decoration for an argument that exists separately; they are themselves an argument."[30] For example, to compare a converted soul to a melted stone (as John Cotton does) instead of to a weather vane (as Roger Williams does) reveals not only a difference in rhetorical style but also fundamental differences in ideas about the logic of salvation, the nature of human agency, and the permanence of spiritual change. Analysis of these kinds of textual moments generates many of the larger arguments constructed in this book.

Although not literature in a strictly traditional sense, Puritan writings lend themselves to literary analysis, in part—as we will see in chapter 2—because the Puritans themselves were so self-conscious about the nature of language. Moreover, careful readings of works by Cotton and Williams and of the transcripts of Hutchinson's trials provide a means to recover the textured particularities of an individual's relationship to institutions, something that is often lost in the haste to generalize about Puritanism. In his famous justification for the lack of exhaustive footnotes in the published version of *The New England Mind*, Perry Miller claims that "it is a matter of complete indifference or chance that a quotation comes from Cotton instead of Hooker, from Winthrop instead of Willard."[31] Miller's bibliographical expediency becomes the foundation for Bercovitch's ideological analysis: it doesn't matter which minister one quotes because they all reflect the same hegemonic consensus.

As scholars such as Alan Heimert, Andrew Delbanco, and Janice Knight have argued, sweeping generalizations about "*the* Puritan mind" often obscure significant tensions and doubts within individual Puritan minds. Thus, in any given textual moment, for example, John Cotton could be struggling with the implications of choosing to emphasize one aspect of covenant theology over another. And over the course of a prolific career, significant changes in interpretation take place, such as those that become startlingly evident when one compares his early and late sermons on the Song of Solomon (see chapter 5). Perhaps, then, the best justification for close literary analysis is that it prevents us from lapsing into predictable generalizations. Every tentative conclusion one draws while reading these Puritan texts must be qualified by the surprise of each new sentence.

2

With the exception of John Winthrop and Anne Bradstreet, minister John Cotton, politician Roger Williams, and congregant Anne Hutchinson are the most studied figures from the first generation of English Puritans to settle in New England.[32] Each of these figures has received sustained individual attention; there has been an astonishing number of biographies of Williams, for example, and both he and Cotton have earned volumes in the Twayne American Author Series. They are also studied in pairs—in books about the Williams–Cotton debates, for example—with one of the pair often cast as the hero (usually Hutchinson or Williams) and the other cast as the villain (almost always Cotton). But they have rarely been taken together. The Harvard scholars tend to ignore Williams in favor of Cotton and Hutchinson, and even in recent studies of Puritan dissent, such as Gura's and Lang's, Williams is largely absent.

This segregation in the scholarship is especially strange in light of the intimate biographical and thematic connections among these three figures. Over a fifteen-year period in New England, their paths crossed and clashed, often in dramatic ways, the most notorious of which was Cotton's role in banishing both Williams and Hutchinson from the Bay Colony. Before that climactic moment, though, Cotton enjoyed sustained, even positive relationships with Williams and especially with Hutchinson. For example, during her trials, Hutchinson claimed that she followed Cotton from England to New England to hear him preach; Cotton at first defended but then repudiated Hutchinson's theological positions. When she was banished from Massachusetts, she briefly stayed in Rhode Island, the colony Roger Williams had helped to settle. Williams himself ended up in Rhode Island after a storied career in Massachusetts. He was offered but declined the job at the First Church of Boston that Cotton eventually took. The two men carried on protracted debates about central questions of their time: standards of church membership, religious persecution, separation of church and state. A focus on this small group of key players, therefore, allows for elaboration on the many implications of institutional individualism.

John Cotton receives a disproportionate share of attention in this elaboration partly because of his involvement with both Hutchinson and Williams and partly because of his general absence in scholarly discussions of Puritan radicalism[33] but mainly because he was one of the most important ministers in New England. By the time he migrated to the New World, Cotton had already established a reputation as a nonconformist preacher of great spiritual conviction.[34] After serving in a number of positions at Emmanuel College, Cambridge, he accepted the post of vicar at St. Botolph's Church in Lincolnshire, where he became even better known for his powerful sermons on conversion. Several times, Cotton got into trouble for his nonconformist practices, the most serious of which required his appearance before the High Court and Bishop William Laud in 1632. Rather than appear before the court, Cotton slipped into the Puritan underground, stopping first in London and then, in 1633 at the age of forty-eight, setting sail for New England. He soon became teacher at the First Church of Boston and gained further respect in both Englands as a major voice for institutional reform.

Cotton's success as a preacher has remained a mystery to a long line of literary and historical scholars who find his sermons dull and his doctrine derivative. In one of the first comprehensive histories of American literature (published in 1878), Moses Coit Tyler recognized Cotton's preeminence, dubbing him "the unmitred pope of a pope-hating commonwealth" but remained puzzled by his popularity: "Let us open, now, any of these old books of John Cotton. At once, the immensity of his contemporaneous influence becomes a riddle to us. . . . There are almost no remarkable merits in thought or style. One wanders through these vast tracts and jungles of Puritanic discourse . . . and is unrewarded by a single passage of eminent force or beauty."[35] Similarly, in the very first sentence of his book about Cotton's writings, Everett Emerson states: "Of the first generation of New England writers, John Cotton is doubtless not the greatest."[36] V. L. Parrington typifies those scholars who cast Cotton as Puritan villain by concluding that "the sins of the oligarchy rest in large measure on the head of John Cotton."[37] While Cotton still has his detractors, he has also been championed as a lone voice of spiritual dissent from his more rigid colleagues in the ministry.[38]

In general, Roger Williams has enjoyed a much better reputation than has Cotton.[39] A pamphlet for the Roger Williams Heritage Trail in Rhode Island trumpets his praise: "Freedom of thought. Perhaps the most central of all American virtues. It was the pursuit of this basic freedom that in 1636 led colonist Roger Williams to break with the Puritans of Massachusetts and found what was to become Rhode Island. A state dedicated to the principle that an individual's beliefs need conform to no one's ideals but his or her own."[40] The pamphlet attributes a historical tourist's version of "unfettered subjectivity" to Williams, but he has been credited with such beliefs in more scholarly precincts as well. "Williams was at the fountainhead of the maturation of liberty in the modern world . . . the notorious maverick of the American religious scene [who] provided a clear path to civil tolerance and freedom for all" writes one scholar; another concludes that "Roger Williams was out to do nothing less than alter the institutional structure of the Western world."[41] While other scholars have wisely qualified Williams's role in establishing democracy, toleration, and separation of church and state in America, he continues to be seen as a radical outsider, the most un-Puritan of Puritans.[42]

This vision of Williams as persecuted exile has largely been handed to us by Williams himself. Even before his first exile from England and his second exile from the Bay Colony, Williams always enjoyed close connections to powerful people and institutions and always suffered about the nature of these connections. His early education benefited from the patronage of Sir Edward Coke, the famous and powerful English lawyer. For a short time he served as chaplain at the manor of Sir William Masham. At age twenty-seven he arrived in New England (three years before Cotton) and was offered the post at the First Church of Boston that Cotton himself eventually filled. He accepted and then vacated ministerial jobs at Salem and Plymouth and even left a church in Providence that he himself helped to found. For Williams, the ministry was among "the best callings but the worst trades in the world."[43] His checkered career as a preacher was accompanied by active involvement in political affairs in both England and Rhode Island.[44] He served twice as president or chief officer of the colony, and his close connections in Parliament helped him secure and protect a colonial charter. It was Williams's questioning of the validity of the Bay Colony charter that led to his banishment in 1636. In 1643 he engaged in the infamous *Bloudy Tenent* exchange with Cotton, a debate that resulted in his reputation as a persecuted champion for religious toleration.

If we have largely been handed Williams's reputation from Williams himself, our knowledge of Anne Hutchinson comes to us almost exclusively from those who banished and excommunicated her.[45] For this reason alone, the history of her reputation becomes more interesting and more complicated than just about any other figure from the first generation. We know very little about Hutchinson other than the information revealed during her trials. Although she was not a member of his Lincolnshire congregation, she heard Cotton preach in England and claimed to have followed him (and her brother-in-law John Wheelwright) to the New World. In her Boston home she held widely attended prophesyings—officially sanctioned meetings to discuss Scripture and sermons. When these meetings became too popular, fear of dissent led by Hutchinson but underwritten by Cotton's preaching grew among the Boston elders. They asked Cotton to clarify his position on salvation, and in 1637 the General Court began to examine those suspected of holding "erroneous opinions" on salvation and resurrection. After her civil trial (in November 1637) and her church trial (March 1638), Hutchinson was banished from the colony and excommunicated from the church.

Her banishment and excommunication at the hands of Puritan ministers and magistrates have earned Hutchinson the reputation of a rebel with a feminist cause. Scholars almost universally agree that she is "the articulate spokeswoman for a strain of radical spiritism," "a rare female voice in a male-dominated history," a "champion of individual liberty," a "feminist before her time," and a "classic American representative of a radical and socially destructive self-trust."[46] Her ideas and her style of presenting them, which one scholar calls "feminist by nature," expressed the "human desire for equal opportunity" and also threatened the "structure of the institutional church" and the "patriarchal hierarchy."[47] Like Williams, Hutchinson has become a tourist attraction. A pamphlet describes the site of the Hutchinson house as the place "where men and women gathered to listen to Anne's dramatic sermons advocating 'preparationism' (a doctrine ascribing some free will to the sinner) in contradiction of the accepted 'covenant of grace' (within which salvation is determined exclusively by the will of God)."[48] Of course, Hutchinson "advocated" antinomianism, not preparationism; but the pamphlet gets it "right" by getting it backward: surely, Anne Hutchinson, the freedom-loving champion of individual autonomy, would *not* deny free will by submitting to the will of God.[49]

Paradoxically, these portraits of Hutchinson as radical rebel stem as much from the original judgment of the General Court as from anything Hutchinson said or did herself. For example, throughout the trials, members of the court accused Hutchinson of "condemninge Authoritie and Magistracie" and "draw[ing] deciples after her." They tag her as "a dayngerous Instrument of the Divell raysed by Sathan amongst us," who, in the end, is "the principal cause of all of our trouble." While no one has recently called Hutchinson an instrument of the devil, assessments by many recent scholars bear a striking resemblance to assessments by the court. One scholar, for example, states that Hutchinson "threatened religious orthodoxy," and John Cotton, a member of that orthodoxy, claims that she "doe the uttermost to rase the foundation of Religion to the Ground."[50] Similarly, the assertion that Hutchinson "revealed her ambition to become the equal of the ordained ministers" echoes John Wilson's statement that "I fear and believe thar was another and greater Cause [of her erroneous opinions], and that is the slightinge of Gods faythfull Ministers and contemninge and cryinge downe them as Nobodies."[51] Both scholar and minister seem to ignore Hutchinson's own statement—"I doe not allow the slightinge of Ministers nor of the Scriptures nor any Thinge that is set up by God"—and her claim that she was distraught when Cotton and Wheelwright migrated because she then had no one to interpret Scripture for her and she felt utterly incompetent to interpret it for herself.[52] So in a great irony of scholarship, critics who wish to champion Hutchinson's cause often end up endorsing the court's judgments of her. They may have reevaluated these judgments, but they have never quite questioned nor challenged the original judgments themselves, thereby overlooking the possibility that the court was fundamentally mistaken in its assessment of Hutchinson's intentions.[53] While the concept of institutional individualism cannot finally bring us any closer to Hutchinson's actual words, it does suggest new ways to conceptualize her relationship to authority. It is the major goal of this book to provide new ways of imagining and articulating institutional affiliations for our understanding of the Puritans and, implicitly, of ourselves.

Chapter 1 examines the history of one of the most common ways to describe relationships between institutions and individuals: the family analogy wherein the affiliations between an institution and its members are compared to the connections between parents and their children. This chapter explores the structural and psychological aspects of such affiliations to suggest that submission to hierarchal authorities offered the Puritans a desirable and useful means for self-definition. Indeed, the family analogy informs some fundamental principles of Puritanism, such as covenant theology and conversion.

While chapter 1 focuses on one important analogy, chapter 2 expands the scope to consider how language in general mediates relationships between individuals and institutions. Through a close reading of John Cotton's sermons and treatises on conversion, this chapter articulates his implicit belief that language itself must undergo a conversion before any change will be realized in institutions and individuals. To a certain extent then, language itself (in the form of sermon rhetoric, conversion relations, or scriptural interpretations) becomes an institution in need of reform; but the goal of this reform is ultimately to dissolve the distinction between institutions and individuals.

Roger Williams firmly believed that such a dissolution was neither possible nor desirable. Chapter 3 demonstrates that, for Williams, language, however purified, and conversion expressed *in* language always remain institutional constructs, often bordering on coercion. Williams thus rejects the converted soul as a model for institutional affiliation and replaces it with the persecuted exile, a form of self-definition that still depends on institutions but by way of negation and difference rather than by affirmation and dissolution.

In chapter 4 the trials of Anne Hutchinson serve as a dramatic case study of the implications of the terms and concepts discussed in previous chapters. For example, Hutchinson essentially accuses certain ministers of failing to meet expectations dictated to them by their place in the family analogy, even as the General Court levels the same charge against Hutchinson herself. By deploying the logic of institutional individualism, this chapter thus addresses the perplexing contradiction between Hutchinson's own claims of pious devotion (she, more than anyone else, believed in Cotton's converted rhetoric) and the court's perception of her as a blasphemous heretic.

Under the general rubric of nostalgia, chapter 5 describes an emotional dynamic that drives many of the religious concepts analyzed throughout the book: a desire to return to or recover a pure ideal and the attendant sense of loss. Dependence on the family analogy, for example, reveals a desire to replace imperfect earthly fathers with ideally perfect, divine institutional fathers. And as much as conversion is driven by a progressive desire for what the self could become, it also betrays a nostalgic sense of loss for what the self never was. All Puritan acts of recovery, then, attempt to return not to the way things were but to the way things could have been.

1

Puritanism and the Family Analogy

> For even in things alike, there is diversitie, and those that doe seeme to accord, doe manifestly disagree. And thus is Man like God, for in the same things that wee resemble him, wee are utterly different from him. There is never any thing so like another, as in all points to concurre; there will ever be some reserved difference slip in, to prevent the Identity, without which two severall things would not be alike, but the same, which is impossible.
>
> THOMAS BROWNE, *Religio Medici*

> Both in nature and in metaphor identity is the vanishing-point of resemblance.
>
> WALLACE STEVENS, *The Necessary Angel*

1. *Affiliation and Individualism*

In 1636 the Massachusetts General Court passed a law prohibiting unmarried people from living alone. Every town had to "dispose of all single persons and inmates within their towne to servise, or otherwise"; that is, unmarried individuals had to live as servants with established families.[1] This law, passed right around the time of the Antinomian Controversy, was partly aimed at minimizing the disruptive influence of outside agitators coming in from other towns allegedly to support Anne Hutchinson. But the law also points to a more general aspect of life in the colonies: individual identity was defined by one's relations to, not independence from, institutions such as church, state, and family. Unless a person was associated with a good family, not to mention a good church, then he or she effectively had no identity.

The Puritans felt that these relations, at least in theory, should follow the contours specified by Ramist logic. As a technical term of this logic, *relative* is defined as "affirmative contraries of which the one exists out of a mutual affection of the other."[2] "Affirmative contraries" suggests an opposition between things in nature, or things positive (husband and wife), in contrast to negative contraries, which is an opposition between something and nothing (husband and not husband). *Relative* indicates a particular mode of association: in relative relations, there is partial agreement, for example, between buyer and seller, husband and wife, governor and governed. The term contrasts with "adverse" relations, which are based on total opposition between terms, such as heat and cold or vice and virtue. As well, *relative* implies mutual cause and effect: a husband causes the woman he marries to be a wife. If a buyer ceases to exist, there can be no seller.

The intricacies of Ramist logic may seem an odd place to begin a discussion of individualism, but this definition of *relative* applies to many forms of association in Puritan culture: between husband and wife, God and believer, minister and congregant. All of these relationships require voluntary consent; no one can be forced to join a particular church or even to enter into a particular covenant with God. Even if a relationship eventually requires a degree of deference and submission, it must initially be entered as an act of free choice. Such relationships also require partial agreement between the members; that is, after generally deciding to enter a given relationship, a person then must agree to at least some of the particulars of that relationship in order for it to be a relative as opposed to an adverse association. Most important, the logic of relations suggests mutual dependence, obligation, and definition. It is the logic of covenants and contracts, where both parties must carry out certain responsibilities even if one is clearly more powerful than the other. And it is the logic of identity that suggests that if you are not in these mutually defining relationships, then you are, in effect, nobody.

Through this logic the Puritans give structure to a fundamental need and desire for association. This need may first be satisfied by filiation, relationships within the family; but it is also realized through affiliation, the many forms of social, cultural, political, and institutional relationships.[3] In fact, the formation and reformation of institutions almost always involves a move from filiative to affiliative relationships. The circumstances of birth, including those institutions that one is "born into," are both involuntary and insufficient: one does not choose one's family, and a family cannot satisfy all of the needs for association. These original associations are left behind not necessarily to claim complete autonomy but rather to search for new and improved relationships through affiliations.[4]

This move from filiation to affiliation and, subsequently, from one form of affiliation to another helps to explain why the Puritans could be so resolutely antipatriarchal in their attacks on the Roman Catholic Church and divine right monarchy and nevertheless rely so heavily on patriarchal models to represent relationships within their own institutions.[5] Both the logical and psychological structures of affiliation call for some form of voluntary submission, but this submission need not turn into oppression. As one recent theorist of patriarchy suggests, "By being so dominated, the self can be incorporated into the other and thus share in its power and strength. This drive toward submission can explain in part the need which people have for leaders. We project onto a human being mythic and superhuman powers, then surrender our selves to that person allowing us to identify with him by being incorporated as means towards his ends."[6] The point here is simple but important: domination and submission can be the result of individual, voluntary choice as much as of institutional coercion.

It is this desire for the best relationships to the best institutions that often motivates the strongest criticism of institutions. Such criticism can take many forms; it can, for example, argue that authority within a given institution is too strong and dominating, with the intent of weakening its stronghold. But critics may also claim that leaders are not strong enough or that they are failing to uphold the duties of office. Such criticism may aim at strengthening a weak patriarchy, rather than weakening a strong one. And such a desire for a stronger, purer patriarchy may well underlie many Puritan attacks on certain forms of patriarchal authority. As David Leverenz has argued, "It was uncontaminated authority, not personal freedom, that every Puritan wanted."[7] Discontent with certain ministers and churches, Puritan or otherwise, stems from the perception that "fathers were often anxious, weak, or failing in their own callings," and so "a call for pure and loving patriarchy became more intense as its absence became more evident."[8] Whatever the motivations—a desire for complete submission, a desire for self-assertion through such submission—in a society where identity derives in large part from affiliations with institutions, the goal becomes to affiliate oneself with the best available institutions.

This dependence on affiliation with and submission to institutions clearly affects the ways in which the Puritans think about what it means to be an individual. Most scholars agree that the concept of individuality underwent a major change right around the time the Puritans were most active.[9] To understand the nature of this change one need only look at the etymology and history of the word *individual* itself. *Individual* derives from the Latin root *dividere* (to divide) and is prefaced by the negative *in-* (not); thus, the word originally meant "not dividable" or "indivisible." As Raymond Williams notes in *Keywords*, this original meaning "now sounds like paradox. 'Individual' stresses a distinction from others; 'indivisible' a necessary connection."[10] In short, *individual* has come to mean its original opposite. Or more precisely—since both definitions were always operative to some degree—one way of thinking about individuality won out over another. Before the seventeenth century, the dominant meaning indicated something or someone that could not be separated or distinguished from a group. To be an individual in the more modern sense of the word would mean that you were eccentric, incomprehensible, because you did not take part in the "common sense." By the end of the seventeenth century and certainly by the nineteenth century (i.e., rugged, self-reliant, Emersonian individualism),[11] the dominant meaning of *individual* came closer to how we now think of the word: something or someone that is unique, special, distinguishable from commonalities. This individual too is indivisible—but only from himself or herself; he or she can be divided from the group but cannot be further divided. Modern individuality is the irreducible unit of identity.

Resemblances and differences play key roles in both the old and new senses of individuality. The older sense of the word clearly emphasizes resemblances over differences. For example, in the seventeenth century a person would most likely think about his identity in terms of his resemblance to other members of the institutions with which he was affiliated. The newer sense of *individual* emphasizes differences over resemblances, so that same person in the twentieth century would derive a sense of identity from the ways in which he distinguishes himself from other members of his institutions. Of course, resemblances and differences always operate simultaneously in forming an identity. People derive their identity from what they are and from what they are not: their resemblances to some *and* their differences from others. But no two people are exactly alike, because, as Thomas Browne points out in the passage that serves as the epigraph for this chapter, some "reserved difference" will always slip in between even the most similar things to prevent complete identity.

Since resemblances and differences are always in play, the shift in the definition of *individual* really amounts to a shift in emphasis: do we derive a sense of individuality primarily from what we share with others or primarily from how we differ from them? Most of the Puritans we will consider generally emphasized resemblances over differences when thinking about individual identity. In fact, the singular goal of Puritanism—conversion—depends on achieving what Thomas Browne describes as an impossibility: total identification of man with God. The ultimate goal for the individual is to become identical to God—not like him, not merely resembling him, but exactly the same. This is a version of the Christian notion of *imitatio Christi*, a "'putting on of Christ,' transforming oneself completely into His image."[12] John Cotton, for example, invokes this principle when he asserts that "seeing Christ in the Gospel, in his ordinances, doth in some manner transform us into his likenesse; this seeing of him shall make us like him."[13] *Imitatio* does not call for physical resemblance, not so much because the Puritans were universally against images (their reputed iconoclasm) but because actually seeing what God looks like, face to face, would mean instant death. Instead, the devout Puritan aspires for resemblance in behavior and attitude, for "walking in a Godly way," for having one's soul inclined toward good and away from evil. And especially in the case of Cotton, one also strives for similarity of linguistic behavior and practice: the converted soul interprets the Bible in a certain way and speaks a special language of salvation.

Difference still has a role in defining an identity based on resemblance, but it is a decidedly negative one. Difference—or deviation—from the Christic ideal is something natural (i.e., it is inborn to the soul) and makes people unique; but the very notions of difference, naturalness, and uniqueness are all associated with sin. Richard Baxter, an English theologian who was a great influence on the New England ministry, writes in *The Christian Directory*: "Man's fall was his turn from God to himself; and his regeneration consisteth in the turning of him from himself to God. . . . The very names of Self and Own, should sound in the watchful Christian's ears as very terrible, wakening words, that are next to the name of sin and satan."[14] Seen in historical terms, conversion requires a turning away from what have come to be considered the positive attributes of modern individuals—uniqueness, difference, self-reliance, personal ownership, and responsibility, the "very names of Self and Own"—and a turning toward what we may now consider the negative attributes of (premodern) individuals: sameness, conformity (i.e., "with the same form"), unanimity (i.e., "of the same soul"), collective ownership and responsibility, submission to and dependence on authority.[15]

2. *The Family Covenant*

Filiation often serves as a model for affiliation; that is, relationships within families provide a basis for describing relationships to other institutions. This comparison between familial and institutional relationships provides both structural and emotional analogues. Institutions, like families, have structures of authority that govern relationships: the boss is like the father, and the workers are like children; or in a Puritan context, the minister is like the father, and the congregants are like children. The family analogy also can govern the emotional dynamics of these relationships: congregants depend on and even idealize ministers, just as children depend on and even idealize parents. While we still think in these terms to a certain extent, the family analogy was especially predominant in the early modern period, where, as we've just seen, individual identity derives in large part from associations with institutions and where the family, not the individual, serves as the irreducible unit of social identity.[16]

Just as the definition of *individual* undergoes a shift in emphasis during the period covered by this book, so too do the terms of the family analogy. Although often compared to institutions such as church and state, the family was not always seen as a private retreat from the public world. Indeed, the idea of privacy as we now know it did not gain ascendancy until later in the seventeenth century, when Locke asserted the central importance of property. Instead, the family was viewed as an extension of, rather than an escape from, all other institutions; it was the first filiation that led to all subsequent affiliations.[17] The analogy also sees another major shift during this period. At first, the family served as a model for thinking about the state, thus transferring feelings of affection from filiative to affiliative fathers and making submission to the king seem like a "natural" duty.[18] Gradually, the emphasis shifts, so that the state is used to describe the family. Familial relationships—especially marriage—come to be thought about more in terms of a legal contract voluntarily joined rather than a divinely or naturally sanctioned arrangement. The Puritans, for example, treated marriage as a civil ceremony officiated by state authority, not as a religious ceremony officiated by a minister.

Robert Filmer, a sixteenth-century English political theorist, gives the most comprehensive articulation of the earlier version of the family analogy in his book *Patriarcha*. In this defense of divine right monarchy, Filmer traces the filial relationships between all kings: "It may seem absurd to maintain that kings now are the fathers of their people, since experience shows the contrary. It is true, all kings be not the natural parents of their subjects, yet they all either are, or are reputed as the next heirs to these progenitors who were at first the natural parents of the whole people, and in their right succeed to the exercise of supreme jurisdiction."[19] Filmer makes an amazing argument here, one that he himself grants may seem absurd. In his attempt to establish the legitimacy of patriarchs he admits that kings cannot claim literal filiation with all of their subjects; they did not actually sire everyone in the kingdom. However, kings can claim direct filiation with the men who were, in fact, "the natural parents of the whole people," namely, Adam (the father of all children; the father of all fathers) and his descendants, the biblical patriarchs. Since we are all children of Adam and since all kings descend directly from Adam, we are also children of those kings. To be absolutely precise, then, Filmer does not posit an analogy between kings and fathers (e.g., the king of a country is like the father of a family); rather, through a series of logical contortions, he posits a direct lineage between kings and fathers: kings are fathers, and fathers are kings.

Filmer then goes on to describe the "natural duties" of these father/kings: "As the father over one family, so the king, as father over many families, extends his care to preserve, feed, clothe, instruct and defend the whole commonwealth . . . all duties of a king are summed up in an universal fatherly care of his people."[20] Although most of *Patriarcha* reads like an unapologetic defense of tyranny, this passage gives us a possible clue to the appeal patriarchy holds for its subjects and followers. Filmer portrays the king as a perfect father, who is both all-powerful and all-loving, one who embodies what Renaissance scholar Debora Shuger has called "a fusion of unlimited, fearful authority and protective love."[21] It is the king's duty not only to rule the commonwealth and wage war but also to provide "an universal fatherly care" of his people: to feed, clothe, and instruct them. Moreover, Filmer continues, "every father is bound by the law of nature to do his best for the preservation of his family."[22] The legal responsibility for providing what we would now call social services—food, shelter, education—falls not to the biological family but to the analogical family of the state. Even in the extreme form that Filmer presents, we can sense the attraction of a guarantee that basic human needs will not go unmet.

Writing directly to refute Filmer, John Locke breaks the link between family and state: "I think it may not be amiss to set down what I take to be political power, that the power of a magistrate over a subject may be distinguished from that of a father over his children, a master over his servant, a husband over his wife, and a lord over his slave."[23] Locke still argues for a kind of patriarchy (magistrates, fathers, masters, husbands, and lords will still have power over subjects, children, servants, wives, and slaves), but he attempts to makes distinctions where Filmer saw continuities. Further, Locke uses a distinction between childhood and adulthood to argue for the difference between family and state.[24] Whereas Filmer insisted that parents maintain control over their offspring for their entire lives, Locke argues that children, born submissive, eventually grow into reason and hence independence: "Children, I confess, are not born in this full state of equality, though they are born to it. Their parents have a sort of rule and jurisdiction over them when they come into the world, and for some time after, but 'tis but a temporary one. . . . Age and reason, as they grow up, loosen them till at length they drop off, and leave a man at his own free disposal."[25] Whereas children involuntarily submit to filiative relationships (they have no choice about which family to be born into or about having their basic needs met by that family) and naturally grow into freedom, adults voluntarily enter into affiliative relationships by way of the social contract and just as voluntarily break those ties should certain conditions arise. After Locke, the family becomes closer to what we think of it today: a collection of free individuals that serves as a private escape from public institutions.

Both chronologically and ideologically, the Puritans reside somewhere between Filmer and Locke.[26] Not only did some of the major events of Puritanism take place during this transition, Puritanism itself helped bring about changes in thinking about familial and institutional relationships. For example, the idea of a covenant—between God and man, between minister and congregation—plays a central role in almost all Puritan thinking about relationships.[27] Here is how John Winthrop describes the marriage covenant between husband and wife:

> This liberty is maintained and exercised in a way of subjection to authority; it is of the same kind of liberty wherewith Christ has made us free. The woman's own choice makes such a man her husband; yet being so chosen, he is her lord, and she is to be subject to him, yet in a way of liberty, not of bondage; and a true wife accounts her subjection to her honor and freedom, and would not think of her condition safe and free, but in her subjection to her husband's authority. Such is the liberty of the church under the authority of Christ, her king and husband; his yoke is so easy and sweet to her as a brides ornament; and if through forwardness and wantonness, etc., she shake it off, at any time, she is at no rest in her spirit, until she takes it up again; and whether her lord smiles upon her, and embraces her in his arms, or whether he frowns, or rebukes, or smites her, she apprehends the sweetness of his love in all, and is refreshed, supported, and instructed by every such dispensation of his authority over her.[28]

Like Filmer, Winthrop relies on a set of linked analogies: the liberty of the wife subjected to her husband is like the liberty of the church subjected to Christ (who is both king and husband), and it is also like the liberty of individuals subjected to the magistrate. All instances of male authority share the traits of the typical patriarch, who is both stern (he frowns, rebukes, and smites) and caring (he smiles and embraces). Again, these dual traits are only superficially contradictory; they are both signs of the "sweetness of his love in all." Winthrop argues another apparent contradiction: false liberty (what he would call license) is actually a kind of slavery, whereas true liberty requires subjection to authority.

Like Locke, Winthrop introduces an element of voluntarism in his description of the marriage covenant: "the woman's own choice makes such a man her husband." If true liberty requires submission to authority, in Winthrop's version at least, one gets to choose the authorities to which one submits.[29] Following the logic of covenant theology, one does not technically "choose" to submit to God. Rather, God makes us an offer we cannot refuse: he "elects" us by deciding to allow us to enter into a contract or covenant with him. But all other affiliations down the Puritan patriarchal chain are elective: wife chooses husband, subjects choose magistrates, congregations choose ministers.[30] This element of choice or election should not, however, be mistaken for incipient liberal democracy. A strict set of religious guidelines, not a quest for individual autonomy, confines (or liberates, depending on one's point of view) the Puritan sense of choice. They must make the choices that bring them to better, purer devotion to the truths of God.[31]

Although the choice of authorities with which to affiliate ultimately aims toward submission, it also contains elements of mutual obligation.[32] While the wife in Winthrop's passage depends on her husband for safety and freedom, the husband is obliged to "support" and "instruct" her, to provide some version of Filmer's "universal fatherly care." This sense of mutuality extends to legal, political, and social arenas as well. Husbands, for example, were held legally responsible for the transgressions of their wives: they would have to appear in court with them and would have to make any necessary financial restitution.[33] The reasoning here is simple: if the wife makes a mistake, it is the husband's responsibility because he failed properly to instruct and care for her. By a similar logic, a wife shares in her husband's successes and failures; she shares by affiliation whatever social and political status her husband happens to enjoy. Although, generally speaking, women were subordinated to men in Puritan culture, a woman married to a man of high standing would outrank a man of low standing.

The logic of covenants depicts Puritan relationships as almost entirely contractual or legalist. Indeed, a number of scholars define this contractualism as a hallmark of Puritan rationality. For a variety of reasons, Puritans attempt to redefine relationships previously thought of as natural, divine, or emotional as "merely" legal; hence, Milton defines marriage as a legal contract so that it can be broken (through divorce) without incurring divine wrath.[34] Similarly, anti–divine right theorists attempt to factor out both the divine and affectionate elements of relationships to the king: one need not think of one's king with the reverence reserved for God or the love reserved for one's biological father.[35] A form of this antiemotionalism even carries over in Cotton's plan for New England congregationalism. He insists, for example, that congregants respect and honor the office of the ministry, regardless of the talents of the individual person occupying that office.

Logical and psychological reformations do not always coincide, and affections do not evaporate at the tweak of an analogy. It may take a long time for institutions to react to the desire for structural change. Conversely, it may take just as long a time for individual desires to catch up with or adapt to institutional changes. Thus, reconfiguring relationships to king or pope—either imaginatively through logic and rhetoric or literally through rebellion, regicide, or migration—does not necessarily put an end to a desire for or dependence on strong patriarchal authority. This residual desire may eventually transform into, say, a desire for individual autonomy, or it may seek new and improved objects. As we will see in the next section, even though John Cotton rejects the aesthetic extravagances of the Roman Catholic Church, this rejection does not end his desire for aesthetic pleasure; instead, he looks for a properly Puritan form to meet these demands. Conversion itself could similarly be thought of as both a logical and psychological redefinition of the father. And as we will see in chapter 5, if desire can find no appropriate new object, it transforms into an intense nostalgia for those objects that have been rejected.

3. Covenants and Conversion

In their 1609 explication of the Proverbs, John Dod and Robert Cleaver, two English Puritan theorists with close ties to the New England Puritans, wrote: "Vicinity and neighborhood will fail, and alliance and kindred will fail but grace and religion will never fail: If we adjoin ourselves unto [godly men] for their virtue and goodness, they will not separate themselves from us for calamities and trouble."[36] This brief passage neatly represents the dynamics of filiation and affiliation: the circumstances of our birth—vicinity, neighborhood, alliance, and kindred—will fail us on a spiritual level, but new and better circumstances—grace, godly men—are available to replace our origins. To represent these new alliances, Puritan ministers rely on the language of family so frequently that its use becomes unremarkable: God becomes father (and sometimes even mother) to his spiritual children, Christ becomes husband to the "wife" of the congregation, ministers become both fathers and husbands to their followers.[37]

But why does the family analogy do such a good job of providing ways to imagine relationships to institutions other than the family? Why are the terms of the analogy so flexible and interchangeable that it is even possible to think of someone other than one's biological parent as a "father"? Renaissance scholar Marie-Hélène Huet provides a helpful clue in her analysis of the role of resemblance in establishing biological paternity: "Short of relying on visible resemblance, paternity could never be proven: that if nothing were more undeniable than maternity, paternity could never be verifiable or physically ascertained. . . . But if resemblance creates a visible connection between father and child, it also conceals the questionable character of all paternities. At the same time that it suggests filiation by instituting a 'natural,' visible, link between the progenitor and his child, resemblance, used as a criterion for establishing paternity, ignores the fact that filiation can never be certain."[38] In the absence of anything like blood or DNA testing, establishing paternal filiation (and all that goes with it, such as legitimacy and inheritance) depends either on resemblances between father and child or on the testimony of the mother. Thus, paternity depends on nothing more than a claim that "he is the father" or the observation that "he looks just like his father." As Huet points out, establishing filiation itself on such grounds is riddled with problems. But when such tenuous paternal filiations, which "can never be certain," also serve as the model for a whole series of paternalistic affiliations, the problems become manifold.

Many of these problems stem from the difficulty of discerning resemblances and differences between father and children. Some children, for example, may not clearly resemble their fathers, and therefore paternity becomes questionable. This lack of discernible resemblance also plagues relationships between analogical fathers and children. Do all true believers genuinely resemble Christ (by way of the *imitatio*), or do they merely feign superficial resemblance without true conversion in order to lay claim to his inheritance? Similarly, do all congregants genuinely embody the preaching of their minister (the "spiritual father"), or do they merely perform the outward signs of grace to gain the benefits of church membership? The structures of institutional order—father over children, king over subject, husband over wife, minister over congregant—rest on the weak foundation of superficial (from the Latin, "surface," or "outer face") resemblances. The fact that these resemblances can be so easily denied, faked, or misunderstood threatens to undermine this order.

But it is precisely the tenuousness and malleability of filiation that allows for patriarchal order in the first place, and it is the related instability of affiliation that allows for the possibility of individual and institutional change.[39] If paternal filiation depends on resemblance, then theoretically it becomes possible to reinvent one's origins by fashioning a likeness to a new father. Since one's paternal origins are always in question, one need not be (in fact, *cannot* be) pinned down to the biological father but can instead establish connections to other "fathers" simply by acting "like" them. By reimagining filiation, by representing oneself as the child of a father other than that of original birth, one gains a new identity, a new way to represent oneself to the world. The Puritans called this process of imitating a new father conversion.

To this end, John Cotton assures his listeners: "You need not feare, nor wonder, if weake beginnings come unto greate issues . . . if you carry along business according to the word, the Lord will carry things an [on] end mightily in your hands beyond all your expectations, or imaginations, for there is no resisting, nor controlling the worke of God." It matters little if beginnings are weak, he argues, because true believers "rest not in first beginnings" since, by definition, natural origins are incomplete and sinful.[40] Once we gain "sight of the sinfull uncleanesse of our natures, from our Mothers wombe," we then "see a need of a better birth then this."[41] This "better birth" (which is exactly the phrase Freud used to describe the family romance) requires a renunciation of the first filiations (one's biological and sinful origins, alliance, and kindred) and first affiliations (vicinity and neighborhood) and then a re-filiation (conversion, with God as the father) and re-affiliation with new and improved church and state fathers. All of these changes are made possible by the reconfiguration of paternal resemblance.[42]

The first step in this reconfiguration demands a renunciation of original filiation and the associated involuntary first affiliations. Cotton wonders if to "cast away our forefathers, that kept such good houses . . . to damne them all to hell: Is it not a cruell, and barbarous opinion?" He answers his own question by citing Luke 14:26: "A man must in this case forsake father and mother."[43] On one level, Cotton merely tells his followers to end those affiliations that they have inherited through filiation, to leave the church they were born into. But as I have been suggesting, to negate affiliation in this way is also to negate filiation; to leave the church of one's parents is also to leave one's parents, in hope of achieving a better birth, of finding the "next fathers."

The next step in the process requires a search for these next fathers, both filiative and affiliative. Conversion depicts God as the new filiative father; one's rebirth results in a new resemblance to God and Christ. Re-filiation then leads to re-affiliation, as the convert associates with the "next Fathers" of a reformed church.[44] Somewhat paradoxically, progress toward the discovery of these next fathers actually takes the form of a return to the past. This return may take shape in attempts to emulate the first church fathers (the apostles) or to establish lineage with previous reform-minded fathers from different historical periods (e.g., Calvin, Beza). Thus, conversion sparks a desire to resemble a timeless ideal (*imitatio Christi*), whereas church reform hinges on a related desire to recover historical ideals. This desire to recover the past often eventuates in a profound sense of loss and nostalgia.[45]

We hear echoes of this nostalgia in Cotton's call to negate all filiative ties by asserting new affiliative resemblances:

> . . . though the bloud of Ancestors run very warme, that a man would chose to live no better life, nor keep a better house then his Father or Grandfather, but wish their souls might be as safe as theirs, when men are once redeemed by the bloud of Christ, and that is sprinkled upon their consciences, then the bloud of Christ is warmer then the bloud of their Ancestors . . . then alasse for our poor Fathers, what is become of them? . . . The Religion of those that taught them, they are gone everlastingly . . . they see a *broad difference between* the Religion of their Ancestors, and that which they see now; but that is the efficacy of the bloud of Christ . . . that it washeth away all relations to Fathers and universality, he is crucified to them all.[46]

Cotton extends a commonplace paradox in Christian doctrine—Christ's blood does not itself stain but instead purifies the stain of sin—to describe what we've been calling a reinvention of filiation as a kind of ancestral transfusion: conversion effectively replaces the blood of the ancestors with the blood of Christ. This act of re-filiation leaves no blood on the convert's hands. It does not require a dramatic or violent break with the ancestors; rather, as Huet suggests, because the bonds of natural filiation are so tenuous to begin with, Cotton can portray this as an efficient process that requires nothing more complicated than a sprinkling of this blood that "washeth away all relations to Fathers."

Cotton also laments the quiet dissolution of filial bonds: "Alasse for our poor Fathers, what is become of them?" It is as if he emerges from the swirl of spiritual experience surprised to discover that the first fathers are gone. But the sentence conveys more than nostalgic sentiment and hints at a more ominous answer to "what is become of them?" As he noted in an earlier passage, the failure of the first fathers to change filiation will "damn them all to hell." The children are saved, but the parents are damned; in fact, the children are saved *because* the parents are damned. Finally, Cotton shifts registers and sounds what by now should be a familiar theme: the imaginative switch of filiation leads to an actual change in affiliation. He no longer is affiliated through resemblance with "the Religion of those that taught" him; he now sees a "broad difference between the Religion of their Ancestors, and that which they see now." Old resemblances—with ancestors and ancestral churches—have become "broad differences." These differences with the past, in turn, help to define new resemblances to the new fathers.

Filiation involves mothers as well as fathers, and it might seem plausible that the Puritans, so intent on escaping certain kinds of patriarchal hierarchies, would attempt to reconfigure institutions following a maternal alternative. While mothers do, in fact, appear in discussions of conversion and church organization almost as frequently as fathers, in the end they seem to raise more questions than even the next fathers. Perhaps the Puritans can reconfigure paternity by repudiating any superficial resemblance to first fathers and by imagining resemblances to new and better next fathers. But maternity is not so easily ignored because it is based not only on resemblance but on direct physical connection between mother and child. The very fact of physicality alone—this direct link to the body—was enough to invalidate the maternal alternative in a religious culture that deemed the flesh as corrupt, an inescapable reminder of original sin.[47] The undeniable physical link to the mother threatens to betray as mere fancy any effort to reimagine filiation.

Moreover, in at least some cases, mothers had power to determine paternity as well as maternity. Thomas Hobbes theorizes, for example, that "in the condition of mere nature, where there are no matrimonial laws, it cannot be known who is the father unless it be declared by the mother; and therefore the right of dominion over the child depends on her will, and is consequently hers."[48] Theory becomes practice in seventeenth-century New England, where, as one scholar notes, "the word of the prospective mother during the agony of 'travail' was normally accepted as incontrovertible." An unmarried pregnant woman could name a man as the father of her child, and even if she were lying, there was no other means, outside of resemblance, to determine paternity.[49] In such cases the power of the father transfers to the mother because she, by naming, "fathers" the child and thus confuses the chain of associations that, however tenuously, establish patriarchal order.

This order works both despite and because of its superficiality because differences and resemblances to the father can, with relative ease, be demarcated and redrawn into traceable lineages or traditions. If the first father is weak, then one need only discern the differences, make the break, and then align oneself with the next father whom one wishes to resemble. If one is not to rest in first beginnings, one needs a pretty clear sense of where such traditions begin and end, of the differences between first fathers and next fathers. For a number of reasons besides the direct physical link to mothers, it is much more difficult to differentiate the boundaries of maternal beginnings and endings, so maternal filiation often gets represented as boundless, uncontrollable, overwhelming, and inescapable.

In this scheme, perhaps, it becomes impossible to imagine "next mothers." The attraction of the first fathers can be denied, but it need not be destroyed. The move from filiation to affiliation is not so much a complete repudiation of one's paternal origins as it is a reconstruction of them into a more acceptable representation: the whole series of paternal analogies used to describe institutions. But there is no analogous culturally legitimate vocabulary one can use to translate the attractions of maternal filiations into maternal affiliations, or institutions. Although the powers of the mother cannot be used to represent individual relationships to institutions, we nevertheless witness in Puritan writings an incredible struggle to find ways to recover and enjoy the powers that in their original form must be rejected.

This struggle is very evident in Cotton's attempts to denounce the Roman Catholic Church. We might expect that an institution steeped in patriarchal tradition—its clerics are called fathers and its chief is called pope (from the Latin word for "father")—would be described in paternal terms. Yet Cotton consistently refers to the Church of Rome as "holy Mother Church" or the "Catholicke Mother Church."[50] This maternal designation describes two important aspects of the institutional structure of the Catholic Church: its universality and its visibility. Like most Christians, the Puritans believed in a universal invisible church: a communion of all saints from all times and places (the universal part) that would be realized only in heaven (the invisible part). But many reformers argued against the Catholic claim that the Church of Rome represented a universal visible church; that it could include all true believers from all over the world, on earth, right now, under the rule of a single leader, the pope. The Puritans argued instead for particular visible churches, local congregations of saved souls, governed by local ministers, with no true overarching worldwide administration.

In terms of the parental analogy, the Puritan congregations, like paternal filiation, could be particularized and differentiated along clearly visible boundaries. But the power structure of the universal Roman Catholic Church exceeds all particular or local boundaries. Thus, Cotton describes it as "a vast roaring sea" where "all Churches must be gathered into one Sea." Since the sea knows no bounds—"all banks are broken down in the Sea, yea there is no distinction, but all is one Sea"—it literally overwhelms (from Old English, "over the helm," [i.e., drowns]) everything in its path: "A Catholick Church . . . beareth sway over so many hundred Churches, and overwhelms them all."[51] To represent this undifferentiated power that cannot be escaped, Cotton uses female images in general (the Catholic Church is a "universal wife," or less euphemistically, a whore) and maternal images in particular: the overbearing, overwhelming "Catholicke Mother Church" or "holy Mother Church" that threatens the particularity of individual churches and believers.

By rejecting this maternal representation of institutional structure, Cotton attempts to reject a religious aesthetic that he also represents as female. All throughout his sermons on Revelation, for example, Cotton notes with barely disguised envy that the Roman Catholic Church has managed

> 1. To satisfie the eyes with goodly Images, and Pictures, and gorgeous Temples, and Vestures, that young and old are taken with, these goodly spectacles.
>
> 2. For the eares; you know in their Cathedralls what curious musique they have, both vocall and instrumentall.
>
> 3. For the smell, you have incense and sweet perfumes to entertaine you.
>
> 4. For the taste, you have double Feasts and solemn Feasts, many Feasts full of luxury and riot.
>
> 5. For the Touch: there is toleration of Stews [an archaic word for brothels].[52]

On the one hand, this list reads like any typical Protestant litany against Catholic overindulgence in sensual experience; indeed, all of the senses are covered: eyes (statues, vestments, cathedrals, pageantry), ears (music, vocal and instrumental), nose (incense), taste (feasts), and perhaps even touch (toleration of brothels). Although it is his Protestant duty to reject these things, Cotton nevertheless comes across like a child with his nose pressed up against the candy store window, repeatedly listing all of the goodies he sees but cannot have, desiring them all the more not only because they are forbidden but also because they are good. Who would not be tempted by "double feasts and solemn feasts, many feasts full of luxury and riot"?[53]

On the other hand, this otherwise standard rejection of luxury is noteworthy because Cotton links it to his rejection of maternal representations of power. If the mother/female represents an overwhelming and undifferentiated power, she also represents the seductive power of luxury and pleasure—a connection Cotton makes quite explicitly in his sermons on the Song of Solomon. On his way to repudiating the institutional structure of the Catholic Church, Cotton transforms its aesthetic attractions (figured as female) from pleasurable to deadly. For example, borrowing an image from Revelation, Cotton describes the Catholic Church (already tagged as Mother) as a leopard: "The Leopard is of the feminine gender, and signifies the female of the Panthers; the she Panther, spotted and ravenous, famous for her speedy race, and yet of a good smell, by which she allures other beasts to her, and as she hath occasion, doth devoure them."[54] Something feminine appeals to the senses, but the allure leads to a deadly consumption of the particular self.

Cotton then elaborates on the comparisons of church to beast and of beast to woman: "The Roman catholicke visible Church is as fitly resembled by a woman as a she Panther. . . . Can a Leopard change his spots, Jer.13.23. Is it not a State full of spots . . . spots of heresie, and spots of Idolatry, and spots of Tyranny, and great variety of all spots of Blasphemy . . . yet of a very sweet and fragrant smel, as they perfume their Temples with incense, and love to please ambitious minds, and to fill covetous hearts; they are sweet also, and faire to voluptuous spirits, with their Brothel houses."[55] The representation of the church mutates from spotted leopard to spotted woman, following a line of references from brothel houses to harlots to the whores of Babylon to the wives of Solomon, who lure the wise man to sin with their luxuries and appeals to ambition. Indelible stains—the leopard's spots, the spots of the church, and the spots of female sensuality/physicality—represent sin and corruption. Cotton then completes the transmutation of church to beast to woman to mother then back to beast: "A Church Catholick that shall have one visible head, and be the Mother Church, verily we look at it as the greatest and ugliest beast, that ever was raised in the world. . . . The Catholick visible Roman Church, is the most monster."[56] Cotton invokes a constellation of images that will be central to our discussion of the Antinomian Controversy—a wrongly headed church, a many-headed monster, woman, beast, mother—to represent undifferentiated power out of control.

Cotton does not banish all female imagery from descriptions of the church. For example, he uses the husband/wife analogy from Canticles (Song of Solomon) to represent the relationship between Christ (the husband) and his followers (the wives). But the wife is a female image with discreet boundaries, defined by relations (in the logical, legal, and spiritual senses) to husband and Christ. It is the lack of boundaries that renders other versions of female imagery inappropriate for representing church hierarchies. Paradoxically, it is precisely this lack of boundaries that makes still other female images highly effective in describing the experience of individual conversion. Cotton's definition of a converted individual hinges on a loss of singularity and particularity, an elision of difference into resemblance. In this famous passage from *The Way of Life* (which Perry Miller has tagged "Wading in Grace"), Cotton describes the experience of being drenched or overwhelmed by grace: "There is such a measure of grace in which a man may swimme as fish in the water, with all readinesse and dexterity, gliding an-end, as if he had water enough to swimme in; such a Christian doth not creep or walk, but he runs the wayes of Gods Commandments; what ever he is to doe or to suffer he is ready for all, so every way drenched in grace, as let God turn him any way, he is never drawn dry."[57] Cotton narrates a progression (started earlier than the quoted passage) from dipping to wading to swimming to gliding (total immersion) with a secondary metaphorical progression from creeping to walking to running.[58] At first cautious, the convert abandons all doubt and surrenders to the water, not to sink or drown but to glide and float. Water both initiates the new birth (a reference to John the Baptist immediately precedes this passage) and represents the feeling of the new spiritual life.

How is this representation of being "drenched in grace" any different from the vast roaring sea of the mother church, where there is "no distinction" and where all are "overwhelmed"? Simply, why does Cotton use similar images to represent the Catholic Church as bad and Puritan conversion as good? One possibility is that he wants to (even if he finally cannot) escape the resemblance asserted by both maternal filiation and affiliations. Thus, on the one hand, "a sight of the sinfull uncleanesse of our natures, from our Mothers wombe" makes us realize that "we are borne in the goare blood of sinfull defilements, and therefore God hath provided the blood of Christ, to wash and cleanse us from our Mothers womb, Col. 2.11, 12 . . . we see what we are from our Cradle, guilty of sin and wrath from the wombe, and stand in need of the blood and Spirit of Christ, to wash us from our sins, John 3.3. . . . [We] see a need of a better birth then this."[59] Cotton follows a logic of transfusion we've already tracked with reference to fathers: our original blood must be replaced with the blood of Christ; the physical stain of birth (blood from the mother) must be washed away in the spiritual cleansing of Christ's blood (sacrifice). Moreover, the physical blood of the mother's womb gets replaced with the spiritual water of the womblike experience of wading in grace. In short, Cotton attempts to obliterate the literal resemblance to mother in the vast ocean of the spirit.

But this explanation still does not account for why oceans are permissible for conversion but not for church structure, or more to the point, why the experience of being overwhelmed is suitable for representing individual identity but not institutional identity. Here we have to consider the relationships between individuals and institutions: an individual identity based on resemblance seems to be contingent upon an institutional identity based on difference. That is, if an individual surrenders control of identity (the sensation of drowning that Cotton describes) it must have something, some structure, to which it can surrender. It will not do for one ocean (the wading in grace of conversion) to be engulfed by another (the vast roaring sea of a church). Only God and grace, not institutions, should have the power to inundate and re-create individual identity. Put another way, maternal affiliation cannot compensate for what is lost when one denounces original filiation. Institutions must simply provide the visible means of support—a strong sense of structure, particularity, difference—that have been surrendered by the individuals within that institution. In this situation, a sense of identity derives both from resemblance (one to another within a particular institution) and difference (between institutions). But once again, the Puritans get caught in a double—if not triple—bind: the church requires this dissolution of the individual for membership, and yet the institution itself can never be restructured in the way that it requires its own members to be restructured.

The struggle between denying and recuperating the power of mother also manifests itself in efforts to assign—and perhaps contain—maternal powers in the figure of the father.[60] Ministers, for example, were often called "nursing fathers" who dispensed "spiritual milk" to their children/congregants. Like many other ministers, Cotton transforms God the Father into God the Mother: "Women, if they were not Mothers, would not take such homely offices up, as to cleane their children from their filth; why if God were not of the like affection to us, he would not cleanse us from our filthinesse, we count it an homely office, to sweep sincks, and scum pots, &c., this is Gods office, if he did not sweep the Sinck, and scum off the scum of our hearts, it would never be done."[61] This passage sounds stereotypically maternal notes in its description of a child so homely only a mother could love it, in its enactment of "If I don't clean up this mess, nobody will." It also echoes other descriptions (e.g., Filmer) of the patriarch as both fearful and loving, responsible for all aspects of "child care." But God does the work only a mother would do in this instance precisely because mothers cannot do it. In fact, the mother is partly responsible for the mess (the scum of our hearts, the blood of defilement) that God must clean up.

Because of weak resemblances the father can be reformed, so he does not have to be denied. Because of strong resemblances (specifically physical) the mother must be denied; she cannot be reformed in maternal terms, but she never goes away. Instead, she reappears in representations of conversion, in reconfigurations of God as mother, and in the always present sense of nostalgic longing for something that has been lost and cannot be recovered. Cotton combines this nostalgia with yet another representation of God as divine domestic in one of his few extant poems:

> In mothers womb thy fingers did me mak,
> And from the womb thou didst me safely take:
> From breast thou hast me nurst my life throughout,
> That I may say I never wanted ought.
>
> In all my meals my table thou hast spread,
> In all my lodgings thou hast [made my] bed:
> Thou hast me clad with changes of array,
> And chang'd my house for better far away.[62]

God must save the child from the conditions of its own creation: God makes and then rescues the infant from the mother's womb. Once again God becomes the mother: he nurses the child from his breast, he makes the meals, sets the tables, provides board and clothing—exactly the list of duties encompassed in Filmer's universal fatherly care. God again enacts the "better birth" of conversion, builds the "better house" of the next fathers, and changes one's "house for the better far away," in the moves—which were often expected to be coincident—from England to New England, from sin to salvation, and from earth to heaven.

4. Orphans and Other Lost Souls

In a letter to John Davenport, Cotton explains that although he discerns serious differences between churches in Old and New England, he still does not want to break all ties to his homeland: "we dare not deny to Blesse the Wombe which bare us, and the Paps which gave us sucke."[63] Even though he has left his native country, even though he has renounced the church of his fathers, even though he has represented the "Wombe" as the site of sin, Cotton nevertheless denies any denial of maternal affiliations. Thomas Edwards, a leading Presbyterian opponent of New England Congregationalism, was not convinced and thus denounced the Puritans for "forsak-[ing] their parents, renouncing the wombe that bare them, and the pappes that gave them sucke, throwing dirt in the face of father and mother."[64] With this image of throwing dirt in the face of the parents, Edwards reduces the entire Puritan movement to a petulant violation of the Fifth Commandment.

And yet Cotton and many of his followers continue to resist the implications of their choices, continue to insist that the choice has not really been a choice, continue to deny their denial of "first beginnings." In a passage from a sermon on Revelation, Cotton dramatizes a potential convert in this vexed position of choosing: "When he looks upon the sonne of the Virgin, he thinks there is perfect salvation; but when he looks upon other things, to the milk of the mother; oh there is more sweetnesse in milk then in blood! when he looks againe to the passion of Christ, then he priseth that; but when he looks to the tendernesse of his mother, hee thinkes there is more in that; And thus doth their blasphemous devotion hang between the milk of the mother, and the blood of the Lamb."[65] The potential convert looks back and forth, tempted by the known attractions of mother (sweet milk) and the promised but as yet unknown attractions of Christ (salvation, blood of the Lamb). Significantly, the convert encounters more confusion in replacing the milk of mother with the blood of the Lamb than he did in replacing the warm blood of paternal ancestors with the blood of Christ. The believer on the brink of conversion becomes so engrossed in spiritual experience that he notices the disappearance of the father only as an afterthought. In this passage, by contrast, the mother does not disappear quietly; instead she asserts a force equal to, if not superior to, the Passion of Christ. Perhaps Cotton depicts this choice as more difficult because, in the terms that he has established, it really *is* a choice. The father is never really denied; he is simply reconfigured into some other form. With mothers, Cotton has imagined a situation where maternal forces that are almost irresistible must nevertheless be denied, even though they may not be restored legitimately elsewhere. One result is that these maternal forces return in "illegitimate" forms: the overwhelming power of the Roman Catholic Church, the gory blood of sinful defilement. Another result is the attempt to legitimate maternal power in terms of the father. Still another result is not so much the denial of the mother but rather a denial of one's own agency in making the choice—that is, the choice to "forsake" the mother, to elect the blood of the Lamb over the milk of the mother, is finally God's and not one's own. Perhaps the most stunning result is a nagging nostalgia, a feeling that something has been taken away and that the promise to replace it with a "better birth" has not been kept.

Conversion thus requires an abandonment of everything that is safe, familiar, and comfortable about the old self—its habits, its language, its family, and even its sins—for the promise of a new and better self, a promise often expressed in the assuring language of paternal care and maternal nurturance. Whether one voluntarily or involuntarily engages in this process, the fear that an old self will be abandoned but will not be replaced remains real, even prohibitive. Cotton addresses this fear in an early sermon on conversion:

> To satisfie the minds of such as are afraid of their friends, wives, or children, brethren and sisters, afraid they should be lost, and be men of another world, if once they become crucified and mortified . . . and dead to the Law and weaned from the world; many a poore soule is apt to thinke it selfe undone, and so will our best friends pity us, and say, alas for us, wee are utterly undone, so many persecutions and afflictions, as we are now subject unto, as men quite cast away, but be not deceived, see what the Apostle saith here, hee would have all the world know, he is not an undone man: Though I bee crucified with Christ, nevertheless . . . I live a bodily life vigourous . . . therefore . . . feare not the livelihood of your selves and yours.[66]

To extricate oneself from all original filiations and affiliations that help to anchor a sense of individual identity—friends, wives, children, brethren, and sisters—is to risk becoming "lost," "cast away," and "undone." If nothing takes the place of these relationships, one does not emerge as a completely free and autonomous individual; instead, one ceases to exist in the world. Following the dictates of religion may result in the loss of all relations and all sense of relatedness: a husband without a wife is not a husband; a father without children is not a father. In the logic of Ramus, conversion threatens to change affirmative contraries—those positive relations with something (here, other people) that in a sense "cause" our identity—into negative contraries, an opposition between something and nothing. If God remains so incomprehensible and vast as to be meaningless, if the promise of salvation cannot be represented in concrete and intelligible terms, then the hopeful convert is forced to locate himself on a blank map.

Both imaginative and literal exile can lead to this sense of dislocation. In Thomas Shepard's notebooks, in which he recorded the conversion relations of many of his congregants, we hear the sense of loss attendant on migrating to the New World.[67] A woman identified only as Katherine, for example, recounts her decision to come to the New World: "And [I] thought here the Lord might be found, and doubtful whether I had a call to come because I was to leave my friends."[68] The absolute prospect of leaving family and friends almost overshadows the by no means absolute prospect of salvation and thus leads her to question her spiritual conviction. Nathaniel Eaton, soon to become head of Harvard College, expresses similar doubts: "I lost my self-assurance. . . . Only since I came hither, I have not found my heart to walk so closely with God as I should." To a certain extent, this loss of self-assurance is exactly what had to happen on the way to conversion. But the next step—the next fathers—has yet to be taken. A woman identified as Brother Crackbone's wife also gives voice to longing and loss: "I forgot the Lord as the Israelites did and when I had a new house yet I thought I had no new heart. . . . So I gave up, and I was afraid to sing because to sing a lie. Lord teach me and I'll follow thee."[69] If in Cotton's poem the promises of conversion and migration had been conflated ("chang'd my house for the better far away"), in Mrs. Crackbone's statement they have been separated: a new heart did not come with the new house. And finally, in a statement that poignantly sums up the dynamic we've been describing, William Ames, son of a famous English minister, speaks of feeling like "orphans which are helpless, heartless and strengthless."[70]

This sense of abandonment suggests that filiation had not been replaced by a sufficiently strong representation of affiliation. The destructiveness of conversion is only tenable if followed by the reconstruction of strong supports outside the self, namely, reformed institutions. If this reconstruction fails to take place, then the converts are left stranded, like so may orphans—relocated but not regenerated. Since individual identity derives in large part from resemblances to institutions, the full achievement of one's individuality depends not on subversion or rebellion from all institutions but rather on affiliation with those institutions that one would most like to resemble. Institutions fail when they do not provide proper forms of affiliation.

Here, for example, is Katherine Chidley, an English defender of Congregationalism, writing about the failures of Presbyterian reform: "I pray you, how can you count the Parish of St. Elens your spirituall children, seeing you are there but an hireling; and as you have not begotten them to the Faith, so you have not taken charge of them, to watch over them as a spiritual Father, and you will onely preach to them as long as any will pay you wages, but no longer; how then, have you converted them to God? from what have you converted them? or what have you converted them to?"[71] What Chidley most laments is not an overbearing, tyrannical minister/spiritual father but an absent father—one who fails to do his duty, fails to "take charge" of his children, or does so only for wages. The word for this absent minister is *sinecure*, which means "without care" or "without cure" (with "of the soul" implied), an officeholder who has abused his office not by excess but by indifference and neglect. Chidley's critique falls most squarely on those ministers who fail to provide the "universal fatherly care" promised by Filmer, who fail to become the next fathers as promised by

Cotton. "It is," she writes elsewhere in her book, quoting the separatist John Robinson, "the stewards duty to make provision for the family; but what if he neglect the duty in the Masters absence? Must the whole family starve, yea and the wife also?"[72] The next fathers have failed to meet the expectation of providing a "better birth" than the first fathers did.

At certain moments, Cotton himself acknowledges that one can never fully escape one's resemblance to first fathers: "Set it home upon our hearts . . . whatever our fathers have been, we their children are not better: Some accidentall difference there may be, but . . . the sustance of prevailing corruptions, they have ruled and reigned in the hearts of men, since the world began, by invincible power unable to be subdued."[73] If Cotton had embraced the truth of this statement for his whole career, there would have been no reason to pursue reform, or at least not to pursue reform as imagined in terms of reconstructed families. If children are "not better" than their fathers, then there would be no hope of "better birth," no hope of better houses; indeed, the entire representational language of conversion would be undone. Conversion, rather than a fundamental and radical reorientation from old to new resemblances, would amount to nothing more than those "accidentall differences," those nonessential deviations, between one's past and one's present. It is this bleak prospect that Cotton most wants to change, that Hutchinson most fears, and that Williams never lets anyone forget.

2

John Cotton and the Conversion of Rhetoric

For John Cotton the most important institutional mission of a reformed ministry and church was conversion.[1] Broadly conceived, conversion requires moves from differences to resemblances and from partialness to completeness.[2] Different individuals, through the *imitatio Christi*, grow to resemble Christ and each other; an imperfect soul reaches for complete apprehension of God's mysteries. Although language serves as the main agent of these changes, they do not take place only in language.[3] For the Puritans and especially for Cotton, spiritual growth and conversion are ideally extralinguistic, an unmediated exchange between God and the essential soul. But in their fallen state, human beings require words to mediate these exchanges between God and soul, between institutions and individuals, between one individual and another. This linguistic mediation assumes many forms: reading and interpreting Scripture, delivering and listening to sermons, narrating the experience of grace in a conversion relation. While God remains the first cause of salvation, language nevertheless operates as both cause and effect of conversion. Hearing sermons and reading Scripture will change the soul, and a changed soul will hear, read, speak, and understand in a new way, with a new language.

Unfortunately, language itself exhibits some of the same traits it seeks to reform. Metaphor, for example, is based both on resemblance and difference; it never achieves complete identification between the elements in a comparison. Similarly, there will always be a difference between the divine intention of Scripture and unregenerate readings or interpretations of that Scripture because both the medium (language) and the means of perception (our understanding) are not complete or perfect. Most troublesome of all, there may always be differences between what one thinks and what one says, between what one says and what one does. Willful deception may account for some of these differences; indeed both Cotton and Roger Williams became preoccupied with hypocrites, those who speak the language of conversion but are not essentially converted.[4] But differences and incompleteness in the structure of language itself also lead to these gaps between understanding, saying, and doing. Since language suffers from some of the same problems as unconverted individuals and institutions and since language serves as the means of conversion, Cotton concludes that language itself must be converted before it can convert. To that end, he posits a direct sequence of events: before institutions, individuals; before individuals, language.[5]

1. Conversion and Language

A famous passage from 1 Corinthians 13 serves as a key text for discussions of knowledge and language during the Renaissance: "For we know in part, and we prophesy in part. But when that which is perfect is come, then that which is part shall be done away. When I was a child, I spake as a child, I understood as a child, I thought as a child: but when I became a man, I put away childish things. For now we see through a glass, darkly; but then face to face: now I know in part; but then shall I know even as also I am known."[6] The "now and then" structure of this passage, framed by the move from childhood to adulthood, narrates a series of changes from partialness to completion, most generally a move from partial to complete knowledge of God and, by reflection, of ourselves. The "dark glass" has often been read as a metaphor for language; both language and the glass reflect the real world, but in both cases imperfections in the medium of reflection lead to a "darkened" understanding of the world.[7] Cotton himself notes that we "cannot properly say of any creature, there is wisdome it selfe, or love it selfe, without a Trope."[8] In our unconverted state, we do not know as we are known. While God knows immediately (both without a time delay and without mediation) and essentially (i.e., what the thing itself *is*), we must settle for knowledge through tropes that tell us not what the thing itself *is* but rather what it is *like*.[9]

While Cotton does not explicitly celebrate the "darkened glass" as a justification for poetic language as some other Renaissance writers do, he does not completely lament the unregenerate state of language either. Mediation through language, in fact, makes us human: "The Angels conceiving things, not by discourse, but by a present view of all things . . . they doe all things with so full resolution, that they cannot alter their mind, or repent: but man conceiving things by discourse, findeth them in the event many times to prove otherwise than he expected, and so may come to alter his mind, and be fit to be brought to repentance."[10] Angels have perfect knowledge of all things; their perception is not hindered by imperfect "discourse," and their judgments need not wait for events to unfold over time because they see everything all at once. This perfect knowledge enables "full resolution"; angels act swiftly and confidently, since there is no need to "wait and see." Further, angels cannot change their minds because they are already perfect, and perfect things, by definition, do not need to change. Similarly, they cannot repent because they make no mistakes for which they need to repent. Cotton offers discourse as a compensation for man's unangelic status. Language slows us down; we must peer patiently into the darkened glass to sort out our perception. Language also buys us time; since all events unfold through words, we may discover that, over time, things prove other than expected, that we have to alter our mind or even repent. For Cotton, the vices of language are also, potentially, its virtues; if it is dark and incomplete, its very darkness affords us time to grow and change. If it can seduce us into evil, it can also persuade us to salvation and repentance. His belief in the transformative power of language makes Cotton's work of conversion both necessary (because language can change us for the worse) and possible (because language can change us at all). Because of his divine calling and because of the nature of language, the minister has no choice but to turn around phrases (the etymology of *trope*) in order to turn around people (the intent of conversion).

But language itself must turn around if it is to persuade us from evil toward good. Ministers and converted souls must learn what Cotton calls the "new tongue"[11] of salvation just as if they were learning a new language.[12] In his reading of Canticles, Cotton describes this new tongue, here as it is spoken by the apostles:

> To goe rightly, or straightly, implyeth the strength and generousnesse of wine, when it sparkleth upward in the cup . . . which here expresseth the lively vigour of the Churches Doctrine, in her preaching of Christ, causing the lips of those that are asleepe to speak. . . . When the Apostles spake (the wonderfull workes of God) in strange tongues, some of the people thought them to be full of new wine (Acts 2.11, 13) but they were deceived, and were willing so to account of them in mockery. But these people shall be full of new wine of the Spirit and Word of God, to open their mouthes to speak as the Apostles did, the wonderfull workes of God.[13]

Cotton compares the new and strange tongue of the apostles to a cup of sparkling wine. First, he suggests that, like wine, the word of God causes spiritual intoxication: the tongue ingests the word/wine, the body transforms it through digestion so that it literally becomes incorporated (i.e., embodied), and then the body itself is transformed into something more vigorous. Specifically, ingesting the word/wine leads to invigorated expression; the "lips of those that [were] asleepe" now speak with lively vigor the wonderful works of God. The wine is not only ingested by the tongue; it also represents the new tongue or new language itself. Although they emanate from the strong and generous wine, the words themselves "sparkleth upward" with a disembodied evanescence. Moreover, the wine/words/bubbles go "rightly or straightly"; this directness describes both the immediate effect of the wine on the body (as in, "it went straight to my head") and also, perhaps, the upward path of the sparkling bubbles. Both possibilities point to an instantaneous reaction carried out without delay. The slow and dark mirror has been supplanted by the quick and sparkly wine.

In *The Way of Life*, Cotton elaborates on his ideal for rhetoric in his description of a soul praying for grace: "In case they doe want utterance, yet they have the livelyest speech of all in point of Prayer, Rom. 8.26. It hath sighes, and groanes, that cannot be uttered. If such a soule cannot speake, it can sighe, and mourne, and weep, what for remembrance of sinnes past, and longing desire after grace."[14] The desire for grace cannot be mediated or expressed by any normal language. As Cotton's reference to Romans indicates, "The Spirit itself maketh intercession for us with groanings which cannot be uttered" (Romans 8:26). Thus, the need for a new language arises out of absence: an absence of desired grace and an absence of an appropriate way to express this desire ("they do *want* utterance"). And yet the soul does not collapse into this void; like the wine-inspired apostle, the hopeful convert has the "livelyest speech of all." Like the sparkling bubbles, this prayer lies beyond normal language and speech; the soul sighs, mourns, and weeps. The language of conversion, then, is a language of unmediated desire; it is soul music without words.

Stated differently, conversion changes the language of the child into the language of the father, with the father representing the move from childhood to adulthood, from unregeneracy to salvation (as expressed by the "next fathers" of the family analogy), and from knowing in part to knowing "even as also I am known" by God the father. If, as Corinthians states, unconverted souls speak, understand, and think "as a child," then the perception, judgment, and language of converted souls reach new levels of insight and maturity. According to Cotton, true converts are able to "see other things they never saw before, judge otherwise then they did before; now they have new thoughts, and judgements, and affections. . . . All things are become new. A new heart, new conference, new imployment, new company, the whole man hath another frame of spirit in him."[15] Again Cotton asserts a chain of events: hearing sermons and reading the Bible in the "new tongue" will lead to conversion (new heart, new frame of spirit), which, in turn, changes one's own way of communicating (new conference) and, ultimately, one's relationships to other people (new company).

From an institutional standpoint, however, this emphasis on newness harbors several potential problems. If the "new tongue" consists of grunts, groans, and sparkly bubbles, then who will understand it? Cotton himself points out the ease with which spiritual wine can be mistaken for literal wine: when the apostles spoke in strange tongues, some people thought they were literally drunk and therefore mocked them. Every profession depends on and perhaps even defines itself by a relatively exclusive language, whether we think of profession in terms of career (i.e., academic jargon, the technical terms used by a physician or a carpenter) or in terms of faith (the prayers and rituals of any organized religion). To a certain extent, then, each institution speaks its own more or less exclusive tongue. But Cotton wants his new language to include as much as exclude; that is, he simultaneously wants the linguistic practices of the converted Puritans to distinguish themselves from the practices of, say, Presbyterians and Catholics, and also to serve an evangelical mission by converting new souls. These somewhat contradictory demands made of institutional language are by no means unique to Puritanism; ideally, individuals learn to master the "new tongue" even if they do not develop "new hearts." But Cotton's vision of a converted rhetoric at times seems so extreme that he runs the risk of preaching to the converted rather than preaching to convert.[16]

At other times his vision does not seem new at all. Clearly, he must use metaphors to describe a language without metaphor, and the wine metaphor particularly brings him back to a Catholic aesthetic he purportedly wants to escape. By comparing wine to the "new tongue," Cotton performs a kind of transubstantiation in reverse. The Catholic Mass transforms wine into the literal blood of Christ; that is, church doctrine holds that the wine does not symbolically represent Christ's blood but that it *becomes* that blood by transubstantiation. Like any good Protestant, Cotton reverses the process: he changes literal wine into a symbol for conversion and a converted rhetoric. Indeed, misreading the symbolic wine for literal wine (i.e., thinking the apostles are drunk) is a sign of unregeneracy.[17] And yet Cotton's reversal and separation from a Catholic aesthetic remain incomplete. Just as he cannot quite break free from Catholic excess even as he denounces it, so too he cannot completely escape the logic of certain institutional metaphors even as he attempts to reverse such logic. The Catholic wafer and wine—the body and blood of Christ—get ingested at Communion; those who take and digest this meal literally become incorporated with the body of Christ. And for Cotton, the "Puritan" wine also gets ingested into the body and makes one incorporated with Christ and with other true converts.

2. *Desire, Conversion, and Institutions*

Cotton's use of drinking wine to represent conversion is just one of many instances where he invokes eating, drinking, hungering, thirsting, longing—in short, desire—to talk about salvation. If language is the agent of conversion, then desire is the object of conversion: "The desire of the righteous is onely good; this affection carries an end all the rest, for as a man desires, so he is; there is nothing but good in a righteous mans desires, it is good to all, onely good."[18] For as a man desires, so he is: if a soul desires good, the soul is good; and if a soul desires Christ, it is itself in some way Christ. Conversion thus aims not so much to change the objects of desire or to put an end to all desire but to redirect desire from the bad to the good, to cultivate "a pronenesse unto that which is good, a backwardnesse unto that which is evil."[19]

Consideration of desire brings us back to the taxonomy of sensual delights Cotton uses to condemn Roman Catholic luxuriousness (see chapter 1). Seeing, hearing, touching, smelling, and tasting in themselves were not corrupt; rather, the Catholic Church wrongly directs individual desires to misguided institutional objects: feasts, statues, brothels, and the like. Cotton attempts to redirect these sensual desires to more acceptable institutional objects. Following the Pauline doctrine that "faith cometh through hearing," for example, the Puritans still emphasized the sensual experience of listening, but the object of attention became sermons rather than ornate music. And for all of their alleged iconoclasm, looking and seeing remained central to their faith, except that the minister replaced statues and stained glass. Indeed, several scholars have suggested that the minister became the new institutional icon, an officially and divinely sanctioned object of visual, aural, and (implicitly) sexual desire.[20] Anne Hutchinson, for example, left England guided by the command from Isaiah: "Thine eyes shall see thy teachers"; she could accept no substitutes—printed books or other ministers—for physical proximity to Cotton.

While seeing and hearing remain central to Puritan doctrine, Cotton views them as necessary but not sufficient conditions for conversion. His taxonomy of the senses also implies a hierarchy in which the tongue outranks the ear, eye, nose, and skin. The tongue represents both speech and the "manner of conveyance" of the Lord's Supper, "which is by eating and drinking; by which, that which is received, tasted and fed upon, is most united to the Receiver. We may see other mens things, and sight maketh them not our own; so we may hear, and smell, and touch, and yet they are not our own: But what we taste and feed upon, is most intimately our own."[21] Sight requires levels of mediation that prevent the kind of spiritual intimacy Cotton desires. Visual perception may distort clear vision—the darkened glass, for example—of the desired object; and no matter how long we stare, sight does not allow us fully to possess an object. Cotton's convert instead resembles a child who learns about his surroundings by putting objects in his mouth; taste affords a less intellectualized, more immediate path to knowledge.

Taste is also the only sense by which the object of apprehension actually enters one's own body, and it is this intimacy of physical ownership/possession that Cotton uses to describe conversion: "All feeding implies a conversion of the aliment into the thing nourished so that in time our meat is so digested that its turned into our own nature . . . to be conformed to him [Christ] in every thing, to be fashioned according to his nature, this is a farther act of life. When a Christian so feeds on Christ, that he is of the same nature with him . . . this is a signe of life. When we are turned into his nature by feeding on him, and he into ours; why, this very feeding on spirituall food, implies a spirituall life."[22] Ingestion and digestion collapse the difference between subject and object of desire: when food is digested, it stops being some other object; it literally becomes part of the molecular makeup of the person who ingests it. Thus, eating and tasting allow Cotton to convey not only unmediated desire but also to depict conversion by way of the *imitatio Christi*. Our desires are turned toward Christ, we incorporate him by the most immediate means available, and he converts us even as we convert him into part of us: "We are turned into his nature by feeding on him, and he into ours."

Finally, hungering and thirsting suggest desires that can never be fully sated; no matter how resplendent the meal, no matter how many feasts, fulfillment remains temporary and does not preclude the need for all future meals. By the same token, Cotton insists that "conversion is a continued act," that although we "are to be thankful for the least measure of grace," we are "not to rest satisfied with that estate we are come unto."[23] This description of grace suggests that conversion does not take place once and for all but rather that it unfolds over time and that it is always partially incomplete. Indeed, this very incompleteness provokes desire for further conversion, a continued desire to reveal the truth obscured by the darkened glass.[24] Desire never ends; it only breeds further desire for grace: "When it is once got, the more a man hath the more he desireth."[25] The true convert becomes spiritually addicted because the desire for good grace defines his identity; for as a man desires, so he is. Following this logic, if he were to cease this desire, he would cease to be.

The desiring convert also grows increasingly attached to and dependent on the sources or suppliers of grace—God, the church, the Bible, the ministry—because they set before him those objects that spark the desires that, in turn, define who he is. Thus, desire serves as the basis for all institutional structures and practices. This desire itself can be neither created nor destroyed; in itself it is neither good nor evil. It exists prior to the formation of any particular institution, and it can outlast the destruction of any given institution. By the same logic, no single institution inspires good or bad desires. Instead, some institutions better encourage desire for the good;

they do a better job of directing, shaping, and controlling the desires of individual members toward a common goal, a common identity.

3. Resemblances and Differences

Up to this point, difference, incompleteness, or partialness have all been inherent characteristics of unregenerate means or media of perception. In general, a fallen language is partial and obscure; in particular, metaphor, by definition, includes differences as well as similarities: "Every metaphor is a short similitude, and it must not be expected that any similitude should agree in all points."[26] There is nothing one can do to fix this imperfect structure of metaphor. As Thomas Browne says, some "reserved difference" must always slip into even the most apt of comparisons, otherwise there would be no true comparison. If the medium introduces difference, so does the means of perception. Borrowing an example from Plato, Cotton writes: "The halting of this comparison lyeth not in the inequality of the things compared, but in the unequal organ or medium, by which they are discerned. A staffe when it is seen partly in the aire, partly in the water, seemeth crooked, though it be never so streight."[27] The stick, in essence, remains identical to itself; the part in the water is not a different stick from the part in the air. Resemblance is mistaken for difference because of the distortions introduced by the change in medium (from water to air) and by the "unequal organ": the means of perception—the eye—is tricked into seeing two different sticks.

Cotton invokes this stick analogy during a discussion of church membership in an attempt to anticipate objections to the practice of conversion narratives.[28] In Cotton's plan, potential church members deliver an original account of their salvation; in their own words, not following any set prayer, they must tell about God's workings in their souls. Church elders assess the validity of these conversion relations and then decide whether or not to admit an applicant to membership. Those who opposed the practice of conversion relations (in both Old and New England) argued that to allow the elders to make such assessments is to place them in the role of God, who alone could know with certainty the state of any individual soul. Through the stick analogy (with the stick now standing for a potential church member, being looked at by church elders), Cotton grants this objection, to a point. Because of a faulty medium (i.e., the language used to compose a conversion relation) and faulty means of perception (i.e., the imperfect faculties and judgment of the elders), it is quite possible to mistake a straight arrow for a crook; that is, through no fault of his own, a true convert may appear to be a hypocrite. However, Cotton's reading of the stick analogy does not account for the possibility that the stick itself may be faking its own integrity, that is, that the potential member may willfully manipulate the means and media of perception to deceive those who judge him.

By placing the blame on language or the faulty perception of the judges and by making the thing judged an inanimate object, Cotton effectively factors out human agency in this particular example. Elsewhere, however, Cotton realizes that only the truly saved soul possesses the integrity of the stick. The sincere (from the Latin: "pure, clean, untainted") convert resembles Christ, but he also resembles himself; that is, there is no difference between what he thinks and what he says, between what he says and what he does. Indeed, Cotton's definition of oratory, or prayer,[29] asserts a continuity between and among thinking, saying, and doing: "*Oratio est* 1. *Mentalis*, to think, a man may say it in his heart, when he thinks so, and that is his opinion; 2. *Vocalis*, to speak, to say in outward words; 3. *Vitalis*, in outward carriage, to make shew and profession in his walking."[30] Speech proves thought, and action proves speech, and all three align in the sincere convert: "If a man say that he knows God and yet keep not his Commandments, his profession is not true, but he that doth saith so, and doth so, his profession is sincere."[31]

Since conversion manifests itself, in part, in language, what is to prevent the hypocrite from fashioning a resemblance to the sincere convert simply by mastering the "new tongue"? Just as all speakers of French are not, by birth, French, so too all speakers of the new tongue may not, by rebirth, be converted. Thus, the hypocrite differs from himself: there is a big difference between what he is and what he says he is. This ability to differ from oneself—to perform one "self" in public and another in private—points to another, more modern definition of individualism. For starters, this definition assumes a distinction between "public" and "private" that was not yet fully in place in the mid-seventeenth century. As well, it assumes that the individual does not reside in a matrix of institutional affiliations but in its *self*. In his essay "Of Simulation and Dissimulation," Francis Bacon talks about the expediency of fully disclosing one's thoughts in a given situation. At times, he argues, it is more expedient to exercise "a power to feign," because each person has a right to "reserve to a man's self a fair retreat."[32] Bacon's "fair retreat" suggests that the essential self exists in a willful removal from or negation of institutional demands, a retreat into a private world of one's own creation, one's own possession.

Bacon's "self" is Cotton's sin. For Cotton, the individual should exist in his affiliations with institutions; for Bacon, the true individual exists despite those affiliations. Both Bacon and Cotton recognize a potential difference between what a man says and what a man does, but Bacon considers this difference a pragmatic expediency at the very least and an opportunity to define and protect a self at the very most. For Cotton, this very same power to feign threatens to undermine the means by which he thinks an "individual" should be created: the integrity of institutions, the integrity of language. Bacon points to the possibility of using language to play an institutional role that does not fully represent one's true self. If, for Cotton, language provides the link between institutional reform and individual conversion, for Bacon it becomes a way to keep them separate. Thus, to preserve a self in Bacon's sense is, in Cotton's sense, to refuse to be converted or, even worse, to pretend to be converted.

Cotton is, of course, not unaware that language can be used to perform institutional roles that may or may not accurately represent an individual's actual relationship to institutions. Performance itself constitutes one of the principal parts of rhetoric: invention, disposition, memory, elocution, and delivery or performance of the oration. The Latin word for "delivery," *actio*, suggests the act of giving a speech but also acting in the sense that the orator must perform a role. Further, the actor/orator must himself perform certain emotions if he wants his audience to feel those emotions; for example, Horace instructs: "If you would have me weep, you must first feel grief yourself."[33] Even if the orator himself does not feel sad, he must appear sad if he wants to provoke genuine sadness in his audience. The Greek word for "delivery," *hypocrisis*, points to the very thing that threatens to undo Cotton's plans for linking language to converted individuals. To be persuasive, a conversion relation must have an effective *hypocrisis*; the potential church member must enact as well as narrate the spiritual struggles he has experienced, and the audience (in this case, the church elders) must also be moved by his story. But this requirement of effective *hypocrisis* also opens the church door wide for hypocrisy.

More so than Roger Williams, Cotton was willing to risk admitting hypocrites into his church. It was better, he felt, to include many false converts through leniency than to exclude even one true convert through excessive stringency. Nevertheless, the possible presence of hypocrites affects the confidence with which judgments get made within the institution. In his earlier writings, Cotton mostly worried about the ways in which the unregenerate outside the church would misunderstand the truly saved—how, for example, the spiritual intoxication of the apostles was misinterpreted as literal drunkenness. Thus, he warns the saved to be prepared for the "misprising of the world" because "the world knows you not. Be willing to go as unknown men in the world."[34] As his career progressed and he came to terms with the inherent contradictions of his plans for conversion, he grew more skeptical even of his own ability to discern the difference between sincere and hypocritical converts: "To distinguish in men between that Sanctification which floweth from the Law and that which is of the Gospel, is a matter so narrow, that the Angels in Heaven have much adoe to discern who differ: a work no fitter for Angels to cut the scantling in it, than for Ministers of the Gospel, though indeed there be great difference of the one from the other. Now though this doe not tend to heale any difference in judgement, yet it is usefull to heale a misprision of sanctification that may be found in all Hypocrites of this Country."[35]

Cotton offers at least four pairs of comparisons: between a covenant of grace (sanctification from the Gospel) and a covenant of works (sanctification from the Law), between angelic and ministerial judgment, between a minister's judgment of a soul and the actual state of that soul, and between a person's own judgment of his soul and the actual state of the soul. A great distance separates the elements of each pair, and yet even the angels from their heavenly perspective cannot accurately discern the difference, for example, between true converts and those who merely do good works under the law. If the angels cannot cut the scantling (literally, split a small stick into even smaller sticks), then how can a minister, who relies on a faulty judgment to evaluate a faulty language, be expected to separate the saved from the damned, the truly saved from the apparently saved? How, for that matter, can we discern this difference in ourselves, for ourselves?

The great difference between works and grace does not "heal" the difference between reality and perception. The word *heal* here implies a wound, a wound so large that it threatens the health of the church. So Cotton must work to heal the "misprision of sanctification" that may be found in "all Hypocrites in the Country." Then as now, the word *misprision* implies a misreading, a misinterpretation of evidence.[36] Whereas Cotton previously worried that the performer would be the hypocrite, he now also stands guard against the hypocrite reader, the ones who misread good works—intentionally or not, in themselves or in others—as a sign of true salvation.

The worst effect of having hypocrite speakers and readers in church, then, is not that members will grow suspicious of each other or even that they will begin to doubt the minister's judgment. The worst effect is that true converts will grow less confident in their own salvation, exactly the opposite of the institutional goal of encouraging people to grow in grace. Cotton writes: "Truly it is hard to perceive when men differ, and therefore it is not an easie matter to make such use of Sanctification, as by it to beare witnesse unto Justification: and it will be a very hard case and much more difficult, when men cannot feele the presence of spirituall gifts, but want spirituall light, and when they doe finde faith in themselves, they doe finde it in hypocrites also for even Eagle-eyed Christians will have much adoe to discerne of sanctification in themselves, before they see their justification, as to cut off all hypocrites from having the like in them."[37] If a person who believes himself to be saved detects a similarity between himself and someone he believes to be a hypocrite, the result could be a loss of faith in his own justification. Cotton makes a sad prophecy: There will come a time when people will no longer be able to discern with confidence the working of the spirit in their own souls—note that he writes "*when* men cannot feele the presence of spirituall gifts," not "if." Real differences—between saved and damned, between the "sanctified frame" and that "which seemeth to be like it"—blend imperceptibly into apparent similarities.[38] Without the visible presence of Christ to serve as the standard for judgment, the ability to evaluate evidence of sanctification (in the form of words, thoughts, and actions) becomes jeopardized. If similitudes ultimately conceal more than they reveal, then Cotton must qualify his confidence in the representational power of metaphor so fundamental to his converted rhetoric.

4. Different Differences

For an institution whose fundamental premise rests on achieving resemblances—between words and essences; thinking, saying, and doing; believers and Christ; one believer and another—members of Cotton's church must spend a good deal of time sorting out their differences. We've already looked at several instances where difference serves a positive function. For example, difference in language—between elements of comparison in a metaphor, between words and essences—defines us as human as opposed to divine; such obscurity may lead us astray, but it also allows for the possibility of conversion. Further, the dark glass of Corinthians acts as an accommodation to our faulty perceptions: since we cannot know as God knows, immediately and essentially, tropes and figurative language mediate between divine and human knowledge. And since the human mind must work hard to "figure out" the literal meaning in the darkened glass, tropes also help us to remember what we have learned.[39]

If the difference embodied in tropes serves as an accommodation to human psychology, it also works to shape this psychology (in the Greek sense of psyche, soul) by sustaining the desire for further knowledge. True converts never settle into complacency; instead they continually seek to clear the medium of the darkened glass and await the final moment of apocalypse, the Greek word for "revelation" or "uncovering." And since Cotton defines conversion as a "continued act," there always remains an implicit difference between the self now and the self yet-to-be.

The desire to turn differences into resemblances and not so much the simple achievement of resemblance itself defines who a true convert is: as a man desires, so he is. But difference plays yet another role in the definition of an individual. Invoking yet once more 1 Corinthians 13, Cotton explains why it would not be a good idea to see God face to face, even if we could do so: "Why cannot we see Gods face and live? The presence of God would swallow us up . . . his glorious presence, which is a consuming fire, would consume us. When Isaiah saw God in a similitude, but in a glimpse of his presence, then he said, Isa. 1.5. Woe is me, for I am undone . . . he was afraid of his life, though he saw God but in a similitude."[40] The incompleteness of similitude preserves us from destruction. Although Cotton frequently uses the language of consumption, he always does so in the context of some mediating force: Christ mediates between God and man; language mediates between man and Christ. An unmediated, direct vision of God would consume us before we had a chance to consume it. Isaiah, in fact, sees God "in a similitude" and still almost loses it, and likewise Moses sees God "in a glorious resemblance" that "did wonderfully affect Moses."[41] Similitudes, resemblances, metaphors all serve double duty: on the one hand, they bring God closer to us so that we may consume him, and on the other hand, they keep him far enough away so that he does not consume us. By balancing resemblances with differences the rhetoric of conversion exhorts its listeners to become undone without becoming unraveled. Thus, difference acts as a form of self-definition by provoking desire for completion and of self-preservation by never finally allowing full completion.

Difference also plays a less productive role in the construction of language, individuals, and institutions. It allows for hypocrite readers and speakers and for the performance of two potentially discontinuous selves: the public institutional self and the private self defined in opposition to the institution. The question now becomes, how is a true believer supposed to tell the difference between differences? If conversion aims for resemblances but must use certain kinds of difference along the way, then how is anyone to distinguish between those differences that encourage conversion and those that enable hypocrisy?

For Cotton, the solution seems simple enough: "a difference in time will grow."[42] Over time a difference between sincere and hypocrite converts will become evident. Waiting allows for the sincere convert to pursue conversion as a continued act and for the hypocrite reader/speaker to be exposed: "Sometimes hypocrisie is spun with so fine a thread, and it is so well dyed, as that you can hardly discern any difference. And sometimes grace is so low in the heart, as that you cannot discern it. This is true, but it is but for a time. . . . Lay hands suddenly on no man; for if he prove not pure, thou shall be partaker of his sins, and all the hurt he doth. Some mens sins lye open before hand, i.e. before the judgment of the Church, others follow after, they cannot be hid, God will have them made manifest in due time, Luke 12.2. There is nothing so secret but it will be discovered."[43] Cotton suggests two time frames, two possible ways of thinking about the "then and now" of conversion. The first and most ideal frame posits an instantaneous switch from the preconverted "then" to the postconverted "now."

There is a flash of light, and the scales drop from Saul's eyes; and he, like all converts, is able to "see other things they never saw before, judge otherwise then they did before." Conversion then continues after this initial burst, as the convert becomes stoked by the desire for further insight. The second time frame posits a gradual shift over a longer period from "then" to "now." This gradual change also allows us to see old things in a new way, simply because those things truly have grown old through the passage of time. Time thus operates like an extended conversion experience; we gain insight through hindsight if not through immediate revelation.

By suggesting that time will accomplish what conversion cannot, Cotton seems to have found a practical solution to many of the problems inherent in the rhetoric of conversion. But this solution also constitutes a compromise of one of the defining traits of salvation: immediacy in both the sense of "without mediation" and "instantaneously." When the soul habitually inclines toward the good and when thought, speech, and action are all properly aligned, then there should be no reason to hesitate. "And why should they not goe fast," writes Cotton, "whom the Spirit of God drives, and improves the liberty they have of God. And therefore it is for us to doe all the good we can."[44] The quickness of the saved extends to political as well as spiritual acts; thus, John Milton initially justifies what may have seemed to some an impulsive regicide, and Andrew Marvell applauds the "Angelic Cromwell who outwings the wind" and laments the "ill delaying what the elected hastes."[45]

The time required to reveal true converts and expose hypocrites also lessens the immediacy of a converted rhetoric that ideally goes straight to the truth, like evanescent sparkling wine. Thomas Browne offers the following example of the ways in which senses that have not been glorified need more words to figure out divine truths: "*Hee that gives to the poore lendeth to the Lord*; there is more Rhetorick in this one sentence than in a Library of Sermons, and indeed if these sentences were understood by the Reader, with the same Emphasis as they are delivered by the Author, wee needed not those Volumes of instructions, but might bee honest by an Epitome."[46] If we understood the full majesty of scriptural assertions such as "he that gives to the poor lends to the Lord," then we could be "honest by an Epitome." Like the angels, we would not need much rhetoric to persuade us, to engage or accommodate our psychology; instead, simple truths could be stated in a simple way, and we would still grasp their complexity and profundity. But we are fallen readers, perhaps even hypocrite readers, so we need a "Library of Sermons" and "Volumes of instructions" to convince us of truths that should be immediately obvious.

Thus, in addition to sustaining a desire for the good, institutions must also provide time for individuals to overcome their own psychological, spiritual, and intellectual limitations. All of this sounds like good news for ministers and churches. The time requirement provides a justification for demanding continued church attendance: if grace is, at times, "so low in the heart as that you cannot discern it," then an individual must be in the presence of those who both encourage and recognize a potential for salvation. The time requirement also justifies the ministerial charge of delivering sermons, many sermons and long sermons.[47] For example, Cotton's sermons on the enigmatic First Epistle of John, a biblical text that runs all of five short chapters, take up about five hundred large folio pages.

But the time requirement also poses many challenges to those who desire to reform institutions. Should church membership, for example, be limited to those who are already saved, or should it include those who can potentially be saved, even if they eventually turn out to be hypocrites? If people are expected to be saved before they become church members, then the time question becomes moot; perfect things, by definition, do not need to grow. A church thus constructed becomes frozen in time at its originary moment, perfect from first to last. Moreover, such a church does not need time on its side; that is, since its members are already saved, they do not need volumes of sermons to understand the Bible; they do not need time to be exposed as hypocrites. Such a plan, by removing the church from earthly time, threatens to remove the church from earth altogether; an institution premised on the already perfect state of its members may never come into existence. By the same token, an institution or church that accepts less than perfect members may find its existence continually threatened. While the presence of such members provides a justification for its continued existence, it also sets up a potentially troublesome contradiction: the leaders of the church must simultaneously find ways to encourage those who are growing in the "right" direction *and* discipline those who are revealing themselves as hypocrites. The rhetoric of conversion and those who preach it must perform double and perhaps even contradictory duties.

5. *Solomon and Universal Fatherly Care*

For Cotton, Solomon stands as the biblical figure who most successfully meets the various demands placed on leaders. Whenever an issue of authority is forced to a crisis, Cotton turns to Solomon as a way of representing his own relationship to institutions. Early in his English career, Cotton preached the first of two sermon series on the Song of Solomon, or Canticles. To establish the canonical status of this Scripture, Cotton argues that Solomon is the legitimate "pen-man." By making this case at a point when his ministerial career is not yet established or secure, Cotton may also be attempting to establish his own legitimacy as a skillful explicator of a difficult text. Shortly after he arrived in the New World (1633), as a minister of great repute, he preached on the sixth book of Canticles in order to gain official admission to the Boston congregation. Again, Solomon serves as his passport into institutional acceptance and legitimacy. Cotton's sermons on Ecclesiastes, delivered shortly after the Antinomian Controversy, implicitly suggest the parallels he sees between himself and Solomon. Both men were considered to be wise and virtuous leaders, but both were led astray by women.[48] Since Cotton's own authority comes under fire during the trials—for his ability both to teach proper doctrine and to control Hutchinson—he looks to Solomon for assurance that a fallen leader may be able to regain a legitimate place in the church. Finally, while he is writing his treatises to promote Congregationalism, Cotton delivers another series of sermons on Canticles, this time reading the text as a prophetic church history that lends divine sanction to the New England Way.

Bibliography aligned with biography clearly indicates that Cotton relies on Solomon to help him think his way through formative institutional questions. His various readings of Solomon's story provide him with a representation of authority that combines in one person the somewhat contradictory mandates of discipline and encouragement, nurturance and enforcement—or what Cotton himself labels as a mixture of rigor with mercy.[49] Solomon represents a scripturally underwritten version of Filmer's patriarch, one who provides the "universal fatherly care" called for by Winthrop and Chidley. At various points in his career, Cotton became more or less skeptical that one leader can embody both modes. His plans for the Congregational Church, for example, call for at least two distinct ministerial offices: the pastor, who enforces church discipline, and the teacher, who preaches for conversion of souls.[50] In his second sermon series on Canticles he speculates that "majesty and love are incompatible": the demands made of universal fatherly care may not only be contradictory, they also may be mutually exclusive.[51] And yet Cotton clings to the possibility that the qualities of Solomon—rigor and mercy, majesty and love—can be found in the same person at the same time and still provide a consistent and coherent form of authority.

For Cotton, Solomon achieved this balance or combination through an aesthetic that, in a sense, renders Solomon as the male version of the Roman Catholic Mother Church. We have already seen Cotton's intense attraction to the aesthetic luxuries of Catholicism and his rejection of the overwhelming boundlessness of these luxuries, a lack of boundaries that he characterizes as female. Through Solomon he is able to recuperate a sense of luxury and at the same time establish the clear and particular boundaries of a paternal tradition. By asserting the institutional and canonical legitimacy of Solomon, Cotton is thus able to enjoy and celebrate an aesthetic excess that he would otherwise have to reject as a threat to the institution. He confidently praises Canticles (and even prefers it to the Psalms of David) for its "luxuriance" and "abundance," the very qualities he condemns in their Catholic form. He argues that any translation of the Song of Solomon should preserve the original meter and verse so "that we might sing the Canticles as the Hebrews did,"[52] and he also supports the singing of psalms during church services.[53] And he urges all ministers to emulate Solomon, the "sweet Singer," to "turn poets of righteousnesse" and to "let thy doctrine drop as honey, preach willingly, freely, sweetly, comfortably."[54] Solomon represents the wise leader and the divinely inspired poet, a successful combination of the pleasure of aesthetics and the rigor of authority.

3

Roger Williams and the Conversion of Persecution

1. Critique of Conversion and the Ministry

In his long invective against George Fox and the Quakers, Roger Williams attacks the idea that outward behavior can serve as evidence of spiritual conversion:[1] "If a notorious Drunkard . . . be convinced, and come to hearken to a Spirit within him, to say, Thou and Thee, and think himself equal and above all his former Superiours, &c. he is Justified, he is Sanctified. . . . Thus they pretend Repentance, Faith, and a change of heart because they have changed their talk, their Garments, &c."[2] Williams relies on a difference between accidentals and essentials. Just as the drunk who appears sober remains essentially a drunk, so too the "convert" who appears saved in the accidentals—how he talks, how he dresses, how he thinks of himself in relation to other people—does not indicate actual salvation. A change of heart is not simply a change of attitude (e.g., simply thinking oneself better than one's former superiors); it cannot be brought about, says Williams, as quickly and easily as a change of clothes.[3] Most significantly, a change of heart is not guaranteed simply because hopeful souls "have changed their talk." While this sentence is directed specifically at the Quaker "thees and thous," it could also be read as a challenge to John Cotton's plan for a converted rhetoric.[4]

It is Williams's suspicion of performance that most distinguishes him from Cotton, whose whole theory of conversion hinges on a series of causal connections between changed talk and changed hearts: a converted rhetoric leads to converted souls who, in turn, speak the "new tongue" of salvation. In his definition of rhetoric or prayer, Cotton combines *mentalis* (what is in the heart and mind), *vocalis* (what one says), and *vitalis* (outward carriage). Although he accounts for possible hypocrisy, Cotton seems more or less certain that only true converts will walk the walk and talk the talk of salvation. Williams is much less confident that these three elements (heart, talk, and behavior) will always be in alignment. For a host of reasons, hopeful converts can exploit the power to feign, the power of *actio/hypocrisis* to perform conversion—to wear the costume and learn the lines—without actually being converted.

While hopeful converts may "perform" conversion out of a genuine desire to join a church or in an effort to deceive, they may also do so as an act of self-preservation. Under the threat of religious persecution, conversion becomes a command performance: "As to the point of true Conversion, and Regeneration by Gods spirit, who can but deny that the body of this and of all other Protestant Nations . . . are unconverted, and (as formerly) ready to be converted and turned forward and backward, as the Weathercock, according as the powerfull wind of a prevailing Sword and Authority, shall blow from the various points and quarters of it."[5] This comparison of conversion to a shifting weather vane neatly undoes the metaphorical logic of salvation. Conversion becomes completely external and transitory compared to, say, depictions of conversion as a heart of stone melted to wax, ready to receive God's imprint or seal, which focus on internal and permanent change. Unlike the heart or soul, the weathercock signals the outside; although it is in the shape of an animal, it is nevertheless inanimate (etymologically, "without breath, spirit, soul"), it is more or less a nonessential decoration, and it must literally be located outside to function. The animus/spirit for the weather vane comes not from divine inspiration but from "the powerfull wind of a prevailing Sword and Authority." Conversion thus becomes a matter of political expediency; the function of the soul-as-weather-vane is to determine which way the wind blows and then momentarily to point in that direction. The weather vane, like the converted soul, still turns; but unlike the converted soul, it does not turn toward anything in particular—it points to the empty sky. In the end, the soul remains, as Williams elsewhere puts it, "unturned turned."

For Cotton, spiritual change serves as the foundation for political reform; for Williams, shifting political alliances serve as the shaky basis for fake spiritual change. When motivated by political force, conversion amounts to little more than a coerced performance or "pretend Repentance." Over and again, Williams insists upon that which Cotton virtually ignores: the *actio* or *hypocrisis* of rhetoric (especially the rhetoric of conversion) invites, if it does not assure, the power to feign. Cotton tries to define away the possibility of feigning by aligning thought, action, and performance. In more practical moments he admits that some hypocrites will still become church members, but he concludes that it is better to admit a few hypocrites than to exclude even one true convert in the name of a rigorous insistence on spiritual purity. Again and again, Williams insists that a church with even one "pretend Repentant" is no true church; that forced conversion to the true religion is at least as bad—and probably worse—than "true" worship of a false religion. "Is there not more danger (in all matters of trust in this world)," he asks, "from a hypocrite, a dissembler, a turncoat in his religion (from the fear or favour of men) then from a restored Jew, Turke or Papist who holds firme unto his principles?"[6]

Williams further argues that hypocrisy cuts both ways; that is, both minister and "convert" participate in a game of mutual deception: "Now counterfeit Spirituall delusions of false and counterfeit Christs, as they are deeper and stronger, so they find more easie possession of the Ears and Souls of men, so wofully prepared by naturall self-deceivings."[7] If Bacon describes the "power to feign" as a kind of dissembling meant to "reserve to a man's self a fair retreat," Williams acknowledges that it takes two to tangle truth with deception: the dissembler (the person who intentionally or unintentionally fakes conversion) and the audience for that dissembler (a minister who intentionally or unintentionally encourages the dissembler to carry on with the delusion or who, in Cotton's term, misprises or misreads sanctification, the hypocrite reader). Williams again emphasizes the negative role of rhetoric; spiritual delusions are both cause and effect of the "easie possession of the Ears and Souls of men." The natural inclination toward self-deception "prepares" man to be deluded by the rhetoric he hears, and such rhetoric only further deepens the delusion of salvation. The word *possession* also echoes the language of captivity, enthrallment, and imprisonment to which Williams objects in another major analogy for conversion, the comparison of sexual and spiritual experiences.

A comparison of sexual to spiritual desire is, of course, typical in the Renaissance. Among the many forms of desire Cotton uses to describe conversion, for example, he includes the idea that a hopeful convert awaits salvation just as the bride in Canticles awaits her husband. In both the sexual union of bride with groom and the spiritual union of soul with God "there is a Recyving," he writes, "to wit, a Passive Reception . . . in that wee are Rejoyced as Paul saith, I am apprehended (that is, taken hold of, and recyved) by Christ Jesus. . . . In this union, the soule Receyveth Christ, as an empty vessell receyveth oyle: but this recyving is not active, but passive."[8] Whatever the actual gender of the individual, the soul is figured in stereotypically female terms (empty vessel, passive and receptive, bride) whereas God is figured in stereotypically male terms (active, taking hold of, apprehending, bridegroom).[9] In a much more famous example, John Donne also underscores the resemblance between sexual and spiritual desire:

> Batter my heart, three-personed God; for, you
> As yet but knock, breathe, shine, and seek to mend;
> That I may rise, and stand, o'erthrow me, and bend

Your force, to break, blow, burn, and make me new.
I, like an usurped town, to another due,
Labour to admit you, but oh, to no end,
Reason your viceroy in me, me should defend,
But is captivated, and proves weak or untrue,
Yet dearly I love you, and would be loved fain,
But am betrothed unto your enemy,
Divorce me, untie, or break that knot again,
Take me to you, imprison me, for I
Except you enthral me, never shall be free,
Nor ever chaste, except you ravish me.[10]

The believer, again figured as female and passive, longs to be overpowered by a divine male force. Just as Cotton's convert is apprehended and taken hold of by God, the speaker in Donne's poem asks God to "o'erthrow me, and bend / Your force, to break, blow, burn, and make me new." In this act of apprehension the speaker undergoes a physical and spiritual transformation. Also like Cotton, Donne deploys the marriage metaphor: the speaker is " betrothed unto your enemy"—a rival in love and belief—and asks God/the husband to "divorce me" or to "break that knot again" to save him/her, literally and figuratively, from an evil marriage or from a marriage to evil. Donne also uses the language of holy paradox: "Except you enthral me, never shall be free / Nor ever chaste, except you ravish me." Presumably, one regains freedom through enthrallment and chastity through ravishment only if one interprets these metaphors in a spirit that properly recognizes similarities (being saved is like being married to God) and differences (but unlike, because one is a physical ravishment and enthrallment while the other is spiritual).

Williams resolutely refutes this reading of the spiritual/sexual analogy and instead interprets the comparison in a radically different way. In his gloss on the marriage analogy from Canticles, for example, he writes:

> . . . the forcing of a Woman, that is, the violent Acting of uncleannesse upon her bodie against her will, we count a Rape: By Proportion that is a Spirituall or Soule-rape, which is a forcing of the Conscience of any Person, to Acts of Worship, which the Scripture entitles by the name of the Marriage bed, Cant. 1. . . .
>
> Indeed, what is this before the flaming eyes of Christ, but as . . . some lustfull Ravisher deales with a beautifull Woman, first using all subtle Arguments and gentle perswasions, to allure unto their spirituall Lust and Filthinesse, and where the Conscience freely cannot yeeld to such Lust and Folly . . . then a forcing and Penalties, Penall Lawes and Statutes?[11]

Williams almost reads the spiritual/sexual analogy literally.[12] He translates "ravishment" into its etymological relative "rape" to underscore and literalize the violence of words such as Cotton's "apprehend" and "taken hold of" and Donne's "batter," "o'erthrow," "break," "blow." The unwilling convert, like the unwilling sexual partner, suffers violent coercion against the will, physically or spiritually. In this regard, Donne's figurative, spiritual ravishment is just as sinful as literal, physical rape, an observation Williams makes very clear with his graphic phrase "soule-rape."

This reading is, as I've suggested, almost a literal interpretation of the metaphor for conversion, but not quite, because Williams, of course, constructs an analogy of his own. His "proportion" (a rhetorical comparison or enthymeme: as A is to B, so X is to Y) states "just as rape is to consensual sex, so conversion against conscience is to consenting acts of worship." So, in fact, the terms of Williams's analogy are exactly the same as the terms of Donne and Cotton; in both cases, sexual experience compares to spiritual experience. And to a certain extent, both cases emphasize the similarities between the terms of the analogies: for Donne and Cotton the similar factor is something like ecstasy experienced through submission; for Williams the similarity lies in being forced to do something against one's will. So what, finally, is the difference between the two cases? It is not really so much that Williams exposes the difference that is hidden by Cotton's resemblances, that an act of conversion actually covers an act of coercion, because in the end they are talking about exactly the same act. And it is not really a matter of direction; both cases use sexual terms to reveal something about salvation, not religious terms to reveal something about sex. That is, Williams is not making a case against actual rape but instead uses rape as a recognized evil to reveal something about conversion. The major difference seems to rest in the way each instance of the analogy evaluates the terms of the comparison. For Williams, ravishment becomes rape, "subtle Arguments and gentle perswasions" become lusty and filthy coercion, rapture becomes imprisonment, and seduction becomes abduction. The difference, then, is not in the structure of the analogy itself but rather in how the analogy is interpreted, evaluated, and judged.

Williams's lack of faith in conversion, then, emerges from a crisis in interpretation. He simply does not trust a potential convert's self-interpretation (the drunkard who presents himself as sober), nor does he trust a minister's ability to interpret correctly the performances of potential converts. Given this lack of trust in interpretation, Williams concludes that ministers have no grounds upon which to base judgments about the state of an individual's soul. "Since there is so much controversie in the World," he writes in his major work, *The Bloudy Tenent*, "where the name of Christ is taken up, concerning the true Church . . . I aske who shall judge in this case, who be they that feare God?"[13] The lack of firm foundation for judgment, in turn, leads to a kind of paralysis when it comes to carrying out the responsibilities of the ministry: "I have no faith to act, nor in the Actings and Ministrings of others."[14]

From every angle, Williams attacks the ways in which ministers both foster and circumscribe the uncertainty surrounding spiritual experience. On the one hand, certain institutional practices lead him to doubt the validity of any claims to conversion because such claims may simply be the product of coercion or fear. On the other hand, while institutions may unintentionally lay the groundwork for uncertainty, they also limit the ways in which this uncertainty can be interpreted. Williams writes: "The most able, diligent and conscionable Readers must pluck forth their own eyes, and be forced to reade by the (which soever praedominant Claergies) Spectacles."[15] This amazing sentence suggests that the kind of reading—or more generally, interpretation—that takes place within institutions is not really reading at all; diligent and conscientious readers are forced to see everything through the eyes of the dominant clergy. Such institutions promote blindness (the plucking out of the eyes) while they promise clarity (the gesture of placing spectacles over the plucked-out eyes).

As a final cruel twist, the blindness is partially self-inflicted: "able, diligent and conscionable" readers must pluck forth their own eyes in order to survive in institutional settings. Although the image of plucking out one's own eyes no doubt suggests a kind of violence, institutional coercion of interpretation can also be much more subtle, especially if it capitalizes on an individual's desire for affiliation. A minister tells his congregation that true converts read the Bible in a certain way. Congregants adopt this reading and thereby persuade both themselves and the minister that conversion has taken place. The minister then persuades himself that he has accomplished God's great work of salvation, mostly because his own congregants have been telling him what he wants to hear. Trapped in this hall of mirrors is the individual and his or her relationship to institutions. Members of a community must affiliate with a church, by whatever means necessary, to have any standing (political, financial, social) in society at large. And ministers must believe they can convert people to justify their own institutional position and even to justify their migration to New England to themselves and to those who remained in England.

By exposing what he believes to be a dance of mutual deception, Williams effectively defines the ministry out of existence. Where Cotton believed that the "one maine intent and end of his [the minister's] Office is to make Disciples, and gather Saints,"[16] Williams sees little reason either to preach to convert or to preach to the converted: "All our professed Ministrations . . . have been carried on . . . for the converting of a converted people . . . how can we pretend to convert the converted, and to preach unto them to convert them? One or the other must be denied, to wit, that they are converted, or if unconverted, that we may offer up Christian and Spirituall Sacrifices with them."[17] If Williams challenges the "pretend Repentance" performed by the insincere convert, he also questions the other main actor in this performance: ministers who "pretend to convert the converted." If someone is already truly saved, then there is no further need for evangelical preaching, which is to say that there is no further need for evangelical ministers. If someone is not converted, then, according to Williams's strict absolutism, they should not be members of a church, taking part in "Christian and Spiritual Sacrifices," including listening to sermons. By thus claiming that ministers need not preach to the converted and should not preach to the unconverted, Williams effectively eliminates the apostolic role that Cotton cherished.[18]

Since a minister has no basis for making spiritual judgments, since he has no reason to preach for conversion, since, in short, he has no sound basis for taking action of any sort, toleration becomes the only acceptable position, even if that position is arrived at by default. In *The Bloudy Tenent*, Williams explains:

> [H]ow fearfull is that wound that no Balme in Gilead can cure? How dreadfull is that blindnesse which for ever to all eye-salve is uncurable? For if persons be wilfully and desparately obstinate (after light shining forth) let them alone saith the Lord . . . what more lamentable condition then when the Lord hath given a poor sinner over as a hopelesse patient, incurable, which we are wont to account a sorer affliction, then if a man were torne and rack'd. . . . I say that all are thus incurable, yet that sometimes that word is spoken by Christ to His Servants to be patient, for neither can corporall or spirituall Balme or Physicke ever heale or cure them.[19]

Yet again, Williams uses a conventional analogy for conversion: ministers are physicians ("soule physician" was a common phrase) who "cure" or "heal" wounded souls. Katherine Chidley, for example, argued that all souls could potentially be saved but the reason this did not happen was that many ministers failed to provide the proper care or cure for their congregants. Thus, she uses the language of healing to criticize ministerial sinecures (*sinecure*, without cure) and to demand more "universal fatherly care," in Filmer's terms. For Williams, the problem is not so much sinecures but incurable souls: some souls cannot be healed no matter how much attention or care they are given. Williams also uses the language of healing to criticize the ministry, but rather than demand more care, as did Chidley, he insists on less attention to the incurable—"let them alone," which has come to be regarded as his call for religious toleration. Ministers should cease trying to convert incurable souls because the cure in those cases is far worse than the disease: "The binding and rebinding of conscience, contrary or without its own perswasion, so weakens and defiles it, that it (as all other faculties) loseth its strength, and the very nature of a common honest conscience."[20] Toleration so conceived becomes a kind of spiritual euthanasia. What we must "tolerate" in the terminally ill, physically or spiritually, is not so much their right to die of an incurable disease (or in Williams's world, their right to be damned because unconvertible) but our own sense of helplessness at not being able to save them.

2. *Infallible Witness in Exile*

If ministers are without power and purpose, then what possible role remains for them in the establishment of churches? If the grounds of evaluation and judgment remain uncertain, then how is it possible for Williams so polemically to criticize the established ministry? That is, what kind of institutional affiliation does he imagine that allows him to judge their inability to judge? How is he able to interpret their misinterpretations? What authority does he have to question their authority? A passage from *The Hireling Ministry* provides the beginnings of an answer to these questions:

> Negatively, wherein they Witnessed against the False, against Usurpations and Abominations of Antichrist; and therein they were the *Infallible Witnesses*, and Prophets of Jesus Christ, Preaching and oft times Suffering to the Death for his Names sake. But View them in their Positive Practice and Worships, as they have assumed and pretended to such and such Ministries, and Titles, and Churches, and Ministrations, and there is not one of them, no not Calvin himself . . . but the Father of Lights, in our times of Light, hath been graciously pleased to discover their great mistakes, and wandrings from the first Patternes and Institutions of Christ Jesus.[21]

Any attempt, including those made by Calvin himself, to recover and institutionalize the "first Patternes and Institutions of Christ Jesus" is doomed to failure. Such attempts fail, in fact, precisely because they try to institutionalize ideals that should resist institutionalization. Truth should not be determined by committee, compromise, nor coercion—all elements of institutional life as Williams sees it.

Further, these truths should resist institutions themselves. Ministers are at their most effective when they play a negative role, when they criticize rather than join or establish institutions, when they serve as "Infallible Witnesses" against the "False, against Usurpations and Abominations of Antichrist." Williams insists that "all . . . that have knowledge & utterance of heavenly Mysteries, & therein are the Lords Prophets & Witnesses against Antichrist, must prophecy against false Worship, and Ministrations, false Hope, and false Heaven, which poor souls in a golden dream expect & look for."[22] To make one's own promises of "golden dreams" is, finally, to "send millions of soules to hell in a secure expectation of a false salvation."[23] Any knowledge of "heavenly Mysteries" and of the first church serves as a grounds for exposing false worship, but it cannot serve as grounds for actually establishing a true church because, in Williams's view, all institutions are inimical to truth.[24]

Nevertheless, criticism remains possible if one can imagine for oneself a place close enough to institutions to witness their errors but far away enough not to be directly affected by those errors. Thus, Williams represents himself as the perpetual exile, a role most clearly defined by the "infallible witness" in Revelation 11.[25] In that scriptural text, to which Williams frequently refers,[26] two infallible witnesses are described as men who stand outside the majority of society; they occupy a lowly station (they are clothed in sackcloth) and are spurned by most men. Yet God gives them great powers; they turn water into blood, and they smite the earth with plagues. The greatest power, though, is the power of prophetic witness: they give testimony that will "torment them that dwelt on the earth." For this testimony they are killed, but after three and a half days, God calls home his witnesses even as an earthquake destroys all nonbelievers.

Just as Solomon serves as a model for Cotton, the role of infallible witness in exile exemplifies for Williams many of the ideals and details of his own relationship to institutions.[27] He was both an outside insider and an inside outsider; that is, he had enormous access to power. From an early age he benefited from patronage; ironically, he was offered but refused the job of minister at the First Church of Boston, a post later filled by Cotton; he spoke several times before Parliament; and he led his own colony. Clearly, he was not as disenfranchised as many or even most members of Puritan New England, not even his fellow exile Anne Hutchinson. And yet Williams never seemed comfortable with authority, even less so with his own than with that of others. His actual banishment was a relatively unimportant factor in his assumption of the role of infallible witness. The banishment may have occasioned his rightful claim to the role, but it was really a role he had been rehearsing for most of his life. In a letter to John Winthrop written shortly after being banished, for example, Williams declares "To all his glorious name I know I have gained the honour of one of his poore witnesses, though in Sackcloth."[28]

Although he assumes this role of witness in exile, Williams does not reject all relationships to institutional authority. In fact, he condemns the Quakers for what he takes as their wholesale rejection of authority and tradition: "They [the Quakers] care no more for the Scriptures then the Papists do, they are forced to make use of them for an end, but all their hope is in their Interpretations, which both Papists and Quakers bend their utmost to secure, viz. the Privilege of Interpretation, and chair of infallibility to themselves, or else down they tumble, for most sure it is the Holy Scriptures, and both Papists and Quakers are at irreconciliable differences, if the one stand the other must fall for ever."[29] For Williams, Papists and Quakers represent opposite extremes with respect to institutional affiliation. One the one hand, the pope is the ultimate institutional man. He claims infallible authority based on direct succession from the apostles, and he is the one individual who speaks for the entire Catholic Church. On the other hand, the Quakers represent the ultimate in individualism. They reject all learned traditions and authority, and instead, by "this rule or rate of being immediately inspired in all they do or say transcend all other Teachers, Translators, Interpreters, Kings and Counsellors, Navigators, Historians, Geographers, Rulers, and Judges."[30]

The "privilege of interpretation"—the authority properly to read Scriptures and use these readings as a basis for judging false worship—belongs neither to an individual so closely affiliated with an institution that the two are synonymous (the pope, readers with their eyes plucked out) or to individuals who pretend to renounce institutional affiliations altogether (the Quakers). Stated in other terms, Williams rejects both the older conception of individualism (one that depends on close identification with institutions to gain authority) and the newer, emergent conception of individualism (one that claims an authority independent of institutional affiliations). Although he rejects both these extremes, unlike Cotton, he does not advocate a convergence of the two. Instead, he maintains a clear difference between the poles because it is precisely in this space between institutionalism and individualism that he locates the interpretive authority of the infallible witness. Seemingly exiled from institutionalism and individualism, Williams purchases a new perspective from which to criticize the limitations of each.

3. Persecution as Conversion

It is from this position of infallible witness in exile that Williams grounds one of his most famous criticisms of institutions, his arguments against persecution and for toleration. In *Yet More Bloudy*, Williams defines persecution as "civill corporall violence and punishment inflicted on the body for some spirituall and religious matter."[31] Persecution is an act of violence to the body (whippings, death) or a punishment inflicted on one's material well-being (imprisonment, disenfranchisement, banishment) committed by the state only in cases of religious conviction. Williams consistently argues elsewhere that the state should punish civil dissent in the name of keeping civic order. Williams also specifies what persecution is not: "I have never heard that disputing, discoursing and examining mens Tenets or Doctrines by the word of God was (in proper English acceptation of the word) persecution for conscience."[32] He excludes verbal attacks from his definition of persecution even if such attacks aim at religious beliefs.[33]

By this definition, Williams's dismissal of Jews, Catholics, and Turks as "false religions" and his attitude and actions toward the Quakers do not constitute persecution. Even though he writes a five-hundred-page treatise refuting what he deems to be the religious errors of the Quakers and even though he condemns them to hell, he nevertheless—in his capacity of civil leader—allows the Quakers to live in Rhode Island unharmed. While such reasoning never leads Williams to acts of persecution, it does assume, a priori, that he is in a position to persecute and that he simply chooses not to do so. In *The Bloudy Tenent of Persecution* he explicitly describes this position through the example of God's toleration for his errant children: "Although he [God] be of pure eyes, and can behold no iniquitie, yet his pure eyes patiently and quietly beholds and permits all the idolatries and prophanations, all the thefts and rapines, all the whoredomes and abominations, all the murthers and poysonings; and yet I say, for his glory sake he is patient and long permits."[34] The logic of toleration hinges on a series of crucial assumptions. First, to label something as idolatry, profanation, theft, abomination, and so on, that is to be tolerated, one needs some notion of right and wrong, truth and falsehood. This is not to suggest that all rationales for toleration require an absolute sense of right and wrong. One could, for example, tolerate all behavior (*a*) because it all makes equally valid claims to the truth or (*b*) because one does not believe in right or wrong. But in its use of the negative labels, this particular passage clearly suggests a strong conviction in absolute truth. Further, one must have confidence in one's abilities to discern the difference between truth and error—an ability here represented by God's "pure eyes." As well, one must assume that one has the power to take action on these judgments; to say that "I will patiently permit such errors to continue" is to assume that one has the authority to punish such behavior (as clearly God does, for Williams) if one so desired. And so Williams's representation of toleration here implicitly defines the tolerator as much as the tolerated: the tolerator possesses a firm conviction of absolute truth; with "pure eyes" he discerns any deviation from that truth, and with authority he decides whether or not to do anything about that deviation.

While Williams never openly declares himself to be in the position of

God, he often does assume the role of infallible witness and thereby arrogates to himself the privileged position of tolerator rather than the one to be tolerated.[35] In *The Bloudy Tenent of Persecution*, for example, he writes:

> [L]et it be seriously considered by such as plead for present corporall punishment, as conceiving that such sinner (though they breake not Civill peace) should not escape punishment, I say, let it be considered, though for the present their punishment is deferred, yet the punishment inflicted on them will be found to amount to an higher pitch then any corporall punishment in the World. . . .
>
> . . . [T]heir end is the Ditch, that bottomlesse pit of everlasting separation from the holy and sweet Presence of the Father of Lights, Goodnesse and Mercy it self, endlesse, easelesse, in extremity, universality, and eternity of torments, which most direfull and lamentable downefall, should strike an holy fear and trembling into all that see the Pit."[36]

In this passage and elsewhere, the arguments for toleration and against persecution are not based on some belief that everyone has the right to worship as they see fit, that all religions share equally valid claims to truth, or even that people should be allowed to make their own mistakes because they will come to see the light. Rather, Williams assumes that there is one true, absolute church and that all other forms of belief—Jewish, popish, Turkish, Quaker—constitute what he constantly calls "false religions." If egalitarianism plays a role in his toleration at all, it is only in his conviction that all other churches are "equally" deviant from the one true church. Further, he will take no steps to correct this deviance either directly by attempting to convert them or indirectly by persecuting them with the intent that they eventually join the true church.

In this formulation, then, toleration is simply persecution deferred. Williams argues for toleration not so much out of religious conviction (other than that he is convinced that he is right and others are wrong) but of political expediency: attempts to inflict corporal punishment for religious belief would lead to civil unrest and therefore should be avoided. But Williams does not then assume that the followers of "false religions" remain unpunished. Instead, he defers his inferior, corporal, earthly punishment to the superior, heavenly wrath of God: "the punishment inflicted on them will be found to amount to an higher pitch then any corporall punishment in the World." Since no earthly punishment could ever match eternal suffering in hell, followers of false religions should be "tolerated" because "their end is the Ditch." Whatever their earthly affiliations, they will be punished by Williams's God; they will burn in his hell.

Of course, Williams does not always speak from the dominant position of the tolerator. In fact, the claims to truth that ground his toleration of error in others also render Williams himself vulnerable to persecution. To assume the role of infallible witness is to put oneself, at once, in the dominant position of tolerating falsehood and in the subordinate position of being attacked for speaking the truth. Williams often points to the dualism of his role by stating that "the wicked are besiegers, the faithfull are besieged."[37] This phrase suggests that the act of persecution itself helps to discern the difference between the saved and the damned. Persecuting others is a good indication of a damned soul, while being persecuted most likely indicates salvation. Williams further explains:

> Gods people have used most to abound with godlinesse and honesty, when they have enjoyed least peace and quitenesse. Then like those spices, Cant. 4. Myrrhe, Frankincense, Saffron, Calamus, &c. they have yeelded the sweetest savour to God and man, when they were pounded and burnt in cruell persecution of the Romane Censors: then are they . . . most sweet when most hunted: Gods Stars shining brightest in the darkest night: more heavenly in conversation, more mortified: more abounding in love each to other, more longing to be with God: when the inhospitable and salvage World have used them like strangers, and forced them to hasten home to another Country which they professe to seeke."[38]

Williams does not quite argue that persecution guarantees truth—that is, if you are persecuted, then you must be telling the truth—but he does imply the converse: if you tell the truth, then you are likely to be persecuted for so doing. Yet rather than lament this close link between truth and persecution, the passage celebrates—almost romanticizes—suffering through its series of paired opposites: most godliness and honesty–least peace and quietness; most sweet–most hunted; brightest–darkest. These pairings suggest that while God may see and know absolute truth in its positive aspects, man can recognize such truth only by the attempts to negate it. Thus, the faithful depend on continued differences with and difference between themselves and those who persecute them. These differences, in effect, legitimate their claims to truth to themselves and to the world. Williams also emphasizes the degree of difference with his series of intensifiers: most sweet when most hunted, brightest in the darkest night. Truth defined by difference works proportionally; the greater the difference or distance between persecuted and persecutor, the stronger and clearer become the faithfuls' claim to truth.

Williams's claim to absolute truth, then, depends on a sustained emphasis on difference that manifests itself in the form of persecution. The need for this process to continue may help explain the fact that Williams seems never to stop representing himself as persecuted, even though he enjoyed a considerable amount of power and privilege in both Old and New England.

Just as he needs to ensure his claims to toleration by being around those whom he must tolerate, so too he secures his status as "the persecuted" by remaining in close contact with those individuals and institutions who had persecuted him. Thus, an odd dynamic informs his lifelong relationship with the leadership of the Bay Colony after they had formally banished him. Although he continues to work with and for Winthrop and others, he seems to do so not to redeem himself, not to rejoin them, but to remind himself and everyone else that, despite the fact that the elders kicked him out, he continues to serve them; and despite his continued service, they continue to punish him. He so strongly identifies himself by means of this relationship to the Bay Colony that he signs the prefatory letter to *Yet More Bloudy* (addressed to the Massachusetts General Court) as "your so long despised Out-cast."[39] And thirty-five years after his banishment he writes of his fourteen-week trek in the winter wilderness as if it happened yesterday: "And surely between those my Friends of the Bay and Plymmouth I was sorely tost for one 14 weekes (in a bitter Winter Season) not knowing what Bread or Bed did meane. . . . It lies upon the Massachus. and me, yea and other Colonies, joyning with them to examine (with feare and trembling before the eys of the flaming Fire) the true Cause of all my Sorrows and Suffrings."[40] By anyone's measure, Williams was never without power. He ran his own colony and had the ear of the top-ranked leaders in Old and New England; he was not a slave, a servant, or a woman. Yet he never stopped thinking about himself as one of the disenfranchised.

If Williams sees conversion as a kind of persecution, it is also possible to see Williams's own depiction of persecution as a form of conversion. Both processes seem to point to a clearly defined end: the point of arguments against persecution would be to end persecution, and the point of the rhetoric of conversion would be to convert souls. But in both Cotton's depiction of conversion and Williams's depiction of persecution we've seen a sense of incompleteness, the feeling that these processes could never—or should never—come to a definite end. Cotton describes conversion as a "continued act" and uses the language of hungering and longing to suggest that the desire for grace, like the desire for food or sex, can be momentarily quenched but never fully sated. And as we've just seen, Williams seems equally invested in perpetuating his role as the persecuted.

Why foster a sense of an ending without ever offering actual completion, especially when both processes seem worth completing? Both conversion and persecution confer a special sanctified status on the converted and persecuted, respectively. If these processes were to end, Cotton and Williams would be forced to find new ways to justify their claims to grace, indeed, to find new narratives in which to locate their identities as religious men. Simply put, who would Cotton be if everyone was finally converted? At best, he would have to become a pastoral rather than an apostolic minister. But to do so would make his entire career up to that point—a career devoted to working out the intricacies of conversion—redundant or beside the point. Likewise, who would Williams be if he were accepted into (or could accept) a secure place in the Bay Colony? He too would have to reimagine his place in the world. So the motivation becomes to sustain the narratives that legitimate and even sanctify one's authority: for Cotton, the narrative of sin and redemption best exemplified by Solomon; for Williams, the narrative of persecution and exile best exemplified by the infallible witness from Revelation.

Both conversion and persecution also depend on difference in that they posit a gap or a distance that both joins and separates the converted and the unconverted, the persecuted and the persecutors. While Cotton clearly emphasizes resemblances (in his definition of metaphor, in his use of the *imitatio Christi*, in his construction of individuality), he grows increasingly aware of the importance of difference, as we shall see in chapter 5. Williams not only objects to Cotton's efforts to erase difference (most obviously in his arguments against conversion) but also takes steps to enforce difference. That is, while he remains justifiably suspicious of any effort to close the gap between saint and sinner, he nevertheless calls attention to this gap because it is precisely this difference that marks him as one of the saved. If he, as one of the persecuted, is "most sweet when most hunted," then he needs to preserve the distinction between hunter and hunted. He clearly does not want to be caught, and he clearly will not become a hunter himself, but he also depends on this antagonism to define his role. Similarly, he cannot claim to be tolerant unless he is in the presence of someone to be tolerated. Hence, he does not see the presence of those with whom he strongly disagrees (the Quakers, for example) as an opportunity for change, to work out or celebrate differences or to reach some common ground. Instead, he loudly calls attention to these disagreements, thereby increasing the sense of distance and difference. In so doing, he strengthens his sense of rightness in his own convictions and confirms his sanctified status as the tolerant one.

Both conversion and persecution, then, aim at sanctification by way of resemblances and differences, but neither one ever quite arrives there. Moreover, they take exactly opposite routes. Cotton defines truth as a positive presence: you can see and feel the workings of Christ in the world (although not quite a millenialist, he believed in the second coming more strongly than Williams did);[41] you can imitate these behaviors by way of conversion; you can discern the difference between hypocrites and true believers; you can establish the true church on earth. Williams, who perhaps is even more zealous about absolutes, nevertheless depicts truth as a negative absence: you cannot convert people to be like Christ; you witness truth only in negation, in the persecution of the faithful; and you know the true church only by its absence, through the failed attempts to institutionalize the first church on earth. Cotton's open declarations of principle ("I am converted," "You are converted," "This is the true church") leave him vulnerable to attack; he can never live up to the expectations his own rhetoric inspires. Williams is more reluctant to declare his principles openly. Instead, his own convictions motivate but remain implicit in his criticism of the open declarations of others. Any attempt to criticize or to negate Williams's arguments only further confirms his sanctified status. The more one disagrees with him, the more one proves his claim that the "faithful are besieged."

4. *Separation of Church and State Reconsidered*

Williams's famous arguments for the separation of church and state can be read as part of his effort to figure out proper relationships between institutions and individuals and between one institution and another. Throughout his career he remains determined to create and protect a place from which the infallible witness can speak the absolute truth, a place that stands outside of Politics (the workings of the state) and politics (the machinations of influence and coercion in both church and state). At the foundation of all of Williams's thought lies the conviction that truth cannot be institutionally determined, whatever the merits of any individual institution: "I should never use an Argument from the Number of Princes (no more then from the Number of any other men) for any truth of Christ Jesus," and more succinctly, "Successe doth not prove causes true."[42] Politically determined truth, then, is not truth at all.

Williams may reject the link between politics and truth because truth created by politics can also be destroyed by politics. He registers this observation in a brief narrative of England's ever-changing religious and political leadership:

> . . . our native Soyle, within a few score of yeeres, how many wonderfull changes in Religion hath the whole Kingdome made, according to the change of the Governours thereof, in the severall Religions which they themselves embraced! Henry the 7 finds and leaves the kingdome absolutely Popish. Henry the 8 casts it into a mould half Popish halfe Protestant. Edward the 6 brings forth an Edition all Protestant. Queene Mary within few yeares defaceth Edwards worke, and renders the Kingdome (after her Grandfather Hen. 7 his pattern) all Popish. Maries short life and Religion ends together: and Elizabeth reviveth her Brother Edwards Modell, all Protestant.[43]

Williams describes changes of religion brought about by contingency, not conviction. He is clearly aware that such changes are transitory (like the weather vane shifting in the wind), but he seems reluctant to submit to the terms of this game because any victory would be equally transitory.

Since Williams clearly did not hide from political or religious controversy, his call for separation of church and state could never be mistaken for a nostalgic desire to return to the days of monks and monasteries. It should also not be mistaken as an effort to diminish the power of the church (as those who see Williams as a forerunner of the Establishment Clause of the U.S. Constitution often claim) or of the state. Williams argues for separation, not so much to protect church from state or to protect state from church but rather to preserve the unique powers of both. Insofar as such arguments are meant to strengthen what is weak or broken, Williams advocates using the right tool for the right job: "To batter downe a strong hold, high wall, fort, tower or castle, men bring not a first and second Admonition, and after obstinacie, Excommunication, which are Spirituall weapons concerning them that be in the Church. . . . But to take a strong hold, men bring Canons, Culverins, Saker, Bullets, Powder, Musquets, Swords, Pikes, &c. and these to this end are weapons effectuall and proportionable."[44] We've already seen a version of this argument in Williams's rejection of the use of political means to achieve spiritual ends. He now adds to this claim the converse proposition: it is equally wrong to use spiritual means to achieve political ends. In both instances, Williams does not base his argument exclusively (or even primarily) on moral or ethical grounds—that it is fundamentally wrong to mix ends and means. Instead, a kind of pragmatism motivates these arguments. One does not use political force to convert people because such force is ineffective; it does not yield the desired results, in this case, true converts. Likewise, spiritual weapons are ineffective in political battle; admonitions are no match for muskets.[45]

Joining church and state, then, leads to bad politics as well as bad religion; it is a "Church-destroying and State-Destroying Doctrine."[46] Separating them preserves the unique powers of each realm precisely by acknowledging the limitations and differences between these powers. Ministers, for example, act most effectively as infallible witnesses when they are least under the power of state authority. For a minister to act as a politician is to dilute, if not surrender, his status as a witness with the privilege of interpretation. In the end, Williams suggests that one cannot mount a truly effective critique of politics if one cannot imagine oneself in a realm outside politics.[47]

Williams's arguments for separation of church and state could be challenged in terms that he himself establishes elsewhere in his writings. For example, if a minister does act as witness and offers political criticism, hasn't that minister himself violated the separation of religious and political issues? Or why should anyone bear witness to falsehood of any kind if Williams has no hope of changing people (his anticonversion arguments) or of establishing pure or true institutions on earth? Perhaps the most interesting problem with these arguments rests in the easy assumption that religious and political issues can be kept separate in the first place. This assumption is especially interesting since it is made during a time when both a regicide and a civil war take place at least partly in the name of religious affiliations. And yet Williams insists that religious causes need not have political effects: "I dare not assent to that assertion, that even originall sinne remotely hurts the civill State."[48] For Williams, religious affiliation has little to do with political conduct; the worst sinners could still make good citizens: "And I aske whether or no such as may hold forth other Worships or Religions, (Jewes, Turkes, or Antichristians) may not be peaceable and quiet Subjects, loving and helpfull neighbours, faire and just dealers, true and loyall to the civill government?"[49]

Roger Williams's concern with hypocrisy—with the difference between performance and essence—runs so deep that he all but dismisses the possibility of genuine conversion. At the same time, he insists that there must be a difference between the spiritual self and the political self—even a Turk could be a good English citizen. It is precisely this ability of the self to differ from itself that enables hypocrisy: the political self may fake a spiritual self solely for political advancement. Paradoxically, it is also this difference that allows for the exposure of hypocrisy: the infallible witness who separates political expediency from spiritual truths and thereby is able to testify against false worship. Individual identity for Williams, then, is never continuous in hypocrites or true believers. Like the hypocrite, the true believer recognizes the differences within himself, the power to feign and perform. But rather than exploit this power for personal gain (especially vis-à-vis institutions) or rather than conflate, deny, or ignore the difference, the true believer works to enforce those differences within himself and within society at large. Thus, Williams insists on protecting the absolute purity of a spiritual self; he works to continue, rather than put an end to, the circumstances that create opportunities for toleration and persecution. And he argues to preserve a separate space from which to criticize falsehood, a criticism that through its very recognition of difference ultimately strengthens both individuals and institutions.

For John Cotton, affiliation serves as a form of criticism (at least insofar as we think of criticism in terms of its Greek roots: *kritikos*, skilled in judging). Choosing an institution with which to affiliate involves a series of value judgments; one's final choice also implies a rejection of other possible choices. Thus, Cotton values the practices of New England Congregationalism for themselves and also because they are not the practices of the Church of England or of Catholicism. For Williams, criticism constitutes a form of affiliation. To evaluate all institutions in the way Williams does, one must be engaged enough to know what's going on and to gain an audience yet detached enough to avoid having one's eyes plucked out. Although he remains resolutely detached from and critical of institutions in his role of infallible witness, Williams also remains highly dependent on institutions for the very grounds of his criticism, the very foundation of his role.

4

The Case of Anne Hutchinson

At the very beginning of her civil trial, Anne Hutchinson asks John Winthrop, "What law have I broken?" Winthrop at first responds rather matter-of-factly, "Why the fifth commandment," but Hutchinson wants to investigate further the charges leveled against herself and her followers:

H: What law do they transgress?
W: The law of God and of the state.
H: In what particular?
W: Why in this among the rest, whereas the Lord doth say honour thy father and thy mother.
H: Ey Sir in the Lord.
W: This honour you have broken in giving countenance to them.

. . . .

W: You have councelled them.
H: Wherein?
W: In entertaining them.
H: What breach of law is that Sir?
W: Why dishonouring of parents.
H: But put the case Sir that I do fear the Lord and my parents, may not I entertain them that fear the Lord because my parents will not give me leave?
W: If they be the fathers of the commonwealth, and they of another religion, if you entertain them then you dishonour your parents and are justly punishable.
H: If I entertain them, as they have dishonoured their parents, I do.
W: No but you by countenancing them above other put honor upon them.
H: I may put honour upon them as the children of God and as they do honor the Lord.
W: We do not mean to discourse with those of your sex but only this; you

do adhere unto them and do endeavour to set forward this faction and so you do dishonour us.

H: I do acknowledge no such thing neither do I think that I ever put any dishonour upon you.[1]

Hutchinson's questioning cuts to the core of a major problem with the family analogy. For the analogy to work in the way that the Puritans want it to work, there must be consistency within institutions and also consistency between institutions. The law of the state, for example, should be consistent with the law of the church, and all of the leaders within a given church should be giving their members a coherent set of rules. If the Fifth Commandment is to be applied to all paternal terms in the family analogy (fathers biological, ministerial, magisterial), then all of these fathers must resemble each other.

It is precisely the difference between fathers that creates problems for Hutchinson. If the fathers fail to provide coherent guidance—if, for example, the religion of the biological father contradicts the religion of the state or if the doctrine of one minister teaches something different from the doctrine of another minister—then which father does she follow without violating the Fifth Commandment?[2] Should she, for example, remain loyal to the example of her own father, Francis Marbury, a reform-minded minister in England? Or should her allegiance be to her family at large, including her brother-in-law, John Wheelwright, a minister who was convicted of sedition for his "antinomian" leanings? Or perhaps she should follow the teachings of the ministers—but which ministers? To obey Cotton is, to a certain extent, to disobey Shepard. Or perhaps honor belongs only to God: the First Commandment trumps the Fifth Commandment in case of a tie between fathers. But it is exactly her professed allegiance to God (through immediate revelation) that results in her banishment and excommunication.

Hutchinson finds herself in a conundrum: damned if she does, damned if she doesn't; obedience to family, church, and state results in the charge that she has disobeyed family, church, and state. And this very act of disobedience brings dishonor even to the fathers whom she does obey. One way out of the bind would be to make the difference between fathers vanish by way of conversion, which is essentially what Cotton does when he replaces old fathers with next fathers. There is no danger of conflict if the differing fathers have disappeared. Hutchinson tries to compensate for difference by pointing out contradictions—between ministers who preach a covenant of works and those who preach a covenant of grace, between one set of fathers and another. By thus pointing out inconsistencies, she implicitly demands consistency. And if the fathers refuse to coordinate, then she can at least force them to tell her which one she must follow. Winthrop begins with a general charge (you have violated the Fifth Commandment), moves to slightly more detailed charges (the law of God and state, dishonoring parents), and concludes with his most specific charge: "You do dishonour us"—not God, not the king, not Cotton, not Mr. Marbury, but *me*, John Winthrop, and my colleagues on the General Court. These, finally, are the fathers she must obey.

1. Be a Man

Despite our general impression of them as a monolithic patriarchy, Puritan leaders were anything but ideal in meeting expectations for consistent and coherent leadership. It is precisely this lack of consistency or coherency, not its overabundance, that creates problems for any individual attempting to derive an identity through affiliation with authority. If authorities keep changing their roles and their rules, then the individual must also reconceive the nature of his or her affiliation with those authorities. Whether these changes happen intentionally or not, one always runs the risk of playing by the old rules when the new rules are in place. Stated in gendered terms, in the eyes of the church elders, Hutchinson clearly fails to live up to their expectations of what it means to "be a woman." Hugh Peter's infamous charges against her—"You have rather bine a Husband than a Wife and a preacher than a Hearer"—attest to this claim.[3] At the same time, the church elders failed to live up to the expectations Hutchinson had for them as authority figures, as spiritual and civic leaders, as men.

During Hutchinson's trials, for example, it is evident that ministers remain at least partly accountable for the actions of wayward congregants. For this reason the Massachusetts General Court turns to John Cotton for an explanation of Anne Hutchinson's behavior and beliefs.[4] In response, he provisionally admits that her "erroneous opinions" are his fault: "I confesse I did not know that you held any of thease Things nor heare till hear of late. But it may be my sleepiness and want of watchfull care over you."[5] In the first sentence of this quotation, Cotton simply attempts to distance himself from the accused, a teacher unaware that his student has misunderstood her lessons. But the second sentence admits the obligation of continued engagement; if he was not aware of Hutchinson's mistakes, Cotton says, he should have been aware simply by virtue of the union between minister and congregant. His "watcfull care over you" recalls Filmer's demand for "universal fatherly care" and Chidley's lament about sinecure, the absence of care. Cotton has failed to play the role established for him in terms of both the family analogy and the Puritan reform of the clergy.[6]

Cotton registers a sense of this failure in a series of sermons on Ecclesiastes delivered shortly after Hutchinson's trials. In these sermons, Cotton explicitly notes a parallel between Solomon, who had been led astray by the luxuries of seductive women, and the leaders of the Bay Colony who had been seduced into error by Anne Hutchinson. He places blame not only, not even primarily, on the seductive women and on Hutchinson but also on Solomon and the church elders for failing to exercise properly their authority as wise leaders, as wise men: "Which yet my soul seeketh, but I finde not: one man among a thousand have I found. [Cotton then cites 1 Corinthians 16:13: "Watch ye, stand fast in the faith, quit you like men, be strong."] . . . There is a great scarcity of men (worthy the name of men, or quitting themselves like men) . . . [with] priestly wisdome, courage, zeal, faithfulnesse."[7] Men have failed to "quit themselves like men" not only in their failure to control Hutchinson but also in their reluctance to stand up to Solomon's follies. They were not "man enough" to confront their leader, and because of their abandonment of duties the whole chain of command becomes unlinked.

For the family analogy to work as a basis for authority, then, consistency must be retained within gendered roles (men must behave like men), and difference must be maintained between gendered roles (men must not behave like women). This failure of one gender to live up to the expectations of the other plays a decisive role in the Antinomian Controversy, although it is by no means unique to it.[8] For example, controversy over gender roles gets played out in Renaissance England in the debates about stage performances and cross-dressing. In 1620 two anonymous pamphlets (*Haec-Vir*, or the female man, and *Hic-Mulier*, or the male woman) observe that too many men are acting and dressing like women, both on and off stage.[9] The author of *Haec-Vir* warns men that "if you walk without difference, you shall live without reverence: if you will contemne order, you must indure the shame of disorder; and if you will have no rulers but your wills, you must have no reward but disdaine and disgrace."[10] Although the pamphlets are somewhat parodic, this particular sentiment—walking without difference, living without reverence—could have been thought (if not written) by Winthrop or Cotton in dead earnestness. If men fail to acknowledge the difference between their roles and the roles of women, the result will be a double irreverence. They fail to pay reverence to God and the divinely sanctioned role he has ordained for them, and they will also live without the reverence of females because they (the men) are not behaving "like men." This lack of reverence is the same kind of disorder feared by Hutchinson's opponents.

By ignoring or even abandoning the differences between male and female roles, men will consistently fail to live up to the demands and expectations of their own unique role. The writer of *Haec-Vir* continues in this vein: "For this you have demolished the noble schooles of hors-manship

. . . hung up your armes to rust, glued up those swords in their scabberds that would shake all Christendome with the brandish, and entertained into your mindes such softnes, dulnesse, and effeminate nicenesse, that it would even make Heraclitus himselfe laugh against his nature to see how pulingly you languish in this weake entertained sinne of wommanish softnesse."[11] Men have neglected their cultural roles and especially their sexual roles; they have hung up their arms to rust, and their "swords" are glued in their "scabberds." In the satiric spirit of the pamphlets, this line could be read in several ways: either *(a)* men are not having sex with women any more or *(b)* men's "swords" are permanently stuck in one "scabberd" (related to the Latin for vagina), which may still suggest an unnatural attachment to women, a lack of virility. This rejection of masculine roles coupled with the usurpation of female roles—"You have gone a world further and even ravisht from us our speech, our actions, sports and recreations"[12]—results in "effeminate nicenesse" and "wommanish softnesse."[13]

In the New England colonies the concern over such feminine luxuries takes many forms, including a sumptuary law passed in 1634 (a year or so before Hutchinson was brought to trial) banning luxurious clothing: "[Because of the] greate, suplfluous and unnecessary expences occasioned by reason of some new and immodest fashions . . . no person, either man or woman, shall hereafter make or buy any apparell, either wollen, silk, or lynnen, with any lace on it, silver, gold, silk, or thread, under penalty of forfeiture of such clothes."[14] Although the law specifically mentions financial reasons for the ban on "immodest fashions," it also points to a general suspicion of luxury as too feminine or not masculine enough. This suspicion also manifests itself in critiques of certain styles of rhetoric thought to be too luxurious and too feminine.[15] Cotton himself exhorts young ministers: "Look that your Seed be Spirituall, that is, the pure Word dispensed in the Spirit and Power, mingle no Traditions or Tricks of your wit with it, if you doe, your Seed is corrupt, and wants vigour, a velvet scabbard dulls the edge of the Sword, so the Word deckt over with Human Eloquence is like a Sword in a velvet scabbard, it hinders the power of it."[16] Although Cotton uttered these sentiments well before the Hutchinson trials, they nicely encapsulate his thinking about rhetoric and gender during the 1630s and 1640s. The word of God is figured as male, as "seed" to be sown into the congregation. Cotton also echoes *Haec-Vir*: if swords (actual swords, phallic swords, verbal swords) are kept in their scabbards (actual scabbards, genital scabbards, rhetorical scabbards), then they lose their power. A preoccupation with feminine things, then, causes men to "lose their edge" as men; even their seed becomes less vigorous, which, as we will see shortly, could lead to the fathering of monstrous births.

To solve the problem of walking without difference, the writer of *Haec-*

Vir demands that men resume their culturally and divinely sanctioned roles: "Cast then from you our ornaments, and put on your owne armours: Be men in shape, men in shew, men in words, men in actions, men in counsell, men in example: then we will love and serve you; then will wee heare and obey you."[17] We've already seen this logic in Winthrop and Cotton and will see it even in Hutchinson. Only if men will "be men" and only if men "be men" consistently in all of their behavior will women then be willing and able to fulfill their culturally and divinely sanctioned roles as women: they will love and serve, hear and obey. The terms of the contract are thus stated: if you (men) behave as men, then we (women) will behave as women, not only because we are negotiating a deal, but also—given that gender roles are defined by difference—because we cannot behave "like women" unless you behave "like men."

The activity of the Massachusetts General Court around the years of the Antinomian Controversy reflects this desire to put men back in their place.[18] Many of the court cases attempt to ensure that men carry out their responsibilities. William Wake, for example, was "councelled to go home to his wife." John Vaughan, having "defiled" a woman and refused to marry her, was committed to prison until he "should give sufficient security to provide both for the mother and the child, or marry her whom hee hath defiled." And James Luxford, having been found to have two wives, was forced to return from England (where apparently he had fled) to have the most recent marriage declared null and void, to find that "all that he hath" had been "appointed to his last [i.e., first] wife and children," and to be "fined and set in the stocks."[19] If a man would not or could not perform his duty, the court would step in as a replacement; in effect, one version of the father/husband would be exchanged for another. When John Stanley died intestate, for example, the court ordered his brother to raise his son. Similarly, the court ordered money for the maintenance of the widow Bosworth and her family.[20] Although my own survey of the court records covers only the ten or so years around the Antinomian Controversy (roughly 1630 to 1640), Mary Beth Norton's extensive research points to similar conclusions. "Men were frequently haled into court," she writes, "to face charges of failing to fulfill their communal duties."[21]

This anxiousness to keep men and women in their respective places is seen even in the slanders used against Hutchinson and her followers. The "antinomians" never labeled themselves as such; it was a slanderous term used by their opponents to underscore perceived transgressions of the law. The term "familist" was used more frequently than "antinomian" mainly because it hinted at the suspicion that this group engaged in the practice of multiple marriages. It was suspected that the familists violated the terms of the marriage covenant and thus of all the other covenants linked to it by way of the family analogy. This logic leads Cotton to predict that Hutchinson, because of her thinking on covenant theology, will eventually commit adultery; "though I have not herd, nayther do I thinke, you have bine unfaythfull to your Husband in his Marriage Covenant, yet that will follow upon it."[22] Although by "husband," Cotton no doubt literally refers to Mr. Hutchinson, the term could also analogically encompass Christ, the magistrates, and even Cotton himself in the role of minister-as-husband.

Acts of adultery, literal and analogical, affect more than just two people in one marriage; the transgression threatens to unravel a system that depends, in so many ways, on union and resemblance. The system works only if all of the "husbands" resemble Christ and in so doing resemble one another as well. The resemblance can be breached if either husband or wife introduces difference in any form; hence the fear of hypocrisy that we have already discussed and hence the absolute demand for consistency between authorities and Christ and between and among all earthly authorities. If one version of the husband or father differs from another, the system breaks down. This need for coherent resemblance in the family analogy may also help to explain why actual adultery was made a crime punishable by death (although, interestingly, adultery was more often punished by "symbolic" death; offenders were made to wear nooses around their necks in public but they were not actually hanged).[23] This fear of the implications of adultery may also help to explain what to us looks like an extremely irrational reaction to the "monstrous births" of Hutchinson and Mary Dyer. As we will soon discuss in greater detail, such births were considered to be a product of adultery because the legitimate father (the instrumental cause of childbirth) had been replaced by someone or something else: a monster, Satan, or even an idolatrous image that the mother had stared at longingly.[24] If the resemblance between father and child is already a tenuous one, then all resemblance breaks down when the child is not even thought to be "human."

2. *Passive Activity: Antinomianism and the Question of Agency*

The theological debates central to the Antinomian Controversy could also be plotted on the graph of actives and passives. On the one hand, Hutchinson could be viewed as actively seeking to participate in the responsibilities and authority of men: she wants to open Scripture, she wants to preach, she wants to lead a band of followers.[25] On the other hand, her extreme dependence on the covenant of grace suggests an inclination toward passivity and submission: she herself can do nothing; God must do it all for her. Indeed, there is an equally strong element of passivity and dependence, not just for Hutchinson but for all Puritans devoted to the idea of regeneration. All converts (male or female) play a female role—metaphorically as bride of Christ, theologically as empty vessels for grace, even politically as colonies of England.[26] In turn, this understanding of conversion influences the Puritan conception of human agency: what human beings can and cannot do for and by themselves. To emphasize this passivity, however, is not to negate the role of action in Puritan thought; it is rather to restore a tension between actives and passives that informs so much of what happens in Puritanism. We've already seen it in the debates about the covenant: do we make the choice to enter a covenant with God? Must we first be chosen by God to enter this covenant? Does God choose us and then allow us to decide?

The play between actives and passives is not, of course, unique to Puritanism. John Donne, in a sermon preached before the king at Whitehall, puns on the theological and grammatical meanings of active and passive: "The Devil's grammar is to apply Actives into Passives: where he sees an inclination, to subminister temptation. . . . And God's grammar is to change Actives into Passives: where a man delights in cursing, to make that man accursed."[27] The temptation of the Devil's grammar resides not so much in the object itself but in the deception that the soul can act to obtain the object; in short, that human beings have the agency to fulfill their own desires. God's grammar turns actives into passives and subjects into objects. The soul no longer does; rather, it is done to, it becomes the passive object of God's active subjection. Even though Cotton talks so much about the soul's inclinations and desires (in hungering and longing after Christ), these actions could still be parsed according to God's grammar. Such desires come from God acting on the soul as object (i.e., he moves the soul to long for Christ), not from the soul actively working by its own volition.

Conversion has a logic—actually several logics—to accompany its rhetoric and grammar. In fact, one could read the Antinomian Controversy as an extended debate—tried out through Hutchinson but not unique to her—about the proper logic of conversion.[28] Most of the members of the Massachusetts General Court that put Hutchinson on trial, especially Thomas Shepard and Peter Bulkeley, emphasized the active role of human agency although certainly never to the exclusion of the primary role played by God. For them, salvation follows a practical syllogism whose minor premise places a great emphasis on human agency:

Major Premise: God will save me if I believe in Scripture and behave in a godly way.
Minor Premise: I believe in Scripture and behave in a godly way.
Conclusion: I am saved.

Salvation still and always comes from God, but here it is premised on conditions that human beings have some control over. By suggesting that human beings could find evidence of their justification in their own thoughts, behaviors, and actions, ministers such as Shepard and Bulkeley display a relatively high amount of trust in the individual's ability to look inward and scrutinize his or her own motives. Some ministers, most notably Cotton, feared that this emphasis on good works as evidence of salvation would be mistaken for good works as a means to salvation, thereby undermining one of the first principles of reform theology: justification by faith alone. By emphasizing the conditional nature of salvation and the role that human agency plays in meeting those conditions, Cotton worried that good works could be read as a cause rather than an effect of salvation. Such an interpretation, taken to the extreme, places altogether too much power in the hands of individuals to affect the state of their own souls.

Cotton shifts emphasis by insisting that God's free gift of salvation, not any act of human agency, must be the cause of salvation. This logic even excludes the ability to scrutinize the inward workings of the soul as evidence of conversion because, as we have seen several times, it is impossible to "discern the difference" between salvation and its mere appearance unless you are already converted. He writes of the apostles, for example: "that unless the Spirit of God set in and clear up the truth and power and grace of God in all those reasonings, their souls will not be able to gather clear of their estates from all they hear."[29] Cotton thus proposes the following logic: the first cause of salvation, as always, is God. The efficient or instrumental cause (that which makes something happen) is the spirit of God; the formal cause (that into which something changes) is the image of Christ (recall how conversion transforms the individual by way of the *imitatio Christi*), and the material cause (the "stuff" upon which a change is wrought) is the "humbled sinner."[30] In this logic, human agency can never be the condition upon which salvation is premised. The human soul is merely the matter—the passive object to which something happens but not the active agent that makes something happen. The human as object cannot even read evidence of its own change; it must instead depend on immediate revelation of its own salvation.[31]

Again, the differences between Cotton and Shepard (which to us may seem so fine as to be nonexistent) are largely a matter of the degree of emphasis each one places on the role of human agency in salvation. This difference can be analyzed along the axes of active and passive, but it would be a grave error to assume that Shepard exclusively advocates active agency while Cotton describes, somewhat oxymoronically, a passive agency. Both ministers keep both ideas suspended in tension—the difference becomes most evident when the ministers are compared to each other—and the balance may shift at any given movement. Cotton himself, for example, never quite articulated a stable position on the question, either over the long haul of his career or during the specific moment of the Hutchinson trials. In fact, very early in his career he was charged with Arminianism, a belief (in the terms we've been using) that ascribes a relatively large role to human agency. In an early English sermon (delivered in the 1620s), Cotton writes: "Go out of your selves, and lay hold on Christ."[32] The active verb construction—with "Christ," not "you," as the object of the action—violates the rules of God's grammar.[33]

About fifteen years later, in New England, Cotton translates the sentence into a logic and grammar more consistent with those he holds during the Hutchinson trials: "If we give up our selves unto the Lord, it is because the Lord hath taken hold upon our hearts first."[34] If we can lay hold of Christ, it is only because he has taken hold of us first, thereby enabling us to act as if we were our own agents of salvation. But in truth, even this act of surrender or submission—the equivalent of the wife submitting to her choice of husband—is not based on genuine human agency. In effect, we cannot surrender our own agency because we lack even the agency to surrender. Instead, in language to which Williams objects, we are "taken." Cotton emphasizes this language of passivity during the Antinomian Controversy: "There is a Recyving, to wit, a Passive Reception . . . in that wee are Rejoyced as Paul saith, I am apprehended (that is, taken hold of, and receyved) by Christ Jesus. . . . In this union, the Soule Receyveth Christ, as an empty vessell receyveth oyle: but this receyving is not active, but passive."[35] This passage exemplifies almost all of the elements of Cotton's portrayal of salvation: the emphasis on passivity, the marriage analogy (union with Christ), the convert in a female role (empty vessel receiving oil), and the erotic desire.

Each of these elements, although clearly emphasizing submission and dependence, nevertheless points to a kind of passive activity. Hungering and longing, for example, are premised on a desire that has not and cannot be fulfilled by one's own means. In fact, one does not even actually hunger and long by one's own means; one is made to hunger for Christ by Christ. And yet, while hungering may not be as active an activity as eating and drinking, it does not suggest that the hopeful convert does absolutely nothing. Hungering for Christ is analogous to waiting for a subway train: one anxiously anticipates the arrival of both, and while this anticipation does absolutely nothing to make Christ or the train arrive, it does imply a faith that there is something worth waiting for and that this something will at some point actually show up. Although relatively passive, then, hungering and waiting are not equivalent to the indifference of not knowing, not caring, or not believing that the train/Christ will arrive.

Immediate revelation works the same way. Hutchinson's claim that she had learned of the Bay Colony's imminent destruction "by immediate revelation" often gets read as a turning point in her trials because she seems to be claiming interpretive authority for herself.[36] That is, she looks inward and depends on a private understanding of Scripture and events to authenticate her claims. This reading of immediate revelation, however, is inconsistent with the debates between Shepard and Cotton, debates in which Hutchinson clearly sides with Cotton and against Shepard. It is Shepard, not Cotton, who believes in the validity of evidence derived from self-scrutiny. Hutchinson, following Cotton, would most likely believe that a turn to "the self" as authority would be a turn to a covenant of works. And after salvation, there is no independent self upon which to rely; the self becomes abjectly dependent on God and is, in effect, replaced with an image of Christ. Hutchinson's claim to immediacy should therefore not be mistaken for personal intimacy. By lack of mediation she means, most likely, that no intermediary—Scripture, minister, prayer, language, and her own thoughts—delivered the revelation from God.

So conceived, immediate revelation can be considered another passive activity premised on belief and expectation: the belief that there is a God who reveals truths to human beings, the expectation that you may be one of those human beings. Hutchinson does not claim actively to reveal anything about herself as an interpretive authority. Nor does she claim to be celebrating her own private inspiration; revelation for her did not mean some Romantic idea of imagination, creativity, or genius.[37] Instead, she claims that God revealed a universal, eternal, absolute, and unchanging truth *to* her. In this context, the word *revelation* suggests (as its etymological link to *apocalypse* also implies) an uncovering or discovery of truth from above, not a self-discovery of truth from within. Hutchinson's stance here recalls, to a certain extent, Williams's role of witness: the "action" derives from the passive reception of truth but not the active creation of truth.

Perhaps the court reacted so strongly against Hutchinson because her claim to immediate revelation challenged its logic of evidence—but not in the way it would appear at first glance. It may seem as if the challenge rests in Hutchinson's recourse to private authority and the implicit rejection of public authority. But in the context we've just set out, it is the court, not Hutchinson, who has more faith in "private" evidence. Hutchinson's rejection of the validity of such evidence as so many "works" implicitly threatens the elders' assurance of their own salvation. Following Shepard, they have been interpreting their own good works as evidence that they have been saved. But Hutchinson insists that this evidence is not valid, that the minor premise of the practical syllogism is unsound. In effect, then, Hutchinson tells the elders that they may not be saved.

It may also be possible that, in the heat of battle, the elders did not have time to click through this line of scholastic reasoning and instead saw Hutchinson's claim to immediate revelation as a direct affront to their earthly authority: perhaps God did speak to her, but she still needed to follow godly intermediaries (namely, them) while on earth. Certainly, whenever anyone claims to have a direct hotline to God, authorities tend to grow a bit uneasy, even if those authorities themselves are believers. The potential for using such revelations as a justification for holy violence only exacerbates the unease. For example, Winthrop seemed afraid that the Antinomian Controversy would erupt into violence, as similar controversies already had in Germany and England; hence, he orders all those in sympathy with Hutchinson and Wheelwright to be disarmed.[38]

The elders clearly feared a loss of control, specifically because of the way Cotton and Hutchinson conceived of human agency and responsibility. Simply put, who is responsible for the actions of a single individual when individualism is based on affiliation with authority, shared participation in a group identity, and passive dependence on God? One line of logic points the finger back at the elders for failing to provide proper guidance. This logic holds husbands accountable for their wives and children, and ministers and magistrates accountable for their followers. Another line of logic points the finger at everyone affiliated with Cotton and Hutchinson, since the individual in this context cannot be differentiated from the group. Thus, dozens of people (mostly men) were suspected, accused, and punished simply by virtue of the fact of their association with or proximity to Hutchinson. Yet another line of logic—the one Hutchinson herself underscores—points the finger at God. We are merely instruments of his agency, and therefore cannot be held primarily responsible for anything we do in his name. None of these fingers points directly and exclusively at Hutchinson. Her infamous question to Winthrop at the start of the civil trial—"What law have I broken?"—can be read with the emphasis on the "I": "What law have I *alone* broken?"

And perhaps it is just this absence of an emphatic "I" and not the authoritative assertion of self that most disturbs the elders.[39] Their own logic of salvation apportions at least some agency to the single (as opposed to communal) individual: he must scrutinize his soul for assurance, and he must behave in a certain way to meet the conditions of the covenant. If individuals are thus somewhat responsible for themselves, they can be singled out and held responsible for their actions (i.e., rewarded or punished) in a public forum. If Hutchinson did in fact claim this kind of responsibility, if, in fact, she saw herself as distinct from a communal identity, then she would have been doing exactly what the elders had wanted her to do all along: "I alone, of my own volition, broke these laws and therefore stand punishable for my transgressions." In this scenario their authority works with, not against, her authority. Their ability to punish her as an individual depends, at least in part, on whether or not she thinks of herself as an individual who alone could be punished for her actions. (I say "in part" because in the end, the court can—and did—punish Hutchinson regardless of how she thought about herself as an individual.) But if she denies accountability by denying agency, then she not only subverts the elders' logic of individualism; she also implies the worst possible thing one could hint at in Puritan New England: that the ministers and magistrates on the court were not among God's elect.

Ironically, the court failed to see, or at least to acknowledge, the fact that Hutchinson openly professed extreme dependence on paternal authorities: first and always God but also ministers such as Cotton and Wheelwright. Perhaps one could argue that the court did not, in fact, object to Hutchinson's stance toward authority but that they simply objected to the authorities she chose to follow. But given that the elders and the antinomians were essentially not speaking in the same language or thinking with the same logic, it is quite possible that the court simply misunderstood the ways in which Hutchinson's passive activities subjected her to all sorts of external controls.[40] Hungering and longing assign her a role in a narrative of desire for salvation, but the direction of this narrative is beyond her control. She herself cannot fulfill her own needs, and even once these needs are met, desire only continues and increases, thus sustaining the narrative.

3. The Trials

In light of the discussions of gender roles and agency, Hutchinson's story becomes not so much a self-reliant quest for a private truth that would somehow also subvert institutional authority but a search for truth within the institutional frameworks available to her at the time. Her testimony at the civil trial gives some of the details of this search:

> Being much troubled to see the falseness of the constitution of the church of England, I had like to have turned separatist; whereupon I kept a solemn humiliation and pondering of the thing; this scripture was brought unto me—he that denies Jesus Christ to come in the flesh is antichrist—This I considered of and in considering found that the papists did not deny him to be come in the flesh, nor we did not deny him—who then was antichrist? Was the Turk antichrist only? The Lord knows that I could not open scripture; he must by his prophetical office open it unto me. So after that being unsatisfied in the thing, the Lord was pleased to bring this scripture out of the Hebrews. He that denies the testament denies the testator, and in this did open unto me and give me to see that those which did not teach the new covenant had the spirit of the antichrist, and upon this he did discover the ministry unto me and ever since. I bless the Lord, he hath let me see which was the clear ministry and which wrong. Since that time I confess I have been more choice and he hath let me to distinguish between the voice of my be-

> loved and the voice of Moses, the voice of John Baptist and the voice of antichrist, for all those voices are spoken of in scripture.[41]

This passage bespeaks a sense of anxiety and even betrayal at the realization that none of the ministers on whom Hutchinson had depended to lead her to salvation "could preach the Lord Jesus aright." This conclusion is also charged with a sense of abandonment on many levels: ministers had abandoned the duties of office; in so doing, they abandon their followers to their own devices. And now Hutchinson herself feels that she must reject or deny these "fathers" with no alternatives in sight: "I was much troubled, I knew not how to bear this." While she seems fairly sure of her conclusion, she nevertheless wants to resist its worst implications. To reject these ministers is to knock out from under herself the props of her religious identity. And if her judgment of them is wrong, if they are not in fact the antichrist, then she pays an even higher price: "I begged of the Lord that this Atheisme might not be in my heart."

She does not portray her break from false ministers as liberating but rather as debilitating. She does not turn to herself for guidance, nor does she consider becoming a minister unto herself. Instead, she turns to God for help in finding new and improved ministerial direction.[42] Her use of passive constructions in this passage reflects this divine dependence: "This scripture was brought unto me [by God]"; "He did discover the ministry unto me"; "The Lord knows that I could not open scripture." The emphasis on hearing over speaking also underscores this dependence. On one level, this emphasis is simply a function of a major tenet of Puritan doctrine derived from Romans 10:17 ("Faith cometh through hearing"): the way to the soul is through the ear. On another level, hearing is another passive activity like Williams's witnessing. Hutchinson wants the ability to discern the difference between truth and the mere rhetorical performance of truth in the sermons that she hears. Such an ability, as we have seen, marks the true convert, the one who does not "misprise" sanctification in herself or in others. Just as the minister must make distinctions between congregants (truly saved or hypocrites), so too the congregants must distinguish between true and false preachers.[43]

Proper listening ultimately leads to proper affiliation. Hutchinson must first choose a voice that speaks *to* her, that consistently preaches a covenant of grace. In turn, that voice will speak *for* her; by associating herself with a minister in whom she believes, she herself shares in the power of that voice. Her search for better ministers thus depends on her declaration that "I have been more choice, and he hath let me to distinguish between" the different available voices. This invocation of "choice" mirrors the logic of covenants: it is Winthrop's description of a wife who chooses a husband to whom she will submit combined with Cotton's logic that God enables us to "choose" to enter into the covenant of grace. Hutchinson, led by God, elects a minister, and just as women share the social status of their husbands by virtue of union, she shares the spiritual status of her minister by virtue of affiliation.

By all accounts, Cotton—and to a lesser extent, Wheelwright—were the ministers with whom Hutchinson most wanted to affiliate. The bond was so strong, in fact, that she followed them to the New World: "When our teacher [Cotton] came to New-England it was a great trouble unto me, my brother Wheelwright being put by also. I was then much troubled concerning the ministry under which I lived, and then that place in the 30th Isaiah was brought to mind. Though the Lord give thee bread of adversity and water of affliction yet shall not thy teachers be removed into corners any more, but thine eyes shall see thy teachers. The Lord giving me this promise and they being gone there was none then left that I was able to hear, and I could not be at rest but I must come hither."[44] Again Hutchinson expresses a sense of abandonment; this time, the "fathers" she has chosen to replace those who had first led to this feeling have now themselves left her, literally and physically by moving to the New World. So again she feels "great trouble," and again she describes this lost affiliation in terms of hearing: "there was none then left that I was able to hear." The citation from Isaiah ("thine eyes shall see thy teachers") underscores the importance of seeing as well as hearing. Like Williams's witness, Hutchinson wants to keep those institutions with whom she affiliates in close range, to see them and to hear them.

Part of this desire for physical proximity is simply a matter of practice: the proper size of a congregation was often defined by the number of people who could hear and see the minister. If the congregation grew too large, a new one was formed. The need to keep Cotton in earshot and seeing distance may also partly stem from the "devoted fan" dynamic that Porterfield describes.[45] Sermons printed in a book cannot substitute for the living, breathing presence of an adored minister. The emphasis on seeing also underscores the dynamic of mutual dependence and mutual watchfulness. Just as Cotton must maintain "watchfull care" over his congregants, so too must they diligently observe him to be sure that he continues to live up to their expectations. This need is especially acute for Hutchinson and people like her, since they have already risked so much on their choice of minister: the wrath of other ministers, atheism, exile, political persecution, and the loss of homeland.

This close relationship between Hutchinson and Cotton, which is always a focus of the trials, receives its most explicit articulation in the words of Thomas Weld: "Whan I spake with her she tould me that Mr. Cotten and she was both of one minde and she held no more than Mr. Cotten did in thease Thinges . . . she affirmed still that thear was no difference betweene Mr. Cotton and She."[46] Of course, by saying that Hutchinson said that "thear was no difference betweene Mr. Cotton and She," Weld and the court may well be putting words in her mouth. Affiliation becomes guilt by association, and the court purchases two antinomians for the price of one. On the other hand, these two quotations together nicely demonstrate how resemblances and differences work to inform Hutchinson's sense of self. The desire for resemblance to Cotton and the attendant differences with other ministers form the axes on which Hutchinson plots her beliefs.[47]

Discussions about gender and agency also inform what, to the modern reader, constitutes one of the most bizarre aspects of the Antinomian Controversy, the so-called monstrous births of Mary Dyer and Anne Hutchinson.[48] Hutchinson was pregnant during the church trial, and after its conclusion she delivered a stillbirth, described as "30 monstrous births . . . few of perfect shape, none at all of them . . . of humane shape."[49] Before the beginning of the trials, Hutchinson was in attendance when Mary Dyer delivered an infant that Weld described as "a woman child, a fish, a beast, and a fowle, all woven together in one, and without a head." At the time, Hutchinson asked Cotton if she should report this birth; Cotton advised against doing so. But news of Dyer's birth—and more important, Hutchinson's presence at the birth—eventually surfaced during the trials. Winthrop had the infant corpse exhumed for all to observe, and Weld used it as an occasion to link the seemingly disparate worlds of unfortunate births and religious dissent: "God himselfe was pleased to step in with his casting voice, and bring in his owne vote and suffrage from heaven . . . as clearly as if he had pointed with his finger, in causing the two fomenting women in the time of the height of the Opinions to produce out of their wombs, as before they had out of their braines, such monstrous births as no Chronicle (I thinke) hardly ever recorded the like."[50] Both Winthrop and Weld make this point even more explicitly by pointing out that the number of "deformed monsters" delivered by Hutchinson happens to equal the number of her "misshapen opinions."[51]

Weld clearly states the two most obvious reasons for bringing in these "monstrous births" as circumstantial evidence against the antinomians: they can be read as yet one more confirmation of the corrupted and corrupting nature of the "two fomenting women," and they can be seen, like everything in the Puritan universe, as a sure sign from God. But the "logic" of the apparently irrational reactions of the court (having the corpse exhumed!) runs parallel to the logic informing much of our analyses of the trials. For example, the same causal logic used to analyze rebirth applies to actual birth as well. The woman/mother serves as the material cause of childbirth, the material or stuff in which a change is wrought. The father/husband stands as both the efficient or instrumental cause (that by which a change is wrought, the agent or secondary cause of change) and the formal cause (the shape or form into which the material is changed). As always,

God is the primary and final cause. According to this logic, if anything is "abnormal" in childbearing or childbirth, the father shares a large part of the blame. A complete lack of children indicates a failure of masculinity. Mary Beth Norton writes "A person who could not father a child was by that criterion alone an unsatisfactory male."[52] Fathering a female child was also considered, if not quite abnormal, then certainly another failure of masculinity. Since the father serves as formal cause, all children should be formed in his image (i.e., men). Females were considered imperfect because incomplete, and such imperfection stems from a father's failure properly to do his job as formal and instrumental causes. By now, we've heard this rhetoric and logic many times: in Cotton's critique of the first fathers, in Chidley's description of sinecural ministers, in *Haec-Vir*'s parody of men who abandoned their role as men, in the court's effort to force men to fulfill their responsibilities, and in Hutchinson's search for "fathers" who will perfectly play their expected role.

Even more than childlessness or female children, monstrous births raise questions about a father's ability to do his job properly. Paternity, as we've seen, is based on resemblance; ideally, a male child should be formed in the image of his father. Since a monstrous birth does not resemble father or mother and in some instances does not even appear to be a human being, the father has clearly failed or abandoned his role as formal cause. Even worse, he has allowed this role to be usurped by the imagination of the mother.[53] Thus, monstrous births represent yet another usurpation of the role of the legitimate father that also takes various other forms from conversion, to charges of adultery, to violations of the Fifth Commandment. In this case, though, the father is replaced not so much by another father but by an image that has aroused the mother's desire. This image need not be another male; it need not even be another person. A statue or a painting that a pregnant woman looks at could also serve as formal cause to deform her infant, as could her "whims and fancy." By this logic, Hutchinson's erroneous opinions could be the cause of her misshapen infant; and Hutchinson herself, in contact with Dyer during her pregnancy, could be viewed as the "father" of those malformed infants.

Whether it is because fathers are weak, have abandoned their roles, have been usurped or denied, or have been made to vanish, or some combination of these options, we have now seen a range of instances where the father has been displaced, replaced, or called back to his place. It may be helpful at this point to summarize at least some of the ways in which Puritan culture sanctioned or punished these acts of paternal displacement. Conversion clearly represents the most legitimate form for this dynamic. The blood of Christ "washeth away all fathers"—in effect, wipes the slate clean—and clears the way for the next fathers. Such replacement is premised on resemblance in several ways: old fathers can be replaced by next fathers because paternal ties are established, broken, and reestablished on resemblance, relatively weak grounds for establishment when compared to those used for maternity. The next fathers are all supposed to resemble Christ (by virtue of *imitatio Christi*) and in so doing resemble each other as well. If this correspondence breaks down, as it did in Hutchinson's trials, then some fathers can be ignored or denied, their authority trumped by the truth claims of the truly Christlike fathers.

Monstrous births represent the inverse of conversion. Both monstrous births and conversion involve the imaginative usurpation and replacement of the first father/husband with something else. In conversion, the minister (husband) unites with the word to produce converted offspring, or Christ (husband) unites with the believer (wife), or God (Father) replaces earthly fathers. In each case, the change simultaneously manifests itself spiritually in the reorientation of the soul and physically in behavior, speech, "walking in a Godly way." In monstrous birth an illegitimate father—an image, a painting, a statue, or a wayward thought, desire, or opinion—joins with the mother. The change primarily manifests itself physically (in a deformed offspring), but this physical evidence also represents spiritual waywardness. But where conversion involves men calling for the replacement of one father with another, monstrous births occur when a woman replaces the legitimate father with something both illegitimate and not male, something perversely luxurious, multiformed, overwhelming, and boundless. More to the point, conversion ultimately reinforces those resemblances upon which the family analogy is based. Monstrous births, with their introduction of radical difference—an offspring that resembles neither mother, father, nor human being—threatens the integrity of the family analogy at worst, and at best, calls attention, yet once more, to the failures of men to "be men."

5

Institutions and Nostalgia

One narrative of New England history, made famous by Perry Miller, tells a story of declension: once upon a time, the institutions of the Bay Colony enjoyed consensus and stability, but gradually this security eroded into conflict, dissent, and secularization. A close cousin of Miller's tale agrees that Puritan institutions enjoyed a period of consensus and stability but renames this security "hegemony." This version of history accepts the "Puritan patriarchy" as a given that is gradually subverted by the radical actions of people such as Williams and Hutchinson. Still another spin on the tale notes that the institutions of New England were being formed at roughly the same time of the Hutchinson and Williams controversies, from 1635 to 1645. Given the timing, it would be impossible for these radicals to subvert institutions that did not yet fully exist; instead, the rules of church and state were forged in the heat of controversy and were intended to suppress any future outbreaks of radical individualism.

Taken separately, each of these narratives is found lacking, but taken together, they form a nicely complicated account of the development of institutions in New England. Rather than read the events as sequential (first consensus, then declension; first consensus, then subversion; first dissent, then oppression), it seems more fruitful to read them as simultaneous. At the same time of the Hutchinson trials (1636–1638) the leaders of the Bay Colony were having initial discussions about the shape of their institutions. Within a few years after the trials, John Cotton wrote a number of sermons and treatises that formulate and defend the "Congregational Way," his plan for church structure and governance that was to be worked out in the colonies and then shipped back home to England. Cotton's debates with Roger Williams about ecclesiastical issues also span this period. Events back home only intensified all of these discussions and controversies: by the early 1640s the English Puritans had gained control of Parliament; in 1646 the Westminster Assembly considered new plans for organizing church and state; and by 1649 the king was dead, and it looked as if the Puritans had finally come to full power. There are many threads here to pursue, but this concluding chapter will focus on the ways in which the plans for institutions in New England—specifically the church and the ministry—were born out of crises that were themselves largely about the problems of institutions. Put another way, the story of institutions in New England does not so much end with declension as begin with it. From the very start we find a sense of longing and loss, a desire to recover from the past the perfect church, the perfect father.[1] Institutions, then, are built on the weak foundation of nostalgia.

Given their antipatriarchalism, the Puritans themselves were partly responsible for destroying those things they then came to desire in different form. These are, after all, the people who attacked paternal power in its various manifestations: the pope, the priest, the presbyter. And these are the people who beheaded a king. In less drastic form, the Puritan emphasis on conversion also demands a denial or repudiation of fathers. Even if strong action has been taken against these figurative fathers and even if such fathers disappear, the desire for strong fathers does not seem to fade away. Perhaps the desire for father is not universal, but it certainly predominates in a culture where individual identity depends so much on affiliation with powerful paternal institutions. This desire takes many shapes, such as the longing for conversion and the search for better ministers and churches. If such new fathers cannot be found, then the desire may take the form of an intense nostalgia, not so much for the old fathers but for the longing that was embodied but never consummated in the desire for new fathers. In the end, nostalgia, as Susan Stewart has noted, is the desire for desire.[2]

Over and again, the next fathers are either not found or they repeatedly fail to live up to expectation and promise. This sense of loss motivates Hutchinson's dependence on and subsequent criticism of the New England clergy: loss of faith in the old fathers (ministers in England), abandonment by the next father (when Wheelwright and Cotton leave for New England), and finally disappointment and even betrayal during her trials. Williams's state of permanent exile and his "negative" truths are also informed by desire and loss. Indeed, all of his attacks on the churches in New England are underwritten by his singular desire to return to the purity and perfection of the "first institutions," that time when Christ walked the earth with his apostles.[3] Although at times Williams's work reads like an extended riff on the joke "I would never join a club that would accept me as a member," it also betrays an almost obsessive desire for a pure and perfect institution, indirectly, through his stance as witness, and directly, in moments such as this: "After all my search and examinations and considerations I said, I do profess to believe, that some [churches] come nearer to the first primitive Churches, and the Institutions and Appointments of Christ Jesus then others. . . . I professed that if my Soul could finde rest in joyning unto any of the Churches professing Christ Jesus now extant, I would readily and gladly do it, yea unto themselves whom I now opposed."[4] And yet there is always an "and yet" that checks Williams's desire to join. In his rejection of almost all forms of the ministry, he as much as declares that the purity of Christ's first institutions will never be recovered nor captured in any institutional form: "[I] cannot, in the presence of God, bring in the result of a satisfying discovery, that either the begetting ministry of the apostles or messengers to the churches, or the feeding and nourishing ministry of pastors and teachers, according to the first institution of the Lord Jesus, are yet restored and extant."[5]

So much of Puritanism seems to hinge on this sense of incompleteness—of a desire that can never be sated, of a longing for something or someone that will never be found. The desire to recover lost origins, to go back to the first church, for example, may help to explain a preoccupation with allegory and typology. As well, this desire manifests itself in the apocalyptic modes of Puritan thought. The forward gesture to the end of the world is really a backward glance to the perfect past, a desire to uncover and restore a former golden age of Christ.[6] This habit of seeking solace in the past leads one to lament present differences (as in "Things are not the same as they used to be"), to long for future resemblances (as in "It will be just *like* when Christ first walked the earth"), and to fear that things finally have come to an unhappy end: "Things will never be the same again."

1. The Absence of Christ

So much of this nostalgia stems from the conviction that Christ was no longer present in New England, so there was nothing left to do but mourn his absence and long for his return. Longing and desire for Christ are always a part of conversion, but the logic of such longing changes depending on whether Christ is believed to be absent or present. If present, then Christ serves as a reminder of the *imitatio*, a model of what converts should desire to become like. Moreover, his felt presence excites a desire (Cotton's use of hungering and thirsting and all of the sexual metaphors) that can be momentarily consummated but never fully sated. The presence of Christ only arouses further and more intense desire to become like Christ. When Christ is thought to be absent, the nature of this desire becomes less intense, less sharp; generally, it switches from a desire to become like Christ to a desire for Christ to return. Alternatively, conversion (and by extension, church structure) becomes more and more based on faith—the need to act as if Christ were present—and faith, even to the best of Puritans, was a compensation for absence rather than a celebration of presence.

This dramatic shift from the presence to the absence of Christ registers in a series of works Cotton wrote in England and in New England, both during and after the Hutchinson trials. Most notable among these are two series of sermons on Canticles, or the Song of Solomon. Cotton delivered the first series in England, around 1625, when he was still a relatively young preacher whose popularity was on the rise. He delivered the second series in New England, around 1642, after the conflicts with Williams and Hutchinson and well after he became "John Cotton," famous and infamous preacher of conversion in Old and New England.[7] These sermon series, written at distinctly different moments in Cotton's career, provide an unparalleled opportunity to chart the changes in his thinking on conversion and the presence of Christ.

He sounds a first note in this sequence with his explication of chapter 4, verse 8 in the English sermons: "Christ still vouchsafes, to be with us, converting soules, feeding his lambes, hearing our prayers; We may also worship Christ in truth without feare of lawes, yea with acceptance. When Christ goes, let all his faithfull spouses goe with him; when there are dens of Lions, and men cannot keepe the profession of Christ, but fall into their mouthes, then it is time to goe; But are there these causes now? doth not Christ dwell here in the simplicity of his ordinances? As long as Christ is here in England, let us not goe away."[8] This reading openly declares that "Christ is here in England," that he "still vouchsafes to be with us." Although Cotton also looks forward to a time "when Christ goes" (incidentally providing a rationale for his migration about eight years before the fact), even this statement strongly implies that Christ has not yet left England.

Eventually, of course, Cotton and thousands of other Puritans concluded that Christ had, in fact, left England and so they followed him to the New World. Even during the heat of the Antinomian Controversy, Cotton confidently affirmed that belief should be based on presence, not absence. In his rejoinder to the elders (1637), for example, he asks this question: "Doth any good Christian take as much comfort from his faith, or from his hope, or from his love, or from his hungering and thirsting after Christ, as he doth from (the object of all of these) Christ himself?"[9] Although the question pretty much implies its own answer, Cotton makes matters even more explicit later in the rejoinder. To prefer thirsting to drinking, he writes, "would make that which is indeed but the way to further fellowship with Christ to be the end of our journey; as if a suitor should satisfie his desire in conversing with the waiting maid, when he longeth for fellowship with her mistress: or as if a man should find his hunger and thirst satisfied, by hearing that hunger and thirst is a sign of a healthful body."[10] This passage points out the folly of fixating on desire itself rather than on the object and consummation of that desire. The person who settles for thirsting over drinking, like the suitor who settles for the waiting maid over the mistress, replaces ends with means. One suffers thirst only as a means to drinking, and one endures polite chatter with the waiting maid only as a way of finally getting to the mistress. To dwell on means over ends is to settle for second prize, a compensation for not being able to achieve the goal actually desired. It also replaces a true object of desire (Christ, a cool drink, the mistress) with a process; the desire here is for desire or longing itself, not for any actual goal. Illogically, then, one satisfies one's thirst with one's thirst—the belief that "thirst is a sign of a healthful body"—a logic that denies the fact that if thirst goes unsated, the body will no longer be healthy.

Of course, Cotton's exhortation not to settle for compensatory longing presupposes, first, that the object of desire is present, and second, that the object can be attained: there is a cool drink available and it is yours; the mistress is still in the house and she is willing to see you, and Christ is still in New England and is willing to save you. If one can confidently assume presence and attainment, then faith becomes an insufficient form of grace—another kind of compensatory second prize—because it is based on absence and unattainability. One resorts to faith only when one has no absolute guarantees. Even at the height of antinomian acrimony, Cotton is unwilling to settle for faith alone: "[Christ] doth not send men that are thirsty, to consider of their thirst, what a gracious disposition it is, and to drink well of their thirsting till they be filled with it, and such satisfaction out of it; No, no, but let them come to me, and drink; not drink their consolation out of their thirst, but out of Christ."[11] Again Cotton underscores the illogic and ill health of satisfying thirst with thirst. Longing souls should not be satisfied nor even consoled by the fact of their longing, especially when Christ is there for the taking. Faith should not be held up as evidence of grace, because it can never replace salvation.

Within just a few years of making these statements, Cotton settled for the consolation. This shift becomes quite clear through a comparison of his Old and New England interpretations of Canticles 5 : 16, "He is altogether lovely, or desirable." In England he wrote: "Now they saw or found nothing in Christ, or in the profession of his name, but what was wholly desirable. The rebukes Christ began [begat?] now to seeme greater riches, then the treasures of Egypt or Babylon in some former ages: they that saw the trueth were often brought to yeeld and recant: but these saw nothing to be more desired then Christ. Besides, hee is now called holy and desirable, because so many generally were stirred up to desire and seeke reformation."[12] Christ is both more desirable and most desired. His visible presence, even when it brings rebukes, outshines the treasures of Egypt and Babylon, and it inspires desire for reformation in many, many people.

About twenty years later, in New England, Cotton interprets the same chapter and verse in the following way: "For she giveth all this large and sweet description of Christ as a just ground of seeking him, and of her charging all the daughters of Hierusalem to help her in her seeking for him. . . . Best affections, and boldest expressions of them are bestowed upon the best object; enjoying him, maketh us like him. 2. Cor.3.18. . . . Christ deserteth us at any time . . . to make himselfe and his ordinances the more sweet and precious to us. . . . Now after long desertion, his Word is most sweet, and himselfe is now altogether lovely."[13] This version emphasizes Christ's absence; he periodically deserts his followers and thereby becomes more sweet and precious. Since believers can no longer see him, they can only long for and talk about him and try to persuade others to do the same. The bride (the "she" in this passage) uses "best affections and boldest expression" to make Christ/her husband seem desirable so that other women (potential believers) will help her look for him. Whereas in the English version his presence alone was enough to convince others of his worth, now—in his absence—others must be persuaded to follow him.

In the New England sermons on Canticles, Cotton also offers a slightly different reading of 2 Corinthians 3:18 ("But we all, with open face beholding as in a glass the glory of the Lord, are changed into the same image from glory to glory, even as by the Spirit of the Lord") than in another series of English sermons. In the English sermons he concludes that "this seeing of him shall make us like him." This claim serves as the basis for the *imitatio Christi*: we see Christ, and then we become like him. But in the New England sermons on Canticles, Cotton glosses the same chapter and verse as "enjoying him, maketh us like him"; "enjoying" replaces "seeing." While it is, of course, quite possible both to see and enjoy something, it is not necessary to see something in order to enjoy it. The passage, in fact, suggests that one could enjoy Christ even more in his absence than in his presence. Cotton says as much elsewhere in the Canticles sermons: "The very earnest desire of such a love of Christ to usward, is a good evidence, that Christ hath set himself as a seal on our hearts and armes."[14] This statement represents an almost complete turnabout from the assertions of 1637 that thirst and hunger alone should not be taken for signs of good health. Cotton now suggests that desire for the love of an absent Christ, rather than consummation of love with a present Christ, provides sufficient evidence of one's salvation.

In still another sermon series from the mid 1640s—this one on the Book of Revelation—Cotton continues to emphasize a faith based on absence: "Hence it comes, That the fathers saw the promise & embraced them, but did not receive them. Heb. 11.39. That is, did not receive them accomplished (for they never saw Christ in his death) but they were perswaded of them, and embraced them, and did verily look for them in expectation, as if they had been present with them."[15] Again we see the hallmarks of absence already discussed: the fathers see the promise, but they never saw Christ; they were persuaded (like the daughters in Canticles) and expectant; they must act as if Christ were present. But this particular instance of the argument introduces a new question: what happens to the authority of the fathers when it is based on an "as if" rather than an "is"? The family analogy works mainly because resemblances can be verified. Anything that calls these resemblances into question could potentially shake the authority of the fathers. This happened during the trials when Hutchinson pointed out (via the Fifth Commandment) that all of the fathers were not telling her to do the same things, that they did not resemble each other. But if Christ is no longer a visible presence, then how could anyone verify that the fathers actually resemble Christ? In this case, authority rests on the shaky foundation of the conditional "as if" rather than the firm bedrock of the essential "is."

This shift in the basis of authority leads to a notable loss of enthusiasm for the rhetoric of conversion and the conversion of rhetoric. Cotton's plan for a converted rhetoric assumed the presence of Christ; he would be held out as the object of desire, the ideal to which and into which everyone must turn. But with Christ absent as a standard, a converted rhetoric risks running out of control, of being misprised, of fathering monsters instead of true converts. During the trials, for example, Winthrop signals this fear of uncontrollable rhetoric when he insists: "The constant language of the Scripture is not unsafe."[16] The elders' emphasis on the safety of constant language and the "unsafety" of other forms of spiritual expression leads Cotton to conclude: "If this kind of arguing seems uncouth and strange to us in these daies, surely it is because these latter daies are perillous times. In Elder times both the Scripture language and the language of our Soundest Divine were wont to expresse it; The Lord must prevent us in every work of Grace or else we shall not follow him."[17] The passage ends with the kind of arguing Cotton describes: "The Lord must prevent us in every work . . . or else we shall not follow him." At first, this statement seems paradoxical: how can we follow the Lord if he prevents us? In the logic of the covenant of grace, the Lord must first stop, or prevent, us from being our degenerate selves before we can follow him. Cotton also plays on an etymological pun: *prevent* means not only to stop but also to "pre-vent," to come before. Now the sentence makes sense: the Lord must come before us (i.e., apprehend us with his grace but also precede us) before we can follow him.

Cotton laments that this intricate play of meaning and logic—essentially the language of holy paradox—is now considered uncouth and strange. *Uncouth* suggests its etymological roots of "unknown" (i.e., people do not know how to engage in this kind of arguing) and "uncertain" (i.e., people are not sure what such arguments actually mean). The word also suggests inappropriateness, a lack of decorum or suitability to the situation or context. In this case, the indecorum stems from the assumption, voiced by Winthrop, that uncertain or inconstant language is not appropriate in unsafe or "perillous times." This concession to dangerous times also brings Cotton to a nostalgic reminiscence of days when such language and arguing was appropriate, safe, and effective. Indeed, in his early sermons on conversion, he encourages his audience "not to be afraid of the word *Revelation*."[18] But after the disastrous consequences of Hutchinson's claim to "immediate revelation," Cotton concludes that "private revelations without the word are out of date now."[19] Revelation was, of course, "in date" in the days of the apostles, the very days that the Puritans hoped to restore. The passage of time does not render revelation doctrinally wrong or humanly impossible. Instead, it renders it old-fashioned, a superannuated (perhaps because politically unsafe) way of communicating with God. If a form of belief can be dismissed simply because it is old-fashioned or politically unsound, then the entire recuperative project of Puritanism is in jeopardy. What remains is a nostalgia for the days when such forms were considered appropriate and acceptable, regardless of their certainty and regardless of their political implications.

A comparison of another pair of readings from the Canticles sermons illustrates Cotton's nostalgia for the lost language of salvation. We have already examined in some detail (see chapter 2) his English gloss on chapter 7, verse 9: "And the roofe of thy mouth like the best wines, for my beloved, that goeth downe sweetly, causing the lips of those that are asleep to speak." Here it is again for ease of comparison:

> To goe rightly, or straightly, implyeth the strength and generousnesse of wine, when it sparkleth upward in the cup, as Prov. 23.31. which here expresseth the lively vigour of the Churches Doctrine, in her preaching of Christ, causing the lips of those that are asleepe to speak. . . . When the Apostles spake (the wonderfull workes of God) in strange tongues, some of the people thought them to be full of new wine (Acts 2.11, 13) but they were deceived, and were willing so to account of them in mockery. But these people shall be full of new wine of the Spirit and Word of God, to open their mouthes to speak as the Apostles did, the wonderfull workes of God.[20]

This passage conveys an optimism afforded by the assurance of Christ's presence. Some people may mistake spiritual drunkenness for literal drunkenness; they may mock the apostles' "strange tongues." But in England, Cotton remains confident that at least some people will understand the language of salvation; these strange tongues, unlike the "uncouth and strange arguing" he describes in New England, are not deemed unsafe or inappropriate; instead, they still carry the promise of redemption.

In New England, Cotton interprets the same passage from Canticles as follows:

> If we be constant in sweet fruitfulnesse; if patient in Burdens, and grow never a whit less sincere and upright; if the righteous flock to us, if our Ministery yield strong and Spirituall Nourishment to strong men in Christ: if our conversation be savoury and cordial: if our conference spirituall and comfortable; if our confidence in Christ be grounded and stedfast; then behold, ye are come to a well growen stature. If otherwise, we are short of our due growth. Time was when it was thus with the New English Churches: but now we cannot bear wrongs, but grow contentious in suites, now few come to us; those that do come, they corrupt us; our conference is not so much like the best Wine sparkling towards Christ, but rather about the best wine where it is. No marvell then, if our confidence be lesse on Christ, and his desire lesse to us.[21]

The passage begins, innocently enough, with a series of conditional statements: if ceretain conditions are met, then we can be confident that we have grown in grace. Up to this point, the statement lacks specificity: it does not say where the conditions need to be met; it does not say if the conditions have been met. Cotton is not directly stating that New England is in trouble, but, unlike his statements in England, he is also not saying that they are not in trouble.

With the phrase "time was"—a phrase that once again signals a sense of nostalgia—the passage takes a turn for the worse. New England does not meet these conditions, and to make matters worse, they used to meet them but no longer do. The time span covered from "time was" to "but now" covers about seven years, but Cotton talks about it as if it were in the distant past. Once again, this shift from confidence to contention has weakened the claims of a converted rhetoric. Cotton, perhaps referring to his English interpretation, notes that conference is no longer "like the best wine" but instead "about the best wine" (i.e., where to purchase the best vintage). The years since the first settlement have witnessed an ironic transubstantiation: the metaphor that formerly compared a converted rhetoric to sparkling wine has degenerated into a literal interpretation. But the metaphoric wine has not become the literal blood of Christ; instead, it has literally become wine. If there was a time when Cotton believed true converts would develop "new tongues," he now worries that critics of the Puritans will ask "If your assemblies were fed by Christ, where are your New

Tongues, gifts of the Holy Ghost and miracles?" Cotton thus concludes "our confidence [is] lesse on Christ, and his desire lesse to us."

2. *Institutional Structures*

Both Williams's and Cotton's plan for church reform are founded on loss and nostalgia. For Cotton, the desire for Christ has been replaced by a desire to regain the intensity of desire. Williams desires to recover the purity and perfection of the first institutions of Christ. Although a similar nostalgic impulse motivates both of them (or perhaps *because* they are motivated by a similar impulse), Williams and Cotton strongly disagree on the forms that should give shape to these desires. Their debates range far and wide, but they really come down to variations on one question: What is the proper relationship between individuals and institutions, between members and a church? Is a group of sound believers sufficient to constitute a true church? Does a true church constitute its members? Does an institution consist of anything other than its members at any given moment, or does it have a general existence beyond a particular constitution?

For Williams, the proper alignment is not causal but coincidental; that is, a group of converted souls cannot cause a corrupt church to become pure. In fact, a corrupt church would most likely threaten to corrupt even saved souls, and so a convert is not truly converted if he or she remains affiliated with a false church. Conversely, no amount of institutional reform will cause true individual conversion. People may feign change to gain membership in a church, but they will do so for other than spiritual reasons. Somehow (and Williams never descends to details here) a group of already converted souls must find an already pure institution, and only then will one have a true church. Cotton offers a much more flexible—one could almost say more tolerant—plan than Williams's. A few good men can cause big institutional change, and strong institutions can help to reform less-than-perfect individuals. Cotton allows for mixtures—of saved and unsaved souls, of good and bad institutional practices—because, even in his darker moments, he remains more confident than Williams of the possibility of change. Good members can purify a corrupt church, and a good church can convert even the most recalcitrant hypocrite.

For Williams the job of the church, quite plainly, is to recover, preserve, and protect the purity and perfection of the first institutions of Christ and the apostles. Churches must prove themselves absolutely free from corruption and hypocrisy in every form, organizational, ministerial, and doctrinal. He settles for nothing more and nothing less. Since such churches must be perfect from the start, there will be no need for change in the form of individual conversion or institutional reform because, by definition, perfect things do not have to change. Williams's strong desire to recover the first church, coupled with his strong desire for affiliation, coupled still with his strong reluctance to affiliate, results in a melancholic nostalgia, an attitude of "I would if I could but I can't" that most clearly manifests itself in the detached stance of the witness in exile. Since he cannot purify the object of desire (i.e., the perfect church), he tries to purify desire itself by his relentless and uncompromising scrutiny of motives: Why does a minister preach such and such? Why does a person claim to be converted? Why does a church meddle in state affairs? And since motives can never be fully known except to God, they can never be fully purified. Truth cannot reside in institutions for Williams because, by their very nature, institutions are inimical to truth.

Cotton had very little patience for what he perceived as Williams's overly fastidious perfectionism. Of Williams's demand that both members and structure be perfect before forming a church, he writes: "I looke at it as an ungrounded distinction, to require more purity to the being of a Church in her first constitution [i.e., when it is first being formed], then is necessary to the being of it, after it is constituted. I should thinke the longer a Church hath enjoyed communion with the Lord Jesus Christ, the more shee ought to grow both in knowledge and purity. Where more hath been given, the more will be required of the Lord."[22] Williams's insistence on such a large down payment of purity threatens to mortgage the future of all churches. To demand purity before a church can form or, for that matter, to demand purity once a church has formed is finally to purify the church out of existence. "Mr. Williams in stead of reforming one Church," writes Cotton, "renounceth all."[23]

Cotton's criticism of Williams also indicates his own basic plan for a church. Like Williams he desires to return to the perfect past, but unlike Williams he views institutions as a means to this perfection, not as a perfect end in themselves. That is, institutions must still hold forth and attempt to preserve the ideal of perfection, but they themselves need not be perfect (at least not initially) to do so. Instead, they must allow for and encourage growth and change toward perfection. By this definition, the church can never expect to reach total purity, because it must always include the unconverted for it to fulfill its institutional mission.

Of course, such contact with the unconverted or hypocrites could threaten the integrity of the institution and perhaps even force a redefinition of its mission. Rather than seek positive fulfillment by conversion, the church may have to settle for minimizing the damage done by its less-than-perfect members. But even in the dark moments following the Antinomian Controversy, Cotton still believed that even if an institution cannot transform all of its members, it can still transcend the limitations of any individual member: "I doe not understand, but that (according to Scripture) those corruptions which doe not destroy a Church constituted, the same do not destroy the constitution of a Church. The Church is constituted, and continued by the same Grace."[24] If the initial constitution of a church has sufficient grace to overcome certain corruptions, then the institution should be able to continue on the strength of that grace and remain unthreatened by future corruption. Thus, to a certain extent, grace resides in the institution itself—in its offices, its forms of worship, and its traditions.

It would be inaccurate to characterize Cotton as an extreme advocate of transcendent institutions and offices; to do so would situate him uncomfortably close to the very papists he denounces. Nevertheless, when compared to Williams, he does express much more faith in the power of institutions to accomplish the "nostalgic" goal of recovering perfection. This faith hinges on two related assumptions. First, while the end goal is complete resemblance of all members with Christ, Cotton recognizes that institutions must be able to tolerate and survive a fair degree of difference (i.e., the unconverted, the corrupt, the hypocrites). He again compares the church to a human body: "The store of malignant and noysome humours in the body, yea the deafnesse and rottenesse of many members in the body, though they make the body an unsound and corrupt body, yet they doe not make the body no body."[25] No amount of internal dissent or difference—from simple ill temper to rotting limbs—can jeopardize the integrity of the body as a body. However sick, it remains a body, but a body in need of cure and healing. Such cure remains possible as long as some part, however small, remains healthy. In terms of churches, then, Cotton argues the holy remnant theory: "It is not a multitude of hypocrites and prophane persons, that maketh a Church (where a remnant of godly persons are found) to become as Sodom or Gomorrah: But it is a remnant, a very small remnant, that preserveth the Church from becoming as Sodom, or Gomorrah."[26] The first church is never completely destroyed, never completely in the past. Instead, some small part of it always remains present and intact. At times this remnant may be small and underground; at other times it may be large and dominant. But as long as it exists, however small, it will overcome all dissent and difference.[27]

Cotton's faith in institutions also rests on both continuity and contingency. Like Williams, Cotton's ultimate goal is a return to the perfection of the first church. This desire drives a narrative that looks both forward and backward: forward, to full growth into this perfection, and backward, because growth is not so much progress as it is return. At the same time, Cotton accounts for historical contingencies. While the master narrative marches on, at any given moment in that narrative the church may be more or less perfect, the remnant may be bigger or smaller. Williams expects a full, complete, and immediate recovery of the patient; since that is virtually impossible, the patient is written off as effectively dead to this world. Cotton allows for progress over time; as long as a small pulse remains, he will continue to try to resuscitate. "The failings of the Churches are not forthwith to be healed by separation," he tells Williams. "It is not Chirurgery, but Butchery, to heale every sore in a member, with not other but Abscission from the Body."[28]

3. History and Conversion

In his sermons on the Book of Revelation, John Cotton warns his readers: "Thou are deceived to think the elder times were better."[29] Similarly, in sermons on Ecclesiastes he chides "old men" who are always "complaining of present times, but praising the former daies of old." He thus sets out to "reprove the fond admiration of elder times . . . to stirre us up to a wise consideration of our present times, and the amendment thereof."[30] Cotton's statements against nostalgia would, of course, seem to contradict a fundamental impulse behind the Puritan desire to return to first institutions. Cotton would no doubt counter this charge by arguing a difference between the past and The Past: by former days and elder times he means everything except the time of Christ on earth. Thus, one should not long to recuperate the glory of the Roman Catholic Church; one should instead push further back to the first institutions as described in the Bible.

This answer still raises an important question: How can one be sure one is not as mistaken about The Past as one was about the past?[31] Given the general tendency to glorify the past over the present, how does one know for sure that the first institutions were, in fact, pure, perfect, and therefore worth recovering? Again, the Puritans would have a simple and ready answer: the Bible says so. One could argue, in response, that the entire Puritan project is based on a delusion or a misreading, but to do so would largely be knocking on an open door. While the Puritans would never claim to be deluded, they were very aware of the fact that they gained their understanding of the past through unregenerate eyes.

Cotton explores the tendency to assume that the past is always better than the present in an amazing sequence of passages in his sermons on Ecclesiastes. He begins by explicating chapter 7, verse 10: "Say not thou, What is the cause that the former days were better then these? for thou dost not inquire wisely concerning this":

> . . . ordinarily men extol the cheapness of former times, their great hospitality, their kind neighbourhood, their honest dealing; their skillful workmanship, none such now adayes; their liberal almes deeds; their devout piety; their deep wisdome, their valiant acts; the reasons which men are wont to give of

> it, are not wise: as, First . . . the decay of the strength and goodnesse of nature, in the world and all the creatures. But this is no good reason; for nature decayed by the flood; yet the times have been better. Secondly, the goodnesse of the old religion, Jer. 44. 17, 18. The Heathen thought the Empire Flourished more under the worship of Jupiter and other false gods, then under the Christian Religion. The devout Papists thinke the same, that it was a better world under their Religion, then ours. . . . Thirdly, the change of time which some thinke are alwayes for the worse. . . . But neither times nor starres were made to rule us.[32]

Here we have someone from late-sixteenth- and early-seventeenth-century England sounding remarkably like a Brooklynite from the 1950s reminiscing about the good old days of the Dodgers and egg creams. Cotton's ode to simpler times sounds strikingly familiar: things cost less, there was a greater sense of neighborhood, people were kinder, braver, wiser, more generous and honest. Although nostalgic in tone, Cotton goes on to reject traditional explanations for this perceived decline. Nature does not go steadily downhill; there may be times of decay, but there are also times of replenishment (certainly a lesson made clear by Ecclesiastes). Old religions appear better than new religions only because people are reluctant to change. Thus, history records a litany of skepticism: heathens skeptical about Christians, papists skeptical about Protestants.

Cotton also categorically rejects a premise that must be anathema to anyone intent on reform: that change is always for the worse. His insistence that "neither the times nor the starres were made to rule us" may initially seem odd coming from someone who believes in predestination. But he most likely refers here not to divine predetermination but to historical determinism (rule by the times) or to a general surrender to fatalism or fortune (rule by the stars). Such rule, in fact, runs counter to divine determination; if one complacently gives oneself over to the dictates of the time, then one may never take action to reform. Even worse, one can become completely paralyzed by an inaccurate vision of the past; if things never get better, then why bother doing anything?

It is just this misperception of the past that lies at the heart of nostalgia. Cotton continues his explication:

> From the cause of the worse appearance of present times, from [form?] fonde mistakings. As, First, In youth want of Judgement to discerne and judge of good or evil. They [their?] Judgement then was green and raw; young mens spirits are green and cheerful, and so looking through a green glasse (as it were) thou sawest all things green and pleasant. Old men are splenetick and sad, and see all things through darke and sad fumes, and so accordingly thinke hardly of them. Besides by better experience, old men now can

> discerne much evil, which before they could not observe. Secondly, through ignorance of history, which speaketh of as bad times as ours. Or else through the choyce that Historians make to tell of notable matters, and neglect common occurrences: besides its pleasant to read in stories of great warres, and exploits; but to feele them would seem Tragical. Thirdly, through following sense in this conceit, evils present seem worst, as in governments so in the whole life of man. Fourthly, through discontentment with a mans own personal condition, and envy of others, and vaine glory in our selves. . . . Fifthly, through curiosity, whilest men looke more at others then themselves, whereas if every man laboured to amend himselfe, the times would soon amend.[33]

Cotton explains the various reasons for our limited perception and points out that in each case this limited perception leads to inaccurate discernment or judgment, which, in turn, leads to inaccurate evaluation of the past. Age plays a big role: the "green tint" of inexperience will inevitably lead us to believe that the time of our youth was simpler, mainly because we were simpler. Similarly, the "dark and sad fumes" of old age cast a shadow over anything new. Cotton also offers some prescient insights into the recording, transmission, and reception of history. The past may look better to us not only because of our own ignorance of certain historical details but also because of a collective ignorance on the part of historians. By choosing notable matters instead of common occurrences, historians further distort a perception of the past that is already distorted by our own limitations and ignorance. Since we "know" most history through stories rather than lived experience, the shift in the means of apprehension or perception changes the entire tone and timbre of the past: the "tragical" experience of wars and exploits becomes "pleasant to read in stories." This distance between experience and recollection also distorts perception of our own personal histories. While "evils present seem worst" precisely because they are present, "evils past" can be selectively considered with a fond remembrance of overcoming them and a willful forgetting of the terror of the moment.

If Cotton warns against allowing history to determine us, he also underscores the equal dangers of how we determine history, not only through direct action but through distorted perception. The last line of this passage—"if every man laboured to amend himselfe, the times would soon amend"—not only echoes an idea we've seen Cotton utter many times (the direct link between personal and societal reform) but also suggests that an accurate understanding of history is both a cause and effect of conversion. To change the present we must change our perception of the past. We cannot get trapped by a nostalgia that allows us to fall into complacency, fatalism, cynicism. And yet, if nostalgia potentially hampers change, it potentially motivates it as well; paradoxically, even the misperception of history could lead to reform. Even if one is inaccurate about how bad the present is or how good the past was, one could still take action to make the present resemble the perceived greatness of the past. In the end, it does not really matter if the past was actually great, as long as one struggles toward some ideal of greatness.

Once again, though, the Puritans would not formulate the question in this way. Instead, they remained firm in the conviction that The Past was, in fact, a time worth recovering. Their goal, as Cotton formulates it, is to discern the difference between disabling nostalgia (the desire to return to "the good old days" that were not, in fact, that good) and enabling nostalgia (the desire to recuperate first institutions). Of course, the ability to discern such differences and to gain such new perspectives are precisely Cotton's goals for conversion. In short, we must become better souls—souls that have overcome "discontentment with a mans own personal condition, and envy of others, and vaine glory in our selves"—to become better readers of history. The process of searching for the truth in history is not an end in itself because the truth is already there for the discovering—a fixed, stable, unmoving target that one could hit if only one could clear away the green tint and dark fumes. Instead, reading history becomes a means to an end, an end that Cotton would call conversion: the acquisition of a new mind, the "new eyes" that one needs to see the truth that has always been there, the clarity of vision and thought needed to discern differences but not be ruled by them. In these ways, then, one's perception of history serves as both a cause (in that it motivates a desire for change) and an effect of conversion (in that we see history in a new way once converted). The chronic danger of such a formulation—and Cotton was well aware of it—is that we search with unconverted eyes for that which will save us.

As part of his understanding of an identity based on resemblance and consistency, Cotton felt that sins against knowledge were the worst sins one could commit. Consciously doing or saying something that you already know to be wrong is far worse than acting out of impulse or ignorance. We sin against knowledge, Cotton writes, "when men sin not in infirmity, nor in pang or passion . . . nor in pang of a lust . . . but when in cool blood, men do reject the word of life."[34] In this instance, Cotton, like Williams, insists on purity of desire as well as pure objects of desire. Thus, a relatively benign act—lying, for example—constitutes a far worse sin if it is done with intentional malice than a far more serious act done out of impulse or ignorance. Once again, Cotton strives for consistency between and among thought, word, and action.

By his own admission he never achieved such consistency in his own career as a minster. His record is spotted with famous—or infamous—

shifts in direction: from a tendency toward Arminianism early in his career to affinities with antinomianism later on, from strong arguments against separation and migration to actual migration and the compromise stance of "non-separation," from support to abandonment of Anne Hutchinson. Cotton explains each of these changes as examples of seeing the light, of throwing off former delusions for a clearer vision of the truth. Even the great Augustine, he notes, published two long books of retractions.[35] His critics respond less generously. Robert Baillie, for example, remarks on his "too precipitant rashnesse . . . both to receive and to send abroad to the world such Tenants whereof after he had cause to repent."[36] Offering mock encouragement to a colleague who has been asked by the court to recant his erroneous beliefs, another of Cotton's opponents notes: "It shal be no disparagement unto you [to recant], for here is our Reverend Elder, Mr. Cotton who ordinarily preacheth that publickly one year, that the next year he publickly repents of, and shows himselfe very sorrowful for it to the Congregation, so that (saith he) it will be no disgrace for you to recant in such a case."[37]

Cotton spends most of his congregational writings defending himself against such charges. For example, he boasts that his drift toward migration anticipated by about ten years the official position of English Parliament or that the Antinomian Controversy only proved the ability of the Congregational Way to correct errant preachers and church members. But in one remarkable moment in *The Way . . . Cleared* he admits that it is virtually impossible to achieve complete consistency, that we are always, in effect, sinning against knowledge: "I shall willingly acknowledge . . . that I am made up of weaknesses and contradictions. The best good in me is but weak at the best: and that which is corrupt, is weakness itself. If there be old and new man in me (as by the grace of Christ I see what I am) verily I cannot but finde a bundle, not only of contradictions, but contrafactions in myself. I believe, I doubt; I allow, I condemn; I hope, I fear; I love, I hate; I rejoice, I grieve; I would, I would not; I do, I undo; the same self, the same thing, at the same time."[38] This passage is uncharacteristic for Cotton in many ways: in its lyricism, its location (it appears in an ecclesiastical treatise, not in a sermon), and its logic of identity. It may be the one place in all of his work where he does approach the "self" described by Whitman ("Do I contradict myself? / Very well then . . . I contradict myself") or Emerson ("A foolish consistency is the hobgoblin of little minds"). The seven pairs of verbs, linked only by a comma, suggest that the self is a delicate mixture of contradictory thoughts and actions.

Missing here is Cotton's insistence that thought, speech, and action should always coincide. Missing also is a sense of progress, that the self, through the process of conversion, moves steadily from hate to love, from fear to hope. Old and new, good and evil, past and present, coexist at the same time, in the same self. The self can never completely resemble Christ, then, because it never completely resembles itself. Some reserved difference slips in to prevent the identity with Christ—indeed, to prevent identity. The individual here described can never enjoy perfect union with others because it can never accomplish perfect unity within the self. Where Emerson may, at times, celebrate this self, Cotton concedes to it as yet another compromise. Just as the diseased body remains an integrated body despite its sickness, so too the multiple self remains "the same self" despite its contradictions. Conversion can never turn all differences into resemblances; at best, it provides perfect insight into one's own imperfection: "by the grace of Christ I see what I am." Nostalgia becomes a longing for something we never fully possess: the self we never were, the self we will never be.

Notes

Introduction

1. A recent and influential version of this model can be found in Stephen Greenblatt's famous epilogue to *Renaissance Self-Fashioning: From More to Shakespeare* (Chicago: U Chicago P, 1980):

   > But as my work progressed, I perceived that fashioning oneself and being fashioned by cultural institutions—family, religion, state—were inseparably intertwined. In all my texts and documents, there were, so far as I could tell, no moments of pure, unfettered subjectivity; indeed, the human subject itself began to seem remarkably unfree, the ideological product of the relations of power in a particular society. Whenever I focused sharply upon a moment of apparently autonomous self-fashioning, I found not an epiphany of identity freely chosen but a cultural artifact. If there remained traces of free choice, the choice was among possibilities whose range was strictly delineated by the social and ideological system in force. (256)

2. Janice Knight also sees the limitations of a margins/center model. She writes: "Important sites of difference within the dominant culture are themselves effaced within this dynamic of margin and center, with the result that dominance is totalized and the possibility of dissent from within the cultural mainstream is precluded" (8). See especially the introduction to *Orthodoxies in Massachusetts: Rereading American Puritanism* (Cambridge, Mass.: Harvard UP, 1994).
3. For histories of the words *individual* and *individualism* see Raymond Williams, *Keyword* (New York: Oxford UP, 1981), and the *Oxford English Dictionary*. Older nuances and definitions of *individual* include "indivisible," "inseparable," "one in substance or essence forming an indivisible entity; that cannot be separated." Newer definitions include "single, as distinct from others of the same kind," "particular," "special," "distinguished from others by attributes of its own," "marked by peculiar and striking character." The first recorded instance of *individualism* is in Alexis de Tocqueville's *Democracy in America* (1835). For a more extensive discussion of the history of these words, see chapter 1.
4. I do not mean to suggest here that Puritan scholars have never engaged in comparative studies of England and New England; a variety of scholars have engaged the terms of this comparison explicitly and productively. Recent examples of such work include Patricia Caldwell, *The Puritan Conversion Narrative: The Beginnings of American Expression* (New York: Cambridge UP, 1983); Andrew

Delbanco, *The Puritan Ordeal* (Cambridge, Mass.: Harvard UP, 1989); Knight, *Orthodoxies in Massachusetts*; David Cressy, *Coming Over: Migration and Communication between England and New England in the Seventeenth Century* (New York: Cambridge UP, 1987); Bernard Bailyn, *Voyagers to the West: A Passage in the Peopling of America on the Eve of the Revolution* (New York: Knopf, 1986); Francis Bremer, *Congregational Communion: Clerical Friendship in the Anglo-American Community, 1610–1692* (Boston: Northeastern UP, 1994); and Stephen Foster, *The Long Argument: English Puritanism and the Shaping of New England Culture, 1570–1700* (Chapel Hill: U North Carolina P, 1991). My own call for comparison differs somewhat in intent and scope. That is, some of these studies (notably Caldwell and Delbanco) engage in comparisons to delineate significant differences between the English and New English Puritan experience. I am not here attempting to argue for something like the rise of "American" individualism as distinct from individualism in England. Further, almost all of these studies keep the scope of the comparison focused almost exclusively on the Puritans themselves. Thus, Knight traces the influence of key English ministers on those who migrated to New England. My own scope includes more general cultural issues that encompass larger segments of early modern England, for example, changes in the family and gender roles.

5. Lawrence Stone, *The Family, Sex and Marriage in England, 1500–1800*, abridged ed. (New York: Harper, 1977/1979). A definition of affective individualism appears on p. 151, of possessive individualism on p. 173.
6. Stone's basic narrative of the rise of modern individualism has been echoed by many New Historical studies of early modern England. In addition to Greenblatt, *Renaissance Self-Fashioning*, see, for example, Nancy Armstrong and Leonard Tennenhouse, *The Imaginary Puritan: Literature, Intellectual Labor, and the Origins of Personal Life* (Berkeley: U California P, 1992); Catherine Belsey, *The Subject of Tragedy: Identity and Difference in Renaissance Drama* (New York: Methuen, 1985); Margaret Ferguson, Maureen Quilligan, and Nancy Vickers, eds., *Rewriting the Renaissance: The Discourse of Sexual Difference in Early Modern Europe* (Chicago: U Chicago P, 1986); and Mary Nyquist and Margaret Ferguson, eds., *Re-membering Milton: Essays in the Texts and Traditions* (New York: Methuen, 1988).
7. Jay Fliegelman, *Prodigals and Pilgrims: The American Revolution against Patriarchal Authority, 1750–1800* (New York: Cambridge UP, 1982), 2–3.
8. For example, Fliegelman argues: "At every opportunity Revolutionary propagandists insisted that the new nation and its people had come of age, had achieved a collective maturity that necessitated them becoming in political fact an independent and self-governing nation" (ibid., 3).
9. Gillian Brown, *Domestic Individualism: Imagining Self in Nineteenth Century America* (Berkeley: U California P, 1990), 1.
10. Christopher Newfield, *The Emerson Effect: Individualism and Submission in America* (Chicago: U Chicago P, 1996), 10.
11. To a greater or lesser extent, Stone, Brown, and Newfield all emphasize material causes—changes in the economic marketplace, ownership and distribution of property and capital, and so on—for these redefinitions of individualism. The lack of discussion of such causes in the present study does not imply a disagree-

ment with these other scholars; rather, my main interest here is how ideas about individuals and institutions shape and are shaped by Puritan religious discourse.

12. Sacvan Bercovitch, *The Puritan Origins of the American Self* (New Haven, Conn.: Yale UP, 1975), 18–19.

13. The fact that Bercovitch's own work on the Puritans constitutes a revision of Perry Miller's compelling paradigms is generally well known among scholars of American culture. This revision has focused largely on how Puritan typology underwrites the mission of a chosen people into a promised land and how this sense of chosenness, in turn, shapes almost all of American culture and history. Miller makes his case, most famously, in the two volumes of *The New England Mind: The Seventeenth Century* (Cambridge, Mass.: Harvard UP, 1939) and *From Colony to Province* (Cambridge, Mass.: Harvard UP, 1953) and in the essay collection *Errand into the Wilderness* (Cambridge, Mass.: Harvard UP, 1956). In most of his arguments, Miller presents the Puritans as unified in their theology and sense of mission. Bercovitch begins his revision of Miller's arguments in an essay about the Cotton–Williams controversy ("Typology in Puritan New England: The Williams-Cotton Controversy Reassessed," *American Quarterly* 16 (1967): 166–91) and expands his ideas in *The American Jeremiad* (Madison: U Wisconsin P, 1978). While he brilliantly reveals the ideological underside of the Puritan mission, he never quite challenges Miller's assumption of consensus and coherence in Puritan thought. For useful accounts of Miller and Bercovitch, see Andrew Delbanco, "The Puritan Errand Reviewed," *Journal of American Studies* 18 (1984): 343–60; the introductory chapter to Janice Knight's *Orthodoxies in Massachusetts*; and Arne Delfs, "Anxieties of Influence: Perry Miller and Sacvan Bercovitch," *The New England Quarterly* 70, no. 4 (December 1997): 601–15. Delfs provides an especially useful bibliography of the debates.

Bercovitch's reliance on a consensus view of Puritan culture has itself come under extensive revision and challenge. The main source of this challenge stems from a number of former students of Alan Heimert (himself a former student of Perry Miller) at Harvard. These scholars and their works include Caldwell, *The Puritan Conversion Narrative*; Delbanco, *The Puritan Ordeal*; Knight, *Orthodoxies in Massachusetts*; and Theresa Toulouse, *The Arte of Prophesying: New England Sermons and the Shaping of Belief* (Athens: U Georgia P, 1987). (The extended headnotes in *The Puritans in America: A Narrative Anthology* [Cambridge, Mass.: Harvard UP, 1985], co-written by Heimert and Andrew Delbanco, are the closest we have to Heimert's published version of his arguments.) To varying degrees, these scholars depict dissensus where Miller and Bercovitch see consensus; that is, they delineate significant differences within the New England ministry on issues such as conversion and the relative importance of the covenants of grace and works. These differences are variously described as a tension between Intellectual Fathers and Spiritual Brethren, Amesians and Sibbesians, preparationists and antinomians, legalists and spiritists. The minister Thomas Hooker is most usually associated with the first set of terms in each pair, and John Cotton represents the second set (Thomas Shepard is always something of a loose cannon). In their analyses these scholars never allow these two sets of terms to become static opposites: Cotton is never portrayed as exclusively antinomian any more than Hooker is exclusively preparationist. Rather, the dramatic tension of these ideas serves as a context for each scholar's particular interests (conversion relations for Caldwell, for example, or immigration and representations of sin for Delbanco).

My own general view of the Puritans has been strongly influenced by this tradition, in part because of the circumstances of my education (attested to in the acknowledgments) but mostly because I think it is correct. This indebtedness holds especially true for my understanding of Cotton's rhetoric and piety, as presented in chapter 2. My differences with this tradition take the form of departures rather than disagreements. That is, it is not my intent to register minor disagreements in interpretations of this or that sermon. Rather, I am using this general view of Puritanism as a point of departure to examine issues such as the role of family and gender in the formation of institutions and individuals or to offer a reading of Hutchinson situated somewhat outside the Hooker/Cotton dualities. Also, although Roger Williams was central to Bercovitch's revision of Miller, he does not receive extensive treatment in the studies listed above.

14. In *A Glimpse of Sion's Glory: Puritan Radicalism in New England, 1620–1660* (Middletown, Conn.: Wesleyan UP, 1984) Philip Gura rightly argues that most scholars of American Puritanism have mistakenly assumed that New England enjoyed a stable religious and political consensus that was occasionally interrupted by minor gestures of radical dissent. Gura argues instead that the range of radical dissent in New England was just as wide as it was in England, and that this radicalism played an important role in the development of the colonies. Based on this more expansive view of radicalism, Gura claims "we have every right to ask why seventeenth-century New England did not become *more* radicalized and *more* democratic than it did" (11–12; Gura's emphasis). This is an interesting question to ask and a difficult one to answer especially if one equates—as Gura often does—religious or spiritual radicalism with political radicalism. That is, Gura and others assume that a challenge to religious consensus implies a challenge to political consensus, and that radical spiritism should translate into radical democracy. My own assumptions differ from Gura's in at least two ways. Some forms of spiritism may appear radical (in that they challenge hierarchies) only if viewed from certain perspectives. For example, Anne Hutchinson's dissent challenges at least some earthly authorities, but it also requires extreme dependence on and submission to divine authority. I am also more reluctant than Gura to see a direct correspondence between politics and religion. For example, Roger Williams's politically progressive call for toleration rests on conservative religious principles.

15. In *Prophetic Woman: Anne Hutchinson and the Problem of Dissent in the Literature of New England* (Berkeley: U California P, 1987), Amy Schrager Lang invokes Bercovitch's model of dissent in her extensive analysis of Anne Hutchinson. Focusing on the idea of antinomianism, Lang also explores other instances of dissent in the New England tradition. Her convincing reading of Emerson, for example, anticipates the contours of Newfield's argument: "Emerson offered a failsafe method for distinguishing true individualism from false: the genuinely self-reliant man would inevitably prove to be the perfect member; true individualism would yield 'union,' not anarchy" (134). Lang further distinguishes

between Hutchinson and Emerson: "However, rather than celebrating the dissenting view implied by this anti tendency or glorying, as Anne Hutchinson in some sense did, in his liberation from the Law, Emerson applied himself to the task of demonstrating how it was that the perfect self-reliance of the American was precisely not antinomianism" (117). My main disagreement with Lang stems from her reading of Hutchinson. To a certain extent, Lang implies a decline of radicalism that hinges on a reading of Hutchinson as radically subversive of institutional authority (in a way that Emerson could never pretend to be): "the problem of individual autonomy is especially problematic when the individual is female. The fact that Anne Hutchinson, the classic American representative of a radical and socially destructive self-trust, is a woman compounds and complicates her heresy" (3). As I argue above and in chapter 4, a desire for individual autonomy should not be asserted as a given fact of the case. I do agree that gender is an important factor in the case but not in the way that Lang suggests (see chapter 4).

16. I do not mean to suggest that no other previous scholar has approached Puritanism in the general spirit of my own approach. My indebtedness to Amanda Porterfield's *Female Piety in Puritan New England: The Emergence of Religious Humanism* (New York: Oxford UP, 1992) will be signaled throughout the book. In addition, David Leverenz has also warned about the dangers of an ahistorical understanding of individualism. In *The Language of Puritan Feeling: An Exploration in Literature, Psychology and Social History* (New Brunswick, N.J.: Rutgers UP, 1980), he writes: "It is easy to misinterpret Puritanism as a first manifestation of individualism, in which solitary pilgrims confront their God. Yet it was primarily a group phenomenon . . . though our more individualistic age has naturally emphasized Puritan repression of the individual" (121); and "Puritans could never conceive of the self the way we do: isolated, individualist, anomic, filled with separable desires, complex personal histories, and uncertain futures. What to us is the norm was to them the essence of sin. In fact, their reaction against the forces precipitating such separate identities helped drive them to New England" (134).

17. For recent arguments against thinking about scholarship as a form of political intervention, see David Simpson, *The Academic Postmodern and the Rule of Literature: A Report on Half-Knowledge* (Chicago: U Chicago P, 1995), and Stanley Fish, *Professional Correctness: Literary Studies and Political Change* (New York: Oxford UP, 1995). Fish, with typical bluntness, states: "The return to literary criticism of political questions does not make literary criticism more political in any active sense" (55).

18. I've borrowed the term and idea of retrojection from Debora Shuger, *Habits of Thought in the English Renaissance: Religion, Politics and the Dominant Culture* (Berkeley: U California P, 1990), 23. Of much recent work in the early modern period she writes: "The result of the contemporary interest in Renaissance ideology with limited concern for its actual articulations is that more familiar modern issues and terms of analysis quietly (or not so quietly) displace historical ones" (3–4).

19. Janice Knight writes: "Perhaps more than other scholarly communities, early Americanists read their subjects as a point of origin for the present day—we

read ourselves against, and we read 'America' out of, the Puritan past" (*Orthodoxies in Massachusetts*, 2).

20. Both projection and retrojection, of course, look from the present to the past. But while retrojection remains rooted in the present, projection attempts to move first from the present to the past and then from the past to the present.
21. I would not count Bercovitch among these scholars. Although he clearly sees a conflation of political and religious convictions, he spends a great deal of time analyzing religious rhetoric in its own terms, and it is the conflation itself that is his main source of concern.
22. See Max Weber, *The Protestant Ethic and the Spirit of Capitalism* (London: Unwin, 1930/1987), and R. H. Tawney, *Religion and the Rise of Capitalism* (London: John Murray, 1926).
23. Ann Kibbey, *The Interpretation of Material Shapes in Puritanism: A Study of Rhetoric, Prejudice and Violence* (New York: Cambridge UP, 1986), 161, n. 11.
24. Ibid., 2.
25. Greenblatt, *Renaissance Self-Fashioning*, 113.
26. For example, Gura asserts that "in place of the spiritual and, by implication, political democracy the radicals demanded, the New Englanders erected only a half-way house on the road to a more democratic society" (*Glimpse of Sion's Glory*, 15); Lang, *Prophetic Woman*, 13–14.
27. Two scholars in particular provide exemplary models for approaching questions of religion. In *Habits of Thought in the English Renaissance*, Debora Shuger writes: "Religion is, first of all, not simply politics in disguise, a set of beliefs that represent and legitimate the social order by grounding it in the Absolute. . . . Religious belief is 'about' God and the soul as much as it is 'about' the sociopolitical order. Whether or not one believes in the former two entities, one gains very little by assuming that the culture under investigation did not itself comprehend the essential nature of its preoccupations. . . . Such subjects are, again, not masked by religious discourse but articulated in it" (6). Other works by Shuger include *Sacred Rhetoric: The Christian Grand Style in the English Renaissance* (Princeton, N.J.: Princeton UP, 1988) and *The Renaissance Bible: Scholarship, Sacrifice, and Subjectivity* (Berkeley: U California P, 1994). Jenny Franchot has brought a similar sensibility (and sensibleness) to bear on the study of religion in American culture. In her forceful essay "Invisible Domain: Religion and American Literary Studies," *American Literature* 67 (December 1995): 833–42, she argues that religion "cannot be looked at as an isolable phenomenon that enjoys explanatory priority over all other experience, as some multiculturalist critics would have us privilege race or some gender theorists sexuality. But neither can we dismiss religion as false consciousness, for aside from it being an objectionable form of condescension, such a dismissal has little analytical power. Religion approached as false consciousness is an exercise in dullness as well as arrogance" (840). See also her book *Roads to Rome: The Antebellum Protestant Encounter with Catholicism* (Berkeley: U California P, 1994).
28. I do not mean to suggest that scholars of the early modern period have found perfect solutions to the problems of projection and retrojection or that they provide a stable ground on which to locate the New England Puritans. Instead, thinking about the Puritans in terms of early modern history provides a useful

check against the temptation of thinking about the Puritans as the first term in American history. Nor do I mean to suggest that the problems of projection and retrojection can ever be completely avoided, even by the most dedicated antiquarians. As William Spengemann has recently argued, "The present is finally inescapable. Because it consists in our linguistic equipment, which we cannot forget, the present unavoidably conditions our reading of any past text, making its statements mean things that they could not possibly have meant when they were written. So long as we go on reading texts amidst circumstances different from those in which the texts were written, a diachronic link will remain intact, implicit in our ability to read—and in our fate to misread—words set down long ago, in other worlds" (38–39). *A New World of Words: Redefining Early American Literature* (New Haven, Conn.: Yale UP, 1994).

29. Of course, many historians also care about the nuances of particular details just as much as do literary scholars. Indeed, it was a desire to clarify and qualify Perry Miller's sweeping generalizations that provoked many of the regional and town studies produced by social historians in the late 1960s and 1970s. This respect for the historical significance of the particular continues to inform works such as Laurel Thatcher Ulrich's *A Midwife's Tale: The Life of Martha Ballard, Based on Her Diary* (New York: Knopf, 1990), wherein much can be learned about the life of colonial women through a reading of this one woman's diary. While this is not the best place to explore the differences between literary and historical approaches to Puritan culture, I would at least suggest a few recent works as points of comparison: Ronald Hoffman, Mechal Sobel, and Fredrika J. Teute, eds., *Through a Glass Darkly: Reflections on Personal Identity in Early America* (Chapel Hill: U North Carolina P, 1997); Mary Beth Norton, *Founding Mothers and Fathers: Gendered Power and the Forming of American Society* (New York: Knopf, 1996); James F. Cooper, "Higher Law, Free Consent, Limited Authority: Church Government and Political Culture in Seventeenth-Century Massachusetts" *New England Quarterly* 69 (June 1996): 201–22. All of these works engage questions that are also central to my own investigations; indeed, the title phrase of the essay collection by Hoffman et al. (taken from Corinthians) plays a central role in my analysis of conversion in chapter 2. Perhaps the most basic difference between these works and works of literary analysis rests in the *kinds* of details each discipline values and the relative balance struck between particular analysis and generalization. To get a sense of institutional values, for example, Cooper examines not the metaphors found in sermons but church membership records and minutes of church meetings. Similarly, Norton builds her arguments about patriarchal authority not by scrutinizing variations on the family analogy (although she does, in fact, discuss them) but by assembling an enormous computer database of almost every available court record. To my mind, the different values assigned to categories of evidence still marks a significantly productive divide between the disciplines.

30. Anne Myles, "Arguments in Milk, Arguments in Blood: Roger Williams, Persecution and the Discourse of the Witness," *Modern Philology* 91 (1993): 154. One model and inspiration for my approach to Puritan texts is Patricia Caldwell's *Puritan Conversion Narrative*. Caldwell focuses on a relatively small number of texts (the conversion relations of Shepard's congregants) and places these

confessions in historical and literary contexts, but she generates her primary arguments from sensitive and nuanced readings that revitalize these otherwise cryptic texts for the modern student.

31. Miller, *New England Mind: The Seventeenth Century*, ix.

32. The "canonical status" of Cotton, Williams, and Hutchinson is somewhat paradoxical. While widely written *about*, very little of their own writing remains readily available. Although the seven volumes of the Narragansett edition of Williams's works total over 2000 pages, only a few snippets of his writing find their way into anthologies, and very little of it can be easily located in modern editions. Students wishing to read the full range of Williams's thought still must rely on the 1963 limited-edition reprint of the Narragansett edition. John Cotton has fared even worse. Like Williams, he was quite prolific, but aside from a few academic reprints the large majority of his works exist only in seventeenth-century editions, now incarcerated in rare book and microform rooms. Unlike Williams, he has not yet enjoyed a modern edition of all of his work. Of the three figures under consideration, Anne Hutchinson (as far as we know) was the only one never to publish a single word. Ironically, she is the only one now readily available in print by way of the Duke University Press reissue of Wesleyan's edition of *The Antinomian Controversy, 1636–1638: A Documentary History*.

33. This is not to suggest that Cotton is a "radical," but it is to suggest that terms such as *radical* and *conservative* are relative; so if one wants to portray Williams as a rebel, for example, it helps to know what he was rebelling against.

34. Useful books on Cotton include Everett Emerson, *John Cotton* (New York: Twayne, 1965), and Larzer Ziff, *The Career of John Cotton: Puritanism and the American Experience* (Princeton, N.J.: Princeton UP, 1962).

35. Moses Coit Tyler, *A History of American Literature during the Colonial Time, 1607–1765*, reprinted as *A History of American Literature, 1607–1783* (Chicago: U Chicago P, 1967), 71.

36. Emerson, *John Cotton*, 17.

37. Vernon Louis Parrington, *Main Currents in American Thought*, vol. 1, *The Colonial Mind* (New York: Harcourt, Brace, 1927), 30.

38. Those who distinguish Cotton from other ministers, such as Thomas Hooker, include Alan Heimert and Andrew Delbanco in *The Puritans in America*; Andrew Delbanco in *The Puritan Ordeal*; and Teresa Toulouse in *The Arte of Prophesying*. In *Orthodoxies in Massachusetts*, Janice Knight provides an important corrective to what she calls "a romanticizing of Cotton's piety as the lost, best part of ourselves" (11). Knight argues that the mainstream Puritan ministry had long had two different modes—Spiritual Brethren (Cotton and the like) and Intellectual Fathers (Hooker and the like), each with a long tradition: "Cottonian piety was a far more ancient and persistent countervoice within 'moderate' Puritanism than has been recognized. It was neither the product of specifically American conditions, nor was it banished to sectarian groups in the aftermath of the Antinomian Controversy" (9).

39. Books on Roger Williams are legion. Among the more useful are Edwin Gaustad, *Liberty of Conscience: Roger Williams in America* (Grand Rapids, Mich.: Eerdmans, 1991); Perry Miller, *Roger Williams: His Contribution to the American Tra-*

dition (New York: Atheneum, 1962); Edmund Morgan, *Roger Williams: The Church and the State* (New York: Harcourt, Brace and World, 1967); Ola Winslow, *Master Roger Williams: A Biography* (New York: Macmillan, 1957).

40. *Roger Williams Heritage Trail* (Providence, R.I., n.d.).

41. Hugh Spurgin, *Roger Williams and Puritan Radicalism in the English Separatist Tradition* (Lewiston, Maine: Edwin Mellen Press, 1989), ix, vii, xiii; Gaustad, *Liberty of Conscience*, 75.

42. Jesper Rosenmeier, for example, argues that "Williams may have believed in religious freedom but this did not make him a political radical. Williams was a rigid conservative" (419). See his essay "The Teacher and the Witness: John Cotton and Roger Williams," *William and Mary Quarterly*, 3rd ser., 25 (1968): 408–31. Perry Miller's portrayal is even more extreme. Dubbing Williams "a menace to society," Miller concludes that he "was exiled as much because he was a nuisance as because he was subversive" (*Roger Williams*, 12, 26–27).

43. Roger Williams to John Cotton, Jr., 25 March 1671, in Glenn LaFantasie, ed., *The Correspondence of Roger Williams* (Hanover, N.H.: Rhode Island Historical Society, 1988), 2:629–30.

44. Edwin Gaustad nicely summarizes Williams's vexed relationship to political authority: "Roger Williams spent much of his time criticizing civil magistrates and trying to circumscribe their activities. The rest of the time he spent assisting such magistrates or becoming one himself. A strong critic of governmental practice, Roger Williams was nonetheless a chief practitioner" (*Liberty of Conscience*, 122).

45. For general information on Hutchinson, see Selma Williams, *Divine Rebel: The Life of Anne Marbury Hutchinson* (New York: Holt, Rinehart, 1981), and Emery Battis, *Saints and Sectaries: Anne Hutchinson and the Antinomian Controversy in the Massachusetts Bay Colony* (Chapel Hill: U North Carolina P, 1962).

46. Gura, *Glimpse of Sion's Glory*, 239; Lad Tobin, "In a Radically Different Voice," *Early American Literature* 25 (1990): 256; Williams, *Divine Rebel*, n.p.; Amy Schrager Lang, *Prophetic Woman*, 3.

47. Tobin, "Radically Different Voice," 254; Lyle Koehler, *A Search for Power: The "Weaker Sex" in Seventeenth-Century New England* (Chicago: U Illinois P, 1980), 233; Carla Mulford, "Colonial Period: to 1700" in Paul Lauter, ed., *The Heath Anthology of American Literature* (Lexington, Mass.: D. C. Heath, 1994), 1:13. I cite this headnote in an anthology because it represents a typical undergraduate's first—and in many cases only—exposure to Hutchinson.

48. The Old Corner Bookstore Building and The Globe Corner Bookstore, Boston, pamphlet, n.d.

49. All quotations are from David Hall, ed., *The Antinomian Controversy, 1636–1638: A Documentary History* (Durham, N.C.: Duke UP, 1990). These quotations are from John Wilson in "A Report of the Trial of Mrs. Anne Hutchinson before the Church in Boston," 384–385 (hereafter cited as "Church Trial"); John Winthrop in "The Examination of Mrs. Anne Hutchinson at the Court at Newtown," 344 (hereafter cited as "Civil Trial").

50. Mulford, Colonial Period: to 1700," 13; John Cotton, "Church Trial," 371.

51. Gura, *Glimpse of Sion's Glory*, 243–44; Wilson, "Church Trial," 380–81.

52. "Church Trial," 376–77.

53. We have many reasons to doubt the court's portrayal of Hutchinson. Many of the charges against her derive from a meeting held at her house about nine months before the civil trial. Several of the ministers in attendance claim to have taken notes on the meeting (already a problem, since Hutchinson thought the meeting was a private visit from the ministers, not a matter of official record), but these notes seem to have disappeared during the trials. As a result, many of the official charges against her cannot be fully substantiated; they depend instead on hearsay, conflicting accounts, and faulty memory. The transcripts of the trials come to us in two forms: a version preserved in Thomas Hutchinson's (Anne's great-grandson) history of the Bay Colony, which is based on the original documents that were destroyed when his house was burned down during the Revolution, and a version presented in Winthrop's *A Short Story of the Rise, reign, and ruine of the Antinomians, Familists, and Libertines* (London, 1644) in Hall, *Antinomian Controversy*. The gaps in each transcript, the conflicts between the versions, and the interested nature of both transcribers should give us pause in making claims about what Hutchinson "really" said. For Cotton and Williams we have thousands of pages of their own writings, published and unpublished, to give us a sense of what they said and how they said it. For Hutchinson we have only her statements at the trials, statements made under a whole range of restrictions. In the absence of her (relatively) unmediated words to balance out the official interpretation of the court, any attempt to talk about Hutchinson runs the risk of putting words into her mouth and of silencing her own story even further.

Chapter 1. Puritanism and the Family Analogy

1. Massachusetts Records, 1:186 (December 13, 1636), quoted in Edmund Morgan, *The Puritan Family: Religion and Domestic Relations in Seventeenth-Century New England* (New York: Harper and Row, 1944/1966), 145.
2. Petrus Ramus, *Dialecticae Libri Duo* (London, 1669), 11–12, quoted in Morgan, *The Puritan Family*, 21. For an extended discussion of the logic of "relative," see Morgan, pp. 21–25. For a general history of Ramist thought, see Walter Ong, S.J., *Ramus, Method, and the Decay of Dialogue* (Cambridge, Mass.: Harvard UP, 1958). For the importance of Ramus to Puritan thought, see Perry Miller, *The New England Mind: The Seventeenth Century* (Cambridge, Mass.: Harvard UP, 1939).
3. Edward Said's discussion of filiation (descent from parents, from the Latin word for "son") and affiliation (to associate with, related to Latin for "adoption") provides a useful vocabulary for analyzing the relationships between institutions and individuals. *The World, the Text, the Critic* (Cambridge, Mass.: Harvard UP, 1983), esp. 16–20.
4. Freud underscores the psychological components of this dynamic in his description of the family romance: "Indeed the whole effort at replacing the real father by a superior one is only an expression of the child's longing for the happy, vanished days when his father seemed to him the noblest and strongest of men

and his mother the dearest and loveliest of women. He is turning away from the father whom he knows to-day to the father in whom he believed in the earlier years of his childhood; and his phantasy is no more than the expression of a regret that those happy days have gone." Sigmund Freud, "The Family Romance," in James Strachey, ed. and trans., *The Standard Edition of the Complete Psychological Works of Sigmund Freud*, vol. 9 (London: Hogarth Press, 1959), 239.

While the present investigation by no means claims to be Freudian or otherwise psychoanalytic, the family romance nevertheless provides a useful model for understanding some of the key emotional aspects of filiation and affiliation as they manifest themselves in Puritanism. For example, Freud's suggestion that the family romance includes a "longing for the happy, vanished days" and a "regret that those happy days have gone" points to the role nostalgia plays in the Puritan conception of history and institutions, the subject of chapter 5 in this volume. As well, the act of "turning away" from one father to a better father motivates descriptions of spiritual conversion, the subject of chapter 2.

5. Lawrence Stone suggests that the confusion that results from the dissolution of one form of patriarchy (here, the Roman Catholic Church) leads to a desire for a stronger, not weaker, sense of paternal order. In *The Family, Sex and Marriage in England, 1500–1800* (New York: Harper, 1979), Stone writes: "The unity of Christendom had been irreparably shattered by the Reformation, and the pieces were never put together again. The result was that from henceforth there were various oppositions in terms of religious ideology, faith and practice, and no one could be completely certain which was right and which was wrong. The first result of this uncertainty was extreme fanaticism. Internal doubts could only be appeased by the most ferocious treatment of those who disagreed. The authoritarian family and the authoritarian nation state were the solutions to an intolerable sense of anxiety and a deep yearning for order" (146).
6. J. C. Smith, *The Psychoanalytic Roots of Patriarchy* (New York: New York UP, 1990), 186–87.
7. David Leverenz, *The Language of Puritan Feeling: An Exploration in Literature, Psychology, and Social History* (New Brunswick, N.J.: Rutgers UP, 1980), 49.
8. Ibid., 101, 103.
9. My general understanding of these historical changes depends heavily on Lawrence Stone's *Family, Sex and Marriage* (esp. chapters 3–6). Stone provides a comprehensive history of the changes in ideas of the family and individualism and pays close attention to the role of the Protestant Reformation in these changes. He narrates a move away from loyalty to kinship and clan toward loyalty to nuclear family and nation-state. Concomitant with this shift is a new emphasis on "affective" or "possessive market" individualism. He explains what may appear to be a paradoxical rise of individualism *and* patriarchy as follows: "Both Church and State provided powerful new theoretical and practical support, while two external checks on patriarchal power declined as kinship ties and clientage weakened. . . . Willing acceptance of the legitimacy of the authority, together with a weakness of competing foci of power, are the keys to the whole system" (109). Stone's narrative has become so widely accepted that a scholar such as Catherine Belsey can confidently assert "the unified subject of liberal

humanism is a product of the second half of the seventeenth century, an effect of the revolution" (*The Subject of Tragedy: Identity and Difference in Renaissance Drama* [New York: Methuen, 1985], 33). For more specific information about the family in Puritan culture, see Morgan, *The Puritan Family*; Philip Greven, *The Protestant Temperament: Patterns of Child-Rearing, Religious Experience, and the Self in Early America* (New York: Alfred A. Knopf, 1977); and Helena M. Wall, *Fierce Communion: Family and Community in Early America* (Cambridge, Mass.: Harvard UP, 1990).

10. Raymond Williams, *Keywords* (New York: Oxford UP, 1981), 161.
11. Williams explains the rise of *individualism*: "*Individuality* has the longer history, and comes out of the complex of meanings in which *individual* developed, stressing both a unique person and his (indivisible) membership of a group. *Individualism* is a 19th century coinage: 'a novel expression, to which a novel idea has given birth,' (tr. Toqueville, 1835): a theory not only of abstract individuals but of the primacy of individual states and interests" (ibid., 164–65).
12. Sacvan Bercovitch, *The Puritan Origins of the American Self* (New Haven, Conn.: Yale UP, 1975), 14. Bercovitch distinguishes Protestantism from Renaissance humanism in general: "Both humanism and Protestantism shift the grounds of private identity from the institution to the individual; and it has been said of each movement that its concept of *imitatio* makes every man his own church. But the humanists considered the true church to be a macrocosm of the self-fulfilled individual. The Reformers demanded that every individual reconstitute himself by grace a reflection of the church" (11). In short, "the model of identity [the humanist] offers posits that no two selves are alike" (12).
13. John Cotton, *A Practicall Commentary, or An Exposition with Observations, Reasons, and Uses upon the First Epistle Generall of John*, 2nd ed. (London, 1658), 226–27 (hereafter cited as *Commentary upon John*). Along the same lines, Bercovitch quotes Richard Mather: "By much beholding of the glory of the Lord in the glass of the Gospel . . . wee are changed into the same image" (*Puritan Origins*, 14).
14. Richard Baxter, *The Christian Directory*, quoted in Bercovitch, *Puritan Origins*, 17.
15. Andrew Delbanco has suggested that "by fear of corruption, the Puritans meant fear of the emergent self. . . . They were in flight from what they themselves were becoming in England—a people fully involved in the pursuit of economic advantage, playing by the new capitalist rules." *The Puritan Ordeal* (Cambridge, Mass.: Harvard UP, 1989), 12.
16. Renaissance scholar Jonathan Goldberg summarizes the findings of historians of the family such as Lawrence Stone and Philippe Ariès as follows: "The modern belief in the family as a retreat, as the place of comfort in an uncomfortable world, would scarcely have been recognized in the Renaissance, at least officially. Rather, the individual derived a sense of self largely from external matrices among which the family and its place in society was paramount. The family was understood as part of the larger world, both as the smallest social unit from which the larger world was composed and as the essential link between persons." "Fatherly Authority: The Politics of Stuart Family Images," in Margaret Ferguson, Maureen Quilligan, and Nancy Vickers, eds., *Rewriting the Renais-*

sance: The Discourse of Sexual Difference in Early Modern Europe (Chicago: Chicago UP, 1986), 7–8.

17. For example, Nancy Armstrong and Leonard Tennenhouse (*The Imaginary Puritan: Literature, Intellectual Labor, and the Origins of Personal Life* [Berkeley: U California P, 1992]) summarize the conclusions of Peter Laslett to suggest that Englishmen understood themselves in relation to the family: either they felt they were part of an integrated, organic whole, or they felt they were broken off from that whole (73). The same basic dynamic holds true for the Puritan family, where, as Edmund Morgan argues, "The Puritans . . . thought of their churches as an organization made up of families rather than individuals" (*Puritan Family*, 135–36). Some scholars give the family analogy a pointedly ideological reading. Catherine Belsey, for example, sees the family as "a training ground for the ready acceptance for the power relations established in the social body" (*Subject of Tragedy*, 146). That is, the family analogy does not so much provide an explicit model for thinking about institutional affiliations as it serves an ideological purpose by making institutional power relations seem "natural," even affectionate, and thus *not* open to explicit articulation and critique. Belsey is especially interested in gendered power relations, made to seem natural by the family analogy: "Once the distinction between public and private, state and family, is established, the position offered to a man is clear, single, and noncontradictory" (154), whereas women had "no single, unified, fixed position from which to speak" (160).

    Debora Shuger challenges such ideological readings by suggesting that "not all patriarchal discourse concerns whitewashing coercive power relations" (*Habits of Thought in the English Renaissance: Religion, Politics and the Dominant Culture* [Berkeley: U California P, 1990]), 233. Mary Beth Norton offers a useful corrective to the reigning ideas of public and private: "The English colonists did not equate private and female or private and family, even though they did largely . . . equate public . . . and male. The public/private dichotomy so frequently discussed by historians of women . . . did not exist in the Filmerian world" (*Founding Mothers and Fathers: Gendered Power and the Forming of American Society* [New York: Knopf, 1996]), 23. Armstrong and Tennenhouse also state that "the puritan family was not infused with the qualities of personal life but was a miniature version of the aristocratic state" (*Imaginary Puritan*, 165).

18. "Familial imagery," writes Michael Walzer, "intensified political bonds and suggested the mystical cult of the political father" (183) and further, "Men who shared the Calvinist distrust of nature, however inarticulately, were not likely to defend kingship by referring to the natural monarchy of the father. Instead, the tendency of Puritan thought was to turn fatherhood into a 'little commonwealth.' . . . Like the state, the family was viewed as a divine institution, established at God's preemptory command, which men entered by contract" (187–88). *The Revolution of Saints: A Study in the Origins of Radical Politics* (Cambridge, Mass.: Harvard UP, 1965).

19. Robert Filmer, *Patriarcha* (c.1640), in Johann Sommerville, ed., *Patriarcha and Other Writings* (New York: Cambridge UP, 1991), 10.

20. Ibid., 12.

21. Shuger, *Habits of Thought*, 191. See also Lynn Hunt, *The Family Romance of the*

French Revolution (Berkeley: U California P, 1992): "The father could still be a source of ambivalent feelings, especially when he vacillated between the roles of stern patriarch and loving father" (24).

22. Filmer, *Patriarcha*, 35.
23. John Locke, *The Second Treatise of Government* (c.1681), in David Wootoon, ed., *Political Writings of John Locke* (New York: Penguin, 1993), 262.
24. Lynn Hunt notes this change in relations between parents and children as a development of the Enlightenment: "The father's power was to end when the child no longer needed his help, and after that moment, father and (male) children were presumed to be equals" (*Family Romance*, 18).
25. Locke, *Second Treatise*, 288. About children, Filmer writes: "I wish that the Jesuit [Suarez] had taught us how and when sons become free. I know no means by the law of nature. It is the favour, I think, of the parents only, who when their children are of age and discretion to ease their parents of part of their fatherly care, are then content to remit some part of their fatherly authority" (*Patriarcha*, 18).
26. Mary Beth Norton has recently used Filmer and Locke to great analytical effect in her book *Founding Mothers and Fathers*. Generally, Norton sees the New England colonies as more Filmerian in their gendered relationships, whereas the southern colonies anticipate Locke. Michael Walzer also locates the Puritans somewhere between Filmer and the post-Enlightenment world of Locke:

    > The Puritan transformation of the family remained incomplete: so long as children were born, instead of appearing voluntarily like colonists in a new country, the family could not become a purely political society. The connection of parents and children, at least, was a natural connection and even Milton, the great theorist of legal divorce, treated nature awkwardly. But if the Puritans thus failed to transform the family into a little commonwealth founded entirely on command and consent, they also made it impossible to imagine the state as an old-fashioned family founded on nature and love. . . . There could not be a more complete reversal of the terms of Filmer's argument. (*Revolution of Saints*, 196–97)

27. The importance of covenant theology to Puritan thought has its own long and complicated history. For a general overview of covenant theology, see Perry Miller, *New England Mind: The Seventeenth Century*, especially book 4. For more specific readings, see Charles Cohen, *God's Caress: The Psychology of Puritan Religious Experience* (New York: Oxford UP, 1986); John von Rohr, *The Covenant of Grace in Puritan Thought* (Atlanta: Scholars Press, 1986); and William Stoever, *"A Faire and Easie Way to Heaven": Covenant Theology and Antinomianism in Early Massachusetts* (Middletown, Conn.: Wesleyan UP, 1978). Cohen provides a useful definition of covenant: "A 'mutual agreement' thus conveyed two senses: a relationship connoted by 'bargain' or 'pact' that emphasized the purely contractual nature of the accord, and one denominated by 'league' or 'alliance' that included amicable personal feelings like those associated with family ties, friendship, and peaceful intentions" (49). Cohen also makes a distinction between covenants (which enforce reciprocal duties) and testaments (which confer

gifts, legacies, or the promise of an inheritance regardless of previous merit). Cohen suggests that ministers did not always keep this distinction precisely and would stress reciprocity or inheritance as the situation demanded (53–55). Stoever further distinguishes the ways in which individual ministers interpreted the idea of covenant. In his taxonomy, covenants work by consent (in that we freely agree to enter into an offer from God) and condition (in that we remain in the covenant only if certain conditions are met) (97–98). I agree with Stoever's argument that, in his view of the covenant of grace, John Cotton virtually dismissed the human capacity to meet its conditions and was almost equally wary of the human capacity to give consent (79).

28. John Winthrop, *Journal*, ed. J. K. Hosmer (New York, 1908) 2:239. Similar statements about the covenant can be found in Thomas Hooker: "Amongst such who by no impression of nature, no rule of providence, or appointment from God, or reason, have power each over other, there must of necessity be a mutuall ingagement, each of the other by their free consent, before by any rule of God they have any right or power, or can exercise either, each towards the other" (*Survey of the Summe of Church Discipline*, pt. 1, p. 69; quoted in Morgan, *Puritan Family*, 26). John Cotton also states: "A wife hath right to her husbands goods not by her chastity or helpfulness to him or observance of him, but by her union with him: So neither have we any right to the blessings of the grace of Christ laid up in any promises, nor can we challenge any assurances thereof, till we can first hold forth and plead our assured union with himself." See "Mr. Cotton's Rejoynder" in David Hall, ed., *The Antinomian Controversy, 1636–1638: A Documentary History* (Durham, N.C.: Duke UP, 1990), 93.

29. The element of choice here is important and should be kept in mind to balance interpretations (such as Belsey's and Kibbey's) that depict patriarchy as a result of ideological or physical coercion (see Ann Kibbey, *The Interpretation of Material Shapes in Puritanism: A Study of Rhetoric, Prejudice and Violence* [New York: Cambridge UP, 1986]). David Leverenz, for example, writes: "Puritan writers took care to say that obedience to the father, like faith in God, must be voluntary, not coerced. In that sense individual decisions, freely made, were to lead to patriarchal order" (*Language of Puritan Feeling*, 46). And Edmund Morgan argues: "Although Puritans believed that a free consent was essential to a covenant, they also believed that freedom consisted in the opportunity to obey the will of God. The freedom of any individual, therefore, lay only in the choice of what state should govern him, what church he should worship in, and to some extent what family he should live in" (*Puritan Family*, 26).

30. For a history of the relationships between ministers and congregants, see David Hall, *The Faithful Shepherd: A History of the New England Ministry in the Seventeenth Century* (New York: Norton, 1974).

31. Lawrence Stone points out a paradox in Puritan ideas about marriage that parallels my interpretation of Winthrop's location between Filmer and Locke. Puritan emphasis on holy matrimony based on affective individualism (rather than, say, kinship demands or economic need) paradoxically results in increased submission to the husband. Stone writes: "Women were now expected to love and cherish their husbands after marriage and were taught that it was their sacred

duty to do so. This love, in those cases where it in fact became internalized and real, made it easier for wives to accept that position of submission to the will of their husbands upon which the preachers were also insisting. By a paradoxical twist, one of the first results of the doctrine of holy matrimony was a strengthening of the authority of the husband over the wife, and an increased readiness of the latter to submit herself to the dictates of the former" (*Family, Sex and Marriage*, 141–42).

32. See, for example, Norton, *Founding Mothers and Fathers*: "The obligation . . . was mutual: fathers protected and cared for their children and servants; in return, such subordinates owed their fathers respect and obedience" (106).

33. The court records of the Bay Colony are replete with instances of husbands assuming legal responsibility for the actions of their wives. For example: "Rich. Cornishe, bound for his wife to appear in court for charges objected against her" (5 August 1634); " Mary Felton: thefts from four men, her husband bound himself to restore the value of the goods taken away to each of them" (29 July 1641). All citations are from Nathaniel Shurtleff, ed., *Records of the Governor and Company of the Massachusetts Bay*, vol. 1 (Boston, 1853).

34. Divorce poses a threat to the integrity of the family analogy. Basing his argument on the premise that marriage is a legal contract and not a divinely sanctioned union, Milton asserts: "For no effect of tyranny can sit more heavy on the commonwealth than this household unhappiness on the family. And farewell all hope of true reformation in the state, while such an evil as this lies undiscerned or unregarded in the house: on the redress whereof depends not only the spiritful and orderly life of our grown men, but the willing and careful education of our children." Milton does not deny the link between the well-being of the family and the well-being of the state; oddly echoing the "family values" arguments of recent presidential elections, Milton polemically insists that if the family harbors evil (here in the form of an unhappy marriage), then the state has no hope for reform. But this same linkage could be used to argue against divorce: if the family is permitted to dissolve its legal bonds, then what is to prevent a similar dissolution of the state? In the logic of affiliation, it is no great leap from divorce to heresy or regicide because each case involves a rejection of paternal submission; and because they are all linked by analogy, undoing one union could—domino-like—undo them all. John Milton, *Doctrine and Discipline of Divorce*, in Merritt Hughes, ed., *John Milton: Complete Poetry and Selected Prose* (New York: Columbia UP, 1957), 700. See also Walzer, *Revolution of Saints*, 193–94.

35. For a distinction between office and office holder, see Walzer: "The denial of any sacramental value in the anointing of a king, for example, successfully pressed by papalist theoreticians, would prove a very incomplete triumph if the king could still be anointed intellectually, as it were, with a mystical fatherhood. For then the king's subjects would still stand in awe of his person and not merely of his office. The relationship between political father and political children would plausibly be described in terms of love alone and by no means as a rational and necessary form of subordination" (*Revolution of Saints*, 183–84).

36. Dod and Cleaver, *A Plain and Familiar Exposition of the Thirteenth and Fourteenth*

Chapters of the Proverbs of Solomon (London, 1609), 119. Quoted in Walzer, *Revolution of Saints*, 187.

37. Norton, *Founding Mothers and Fathers*, argues that the Puritans actually favor the husband/wife comparison over the mother/father comparison because, in a Filmerian world, the Fifth Commandment permits (at least theoretically) the same authority to both mothers and fathers (widows, fictive widows, etc.). The husband/wife analogy makes the conditions of submission much more fixed and explicit. Amanda Porterfield, in *Female Piety in Puritan New England: The Emergence of Religious Humanism* (New York: Oxford UP, 1992), argues that "the image of the church as bride of Christ became even more humanly concrete as a result of a growing preponderance of female church members after 1650. By the 1680s women outnumbered men three to one. As the compositions of New England congregations became increasingly female, the image of the bride of Christ became increasingly realistic in an empirical, social sense and provided an important referent for images of New England as a woman" (8).

38. Marie-Hélène Huet, *Monstrous Imagination* (Cambridge, Mass.: Harvard UP, 1993), 33–34.

39. Philip Greven has argued that conversion allows for not only a change of fathers, but also return to childhood: "The imagery characteristically associated by evangelicals with self-denial suggests the unconscious restoration of the feelings of childhood, when individuals were small and low to the ground, while parents and other adults loomed big and tall above them. Self-denial was part of becoming a child again, for it meant being 'low' and 'nothing' (*Protestant Temperament*, 79). Lawrence Stone points out that these shifts of familial affiliations were not restricted to the imagination. For a variety of reasons, actual "family relationships were characterized by interchangeability. . . . It was a structure held together not by affective bonds but by mutual economic interests. It was, moreover, an institution that lacked firm boundaries" (*Family, Sex and Marriage*, 88–89).

40. John Cotton, *The Powring Out of the Seven Vials* (London, 1642), vial 7, p. 18.

41. John Cotton, *The Way of Life, or Gods Way and Course, in Bringing the Soule into, Keeping it in, and Carrying it on, in the Wayes of Life and Peace* (London, 1641), 379–80 (hereafter cited as *Way of Life*).

42. Edward Said briefly mentions the Protestant reformation in his discussion of T. S. Eliot's essay on Lancelot Andrewes, saying that "Andrewes and others like him were unable to harness the old paternal authority to an insurgent Protestant and national culture, thereby creating a new institution based not on direct genealogical descent but on what we may call, barbarously, horizontal affiliation. According to Eliot, Andrewes' language does not simply express the anguished distance from an originating but now unrecoverable father that a protesting orphan might feel; on the contrary, it converts that language into the expression of an emerging affiliative corporation—the English church. . . . For Eliot the church stands in for the lost family mourned throughout his earlier poetry" (*The World, the Text, the Critic*, 18). Stephen Greenblatt, in *Renaissance Self-Fashioning: From More to Shakespeare* (Chicago: U Chicago P, 1980), describes reform in similar terms: "Such is the individual's relation to the great patriarchal

institutions of the world: one father must be destroyed; the other exalted to supreme temporal authority. In the individual's relation to God, the split is resolved by the transformation of rebellion into proper boldness and of submission into proper observance" (90).

43. John Cotton, *An Exposition Upon the Thirteenth Chapter of the Revelation* (London 1655), 215 (hereafter cited as *Exposition upon Revelation*).
44. The term "next Father" comes from Cotton, *Exposition upon Revelation*, 216.
45. For a comprehensive discussion of the notion of progress through regress, see Theodore Dwight Bozeman, *To Live Ancient Lives: The Primitivist Dimension in Puritanism* (Chapel Hill: U North Carolina P, 1988).
46. *Exposition upon Revelation*, 141.
47. For discussions of Renaissance notions of women, see Ian Maclean, *The Renaissance Notion of Woman: A Study in the Fortunes of Scholasticism and Medical Science in European Intellectual Life* (New York: Cambridge UP, 1980); Linda Woodbridge, *Women in the English Renaissance: Literature and the Nature of Womankind, 1540–1620* (Chicago: U Illinois P, 1984); Hilda Smith, *Reason's Disciples: Seventeenth-Century English Feminists* (Chicago: U Chicago P, 1982); Margaret Olofson Thickstun, *Fictions of the Feminine: Puritan Doctrine and the Representation of Women* (Ithaca, N.Y.: Cornell UP, 1988). Charles Cohen rightfully points out that we should not lean too heavily on a distinction between flesh and spirit, since the spirit itself was also thought to be a physical entity, like oil lubricating the soul. *God's Caress*, 26–34.
48. Thomas Hobbes, *Leviathan*, quoted in Norton, *Founding Mothers and Fathers*, 141.
49. Roger Thompson, *Sex in Middlesex: Popular Mores in a Massachusetts County, 1649–1699* (Amherst: U Massachusetts P, 1986), 22.
50. "Catholicke Mother" is from John Cotton, *The Churches Resurrection* (London, 1642), 17; "holy Mother" is from *Exposition upon Revelation*, 18.
51. *Exposition upon Revelation*, 8–9, 30.
52. Ibid., 117–18.
53. Lawrence Stone has made a general argument along the lines I am arguing here for Cotton: "Sometimes slowly, more often quickly and violently, the Reformation destroyed the social and psychological supports upon which both the community and the individual had depended for comfort and to give symbolic meaning to their existence. . . . Man now stood alone before his Maker . . . deprived of all of the old psychological props, collective rituals, and opportunities for blowing off steam" (*Family, Sex and Marriage*, 103–4). A number of scholars have noted Cotton's complicated relationship to Catholicism. See, for example, Delbanco, *Puritan Ordeal*, 127–29.
54. *Exposition upon Revelation*, 2.
55. Ibid., 11.
56. Ibid., 29.
57. *Way of Life*, 104–5.
58. On the relationship between this mixed metaphor and the mixed audience in Cotton's congregation, see Teresa Toulouse, *The Arte of Prophesying: New England Sermons and the Shaping of Belief* (Athens: U Georgia P, 1987), chapter 1, esp. pp. 35–38.

59. *Way of Life*, 379–80.
60. For extensive discussions of the transfer of female imagery to male roles, see Porterfield: "The authority associated with motherhood in Puritan culture was represented in Puritan theology by images of God's maternal care, most commonly through the attribution of nursing breasts to God" (*Female Piety*, 80). See also Leverenz: "The Puritan version of the Family Romance offered the possibility that sons could rescue the father's authority by being reborn of the greater Father, without a mother's help, and suckled and raised by Him alone (*Language of Puritan Feeling*, 4). Thickstun speculates about a possible social consequence of the use of such metaphors: "When the realities of women's experience are spiritualized to create metaphors for male spirituality, the actual earthly activities of childbirth and mothering become devalued" (*Fictions of the Feminine*, 20).
61. *Commentary upon John*, 41.
62. Cotton's poem can be found in Harrison Meserole, ed., *Seventeenth-Century American Poetry* (New York: New York UP, 1968), 383. Leverenz has noted Cotton's propensity for the maternal: "Cotton's God remains, like Cotton himself, a mother hen. Cotton's best prose style gives the feeling of a mother tucking a child into bed, or of the child being tucked into the womb of God's spiritual obedience" (*Language of Puritan Feeling*, 185).
63. John Cotton, "A Coppy of a Letter Mr. Cotton of Boston, in New England, sent in answer of certaine Questions made against their Disciplines and Orders there, directed to a Friend" (London, 1641), 3.
64. Thomas Edwards, quoted in Katherine Chidley, *The Justification of the Independent Churches of Christ* (London, 1641), 67.
65. *Exposition upon Revelation*, 201–2.
66. *Way of Life*, 266.
67. For a reading of these relations see Patricia Caldwell, *The Puritan Conversion Narrative: The Beginnings of American Expression* (New York: Cambridge UP, 1983).
68. *Thomas Shepard's "Confessions,"* in George Selement and Bruce C. Woolley, eds., *Collections of the Colonial Society of Massachusetts*, vol. 58 (Boston: The Society, 1981), 100.
69. Ibid., 57, 140.
70. Ibid., 212.
71. Chidley, *Justification*, 67.
72. Ibid., 3.
73. *Exposition upon Revelation*, 199.

Chapter 2. John Cotton and the Conversion of Rhetoric

1. For a contemporary biography of John Cotton, see John Norton, *Abel Being Dead Yet Speaketh; or, the Life and Death of . . . Mr. John Cotton* (London, 1658). The best full-scale account of Cotton's life remains Larzer Ziff, *The Career of John Cotton: Puritanism and the American Experience* (Princeton, N.J.: Princeton UP, 1962). For a chronological summary of most of Cotton's writings, see Everett Emerson, *John Cotton* (New York: Twayne, 1965).

2. For overviews of Puritan conceptions of conversion see Perry Miller, *The New England Mind: The Seventeenth Century* (Cambridge, Mass.: Harvard UP, 1939); Edmund Morgan, *Visible Saints: The History of a Puritan Idea* (Ithaca, N.Y.: Cornell UP, 1963); and the introduction to Charles Lloyd Cohen, *God's Caress: The Psychology of Puritan Religious Experience* (New York: Oxford UP, 1986). Cohen traces the historical and etymological roots of conversion to its original meaning of "to go back again" or "to return" and then suggests that for the Puritans "true piety consists in consciously turning back from sin to embrace God, reversing one's earlier path" (5).
3. For a very different reading of Cotton than the one offered in this chapter, see, in general, Ann Kibbey, *The Interpretation of Material Shapes in Puritanism: A Study of Rhetoric, Prejudice and Violence* (New York: Cambridge UP, 1986). Kibbey strongly emphasizes the linguistic aspect of conversion, which she defines as "an alteration of the hearer's system of reference in response to the preacher's words, a conversion from one system of meaning to another. . . . Puritan preachers sought mainly to produce converts who would speak differently because they had come to think differently about the meanings of words and things" (7–8). While I very much agree with Kibbey's emphasis on language, I do not share her feelings that conversion borders on hypnosis or brainwashing (22) or that the Puritans' systems of belief and faith involved no critical thought (31).
4. Stephen Greenblatt has described this danger of hypocrisy as follows: "It is the cross of power that it can only know the inner state it has brought into being through outer gestures; even as it asserts the incorporeality of the soul, it must accept a physical sign." *Renaissance Self-Fashioning: From More to Shakespeare* (Chicago: Chicago UP, 1980), 81.
5. David Leverenz has also remarked on this link between the need to reform language and the need to reform the self: "Puritans suspected the unbounded self in all its forms, and the suspicion extended to language itself." *The Language of Puritan Feeling: An Exploration in Literature, Psychology, and Social History* (New Brunswick, N.J.: Rutgers UP, 1980), 9.
6. 1 Corinthians 13:9–12. All scriptural citations are from the King James Version.
7. For discussions of the relationships between Puritan aesthetics and theology, see Norman Grabo, "The Veiled Vision: The Role of Aesthetics in Early American Intellectual History," *William and Mary Quarterly* 19 (1962): 493–510 (reprinted in Sacvan Bercovitch, ed., *The American Puritan Imagination* [New York: Cambridge UP, 1974]), and Jesper Rosenmeier, "Clearing the Medium: A Reevaluation of the Puritan Plain Style in Light of John Cotton's *A Practicall Commentary Upon The First Epistle Generall of John*," *William and Mary Quarterly*, 3d ser., vol. 37 (1980): 555–91.
8. Cotton, *A Practicall Commentary, or An Exposition with Observations, Reasons, and Uses upon the First Epistle Generall of John*, 2nd ed. (London, 1658), 397 (heafter cited as *Commentary upon John*).
9. For a description of Puritan conceptions of knowledge, see Miller, *The New England Mind: The Seventeenth Century*, esp. books 1 and 2.
10. *Commentary upon John*, 6.
11. *The Way of Life, or Gods Way and Course, in Bringing the Soule into, Keeping it in,*

and Carrying it on, in the Wayes of Life and Peace (London, 1641), 137 (hereafter cited as *Way of Life*).

12. In this reading of Cotton's understanding of conversion as an aesthetic experience made manifest in new perceptions and in a new language, I am in agreement with readings forwarded by scholars such as Andrew Delbanco in *The Puritan Ordeal* (Cambridge, Mass.: Harvard UP, 1989) and Janice Knight in *Orthodoxies in Massachusetts: Rereading American Puritanism* (Cambridge, Mass.: Harvard UP, 1994). Delbanco writes: "The experience of conversion, then, involves a totally reorganized perception of the world, which in turn requires a new mode of expression" (127). Similarly, Knight points out that Cotton "never retreated . . . from an insistence on grace as a new aesthetic and spiritual sense passively infused" (21). Both Delbanco and Knight also suggest a link between Cotton's aesthetics and his interpretation of the covenant of grace. The state of heightened perception, Delbanco argues, is "a frame of mind opposed to the idea of stepped progress and open to the hope of sudden illumination" (125). Similarly, Knight argues that "Cotton's conception of grace as a new perception or sensibility, a new relish for divine things, really could not be reconciled with the gradualist processes of preparationism" (21). I will take up Cotton's relationship to the covenant of grace more fully in chapter 4.
13. Cotton, *A Brief Exposition upon the Whole Book of Canticles* (London, 1648), 229–30. Cotton preached on the Song of Solomon twice in his career, once in England (*A Brief Exposition upon the Whole Book of Canticles*, hereafter cited as *Canticles*, England) and once in New England (*A Brief Exposition with Practical Observations Upon the whole Book of Canticles* [London, 1655], hereafter cited as *Canticles*, New England). Some of the differences between these two sermon series will be discussed in chapter 5.
14. *Way of Life* , 8.
15. *Commentary upon John*, 397.
16. For a useful account of Cotton's relationship to his audience see Teresa Toulouse, *The Arte of Prophesying: New England Sermons and the Shaping of Belief* (Athens: U Georgia P, 1987), chapter 1. Knight suggests that the sermon style of Spiritual Brethren such as Cotton—"opening biblical texts word by word, meditating on single phrases and tropes, collating like texts, and privileging exegesis over applications"—makes best sense to a regenerate audience (*Orthodoxies in Massachusetts*, 146–48), whereas the style of the Intellectual Fathers (such as Hooker) has "an unregenerate but educable audience in mind" (173).
17. Kibbey also discusses the importance of the right reading of metaphors: "The hearer accomplishes initiation into the spiritual life portrayed by understanding the metaphor that describes it" (*Interpretation of Material Shapes*, 24). However, she also argues that this emphasis on correct interpretation constitutes not just a foundation for building institutions, as I'm suggesting here, but also a form a social control: "Preaching an idea overtly implies a sense of contingency, a need to persuade. The use of metaphor, however, asserts that persuading is not necessary, for the figure is understood to rely on already accepted conventions. Cotton thus indirectly defines social consensus by his choice of metaphors . . . co-opting the collective agreement implied by consensus" (30). Andrew Delbanco agrees that the correct reading of metaphor marks the true convert: "To

be a Christian is to grasp the essence of metaphor. . . . It is to avoid confusing figurative with denotative language." Unlike Kibbey, however, Delbanco argues that Cotton attempts to open up, rather than limit, interpretative possibilities. For example, for Cotton, "the real failure of Catholic practice is that is shackles the imagination. To conceive wine and bread literally as blood and body is not an imaginative triumph, but a failure" (*Puritan Ordeal*, 127–29).

18. *Way of Life*, 214.
19. John Cotton, *The New Covenant* (London, 1655), 35.
20. On the relationship between minsters and congregants, see Amanda Porterfield, *Female Piety in Puritan New England: The Emergence of Religious Humanism* (New York: Oxford UP, 1992):

> Women complied in this arrangement and became involved in relationships with men that celebrated male potency and female submission not only because of the indirect authority they often enjoyed as exemplars of female piety, but also because of the seductiveness of Puritan theology and Puritan ministers. Especially when delivered by an inspired preacher, Puritan theology offered women imaginary experiences of erotic satisfaction and emotional security. Images of God as omnipotent Father and Christ as ravishing Bridegroom created imaginary objects of desire that answered women's desires for powerful love objects, channeled those desires into emotional and behavioral patterns essential to the stability of Puritan society, and established the basis of women's indirect influence and authority. (90)

Kibbey provocatively suggests that the minister takes the place of Catholic idols: "Protestant iconoclasts were true idols, 'living images' who were counterparts of the 'dead idols' of Catholic art" (*Interpretation of Material Shapes*, 44).

21. *Canticles*, New England, 197.
22. *Commentary upon John*, 402–3.
23. *Way of Life*, 341; 103–4.
24. This is a version of the argument Sacvan Bercovitch makes about the ways in which Puritan ministers sustain a gap between the real and the ideal as a way to gain ideological control. See *The American Jeremiad* (Madison: U Wisconsin P, 1978).
25. *Commentary upon John*, 137.
26. Ibid., 8.
27. Cotton, *Of the Holinesse of Church-Members* (London, 1650), 94–95.
28. For descriptions of conversion narratives, see Morgan, *Visible Saints*, and Patricia Caldwell, *The Puritan Conversion Narrative: The Beginnings of American Expression* (New York: Cambridge UP, 1983).
29. The word *oratorio* could refer to oratory in general or to prayer in particular.
30. *Commentary upon John*, 26.
31. Ibid., 65.
32. Francis Bacon, "Of Simulation and Dissimulation" (1625), in John Pitcher, ed., *Francis Bacon: The Essays* (New York: Penguin, 1985), 78.

33. Horace, *Ars Poetica*, line 102, in H. Rushton Fairclough, trans. *Satires, Epistles and Ars Poetica*, Loeb Classic Library (Cambridge, Mass.: Harvard UP, 1926).
34. *Commentary upon John*, 222; 221.
35. Cotton, *The New Covenant*, 59–60.
36. The word *misprision* also refers to the lack of consideration for the terms of an agreement, roughly, breaking the law by a breach of contract.
37. Cotton, *The New Covenant*, 64–65.
38. Ibid., 65.
39. Greenblatt describes the role of figural language as an accommodation to human psychology: "Allegory, along with the related forms of similitude, example, and figure, are not used to express a dark mystery but rather to heighten the effect upon the reader, for such indirect or metaphorical speech 'doth print a thing much deeper in the wits of a man than doth a plain speaking, and leaveth behind him as it were a sting to prick him forward, and to awake him withal'" (*Renaissance Self-Fashioning*, 101–2). For further discussion of the links between rhetoric, memory, and psychology, see Frances Yates, *The Art of Memory* (Chicago: U Chicago P, 1966).
40. *Commentary upon John*, 306.
41. Ibid.
42. Cotton, *The New Covenant*, 69.
43. *Commentary upon John*, 249.
44. *An Exposition Upon the Thirteenth Chapter of the Revelation* (London, 1655), 77.
45. See John Milton, *The Tenure of Kings and Magistrates* (1649), in Merritt Hughes, ed., *John Milton: Complete Poetry and Selected Prose* (New York: Columbia UP, 1957), 750–80; Andrew Marvell, "The First Anniversary of the Government under His Highness the Lord Protector, 1655," in Elizabeth Story Donno, *Andrew Marvell: The Complete Poems* (New York: Penguin, 1972): "Angelic Cromwell" is on p. 129; "ill delaying" is on p. 130.
46. Thomas Browne, *Religio Medici* (1643), in Sir Geoffrey Keynes, ed., *Sir Thomas Browne: Selected Writings* (Chicago: U Chicago P, 1968), 87.
47. Based on the premise that ministers preached twice on Sunday and once during the week and that the average sermon lasted between one and two hours, Harry Stout has estimated that the average Puritan churchgoer heard about seven thousand sermons—about fifteen thousand hours of preaching—over a lifetime. *The New England Soul: Preaching and Religious Culture in Colonial New England* (New York: Oxford UP, 1986), 3–4.
48. *Brief Exposition with Practical Observations upon the whole Book of Ecclesiastes* (London, 1654), n.p. (hereafter cited as *Exposition upon Ecclesiastes*).
49. The actual quotation comes from the sermons on Ecclesiastes. Cotton argues that Solomon's fall may "teach us not to wonder, if we finde sometime like errours here in our Courts. We are to humble ourselves for the sins of our Courts. . . . But is it not a wickednesse to suffer blasphemy to passe unpublished? . . . What will become of rigour without mercy, is yet unknown" (Ibid., 69).
50. For a detailed history of the various ministerial offices, see David Hall, *The Faithful Shepherd: A History of the New England Ministry in the Seventeenth Century* (New York: Norton, 1974).

51. *Canticles*, New England, 141.
52. *Canticles*, England, 128.
53. For Cotton on the psalms, see *Singing of Psalms: A Gospel Ordinance* (London, 1647). Cotton's advocacy of psalm singing was itself somewhat controversial. For an account of this controversy, see Theodore Dwight Bozeman, *To Live Ancient Lives: The Primitivist Dimension in Puritanism* (Chapel Hill: U North Carolina P, 1988), 139–50.
54. *Commentary upon John*, 250.

Chapter 3. Roger Williams and the Conversion of Persecution

1. Book-length studies of Williams are legion. To gain a sense of Williams's evolving scholarly reputation, I have consulted studies ranging over the past century. These include Oscar S. Straus, *Roger Williams: The Pioneer of Religious Liberty* (New York: Century Co., 1899); James Ernst, *Roger Williams: New England Firebrand* (New York: Macmillan, 1932); Ola Winslow, *Master Roger Williams: A Biography* (New York: Macmillan, 1957); Perry Miller, *Roger Williams: His Contributions to the American Tradition* (New York: Atheneum, 1962); Cyclone Covey, *The Gentle Radical: A Biography of Roger Williams* (New York: Macmillan, 1966); Edmund Morgan, *Roger Williams: The Church and the State* (New York: Harcourt, Brace and World, 1967); Irwin H. Polishook, *Roger Williams, John Cotton and Religious Freedom: A Controversy in New and Old England* (Englewood Cliffs, N.J.: Prentice-Hall, 1967); John Garrett, *Roger Williams: Witness beyond Christendom, 1603–1683* (New York: Macmillan, 1970); Henry Chupack, *Roger Williams* (New York: Twayne, 1969); L. Raymond Camp, *Roger Williams, God's Apostle of Advocacy: Biography and Rhetoric*, Studies in American Religion, vol. 36 (Lewiston, Maine: Edward Mellen Press, 1989); Hugh Spurgin, *Roger Williams and Puritan Radicalism in the English Separatist Tradition*, Studies in American Religion, vol. 34 (Lewiston, Maine: Edwin Mellen Press, 1989); Edwin Gaustad, *Liberty of Conscience: Roger Williams in America* (Grand Rapids, Mich.: Eerdmans, 1991). Of these many books, I have found that Winslow is most helpful on Williams's early career, Gaustad on his New England career, Morgan on the issue of separation of church and state, and Chupack for a broad overview of his writings.
2. *George Fox Digg'd Out of his Burrowes* (Boston, 1676), 235–36 (hereafter cited as *Fox*). All Williams texts are from *The Complete Writings of Roger Williams* (New York: Russell & Russell, 1963).
3. Williams also uses the comparison to clothing in *The Bloudy Tenant*: "An unbelieving Soule being dead in sinne (although he be changed from one worship to another, like a dead man shifted into severall changes of apparell) cannot please God, Heb.11. and consequently, whatever such an unbelieving and unregenerate person acts in Worship or Religion, it is but sinne" (138). *The Bloudy Tenent, of Persecution, for cause of Conscience, discussed in A Conference betweene Truth and Peace* (London, 1644) (hereafter cited as *Bloudy Tenent*).
4. Cotton feared that spiritual intoxication of the apostles would be mistaken or "misprised" for actual drunkenness by hypocrite readers. Williams, on the

other hand, remains entirely in the literal realm: an actual drunk can misrepresent himself merely by staging a convincing performance of sobriety. In Cotton's example the fault lies with the readers; in Williams's the fault lies with our "selves." Stated differently, Williams would most likely agree with Cotton's assertion that saved souls speak a new language, but he clearly disagrees that there is any chance of this happening or of genuinely judging that it has happened on earth. Jesper Rosenmeier similarly characterizes Williams's stance on the issue: "Until Christ sends His new apostles with the spiritual language of the millennium, no man can speak in a tongue pure enough to make other men anything but members in the congregation of Antichrist" (420). "The Teacher and the Witness: John Cotton and Roger Williams," *William and Mary Quarterly*, 3rd ser., 25 (1968): 408–31. As Anne Myles points out, Williams would also agree with Cotton's belief that language is imperfect and therefore dangerous ("These strictures suggest that impurity infects language in particular, or more precisely, that speech itself represents a primary danger" [137]) but would strongly disagree with Cotton's hope that language can somehow be purified. "Arguments in Milk, Arguments in Blood: Roger Williams, Persecution, and the Discourse of the Witness," *Modern Philology* 91 (1993): 133–60.

5. *The Hireling Ministry None of Christs* (London, 1652), 168 (hereafter cited as *Hireling*).
6. *The Bloody Tenent, Yet More Bloody: by Mr. Cottons endevour to wash it white in the Blood of the Lambe* (London, 1652), 208 (hereafter cited as *Yet More Bloody*).
7. Ibid., 21.
8. Cotton to Bulkeley (c. 1636), in David Hall, ed., *The Antinomian Controversy, 1636–1638: A Documentary History* (Durham, N.C.: Duke UP, 1990), 37.
9. For a more complete discussion of active/passive, male/female depictions of conversion, see chapter 4.
10. John Donne, Meditation 14, in A. J. Smith, ed., *John Donne: The Complete English Poems* (New York: Penguin, 1971), 314.
11. *Yet More Bloody*, 325–26.
12. Several scholars have noted differences between the ways in which Cotton and Williams interpret metaphorical, literal, and spiritual language. For example, in his important essay on Cotton and Williams ("Typology in Puritan New England: The Williams-Cotton Controversy Reassessed," *American Quarterly* 19 [1967], 166–91), Sacvan Bercovitch delineates their very different understandings of typology, and concludes that "Williams . . . insists on an absolute separation of the literal and the spiritual" (177). Anne Myles further argues that Williams tends not only to keep separate all literal meanings but also, as I'm suggesting here, to literalize metaphorical meaning: "Even at the level of argument, Williams's literalization of the metaphors of milk and blood points to a fundamental incommensurability in how he and Cotton describe and categorize the world. . . . In their underlying appeals, then, Williams and Cotton speak different languages regarding not just the validity of persecution but also the dimension in which truth itself resides" ("Arguments in Milk," 152–53). Myles's suggestion that Cotton and Williams speak different languages goes a long way toward accounting for the rancor of their disagreements.
13. *Bloody Tenent*, 214. Williams is not alone in voicing this criticism. For a useful

discussion of the controversy over the New England practice of conversion narratives, see Patricia Caldwell, *The Puritan Conversion Narrative: The Beginnings of American Expression* (New York: Cambridge UP, 1983).

14. *Hireling*, 176.
15. *Yet More Bloody*, 496.
16. Cotton, "A Reply to Mr. Williams his Examination; And Answer of the Letters sent to him by John Cotton," or "John Cotton's Answer to Roger Williams," *Complete Writings of Roger Williams*, 2:213.
17. *Hireling*, 163.
18. There were basically two kinds of ministers: apostolic and pastoral. Pastoral ministers were the church elders—teachers and pastors charged with the care of those souls that were already converted. Apostolic ministers were evangelical preachers whose goal was to convert. Edmund Morgan argues that Williams wanted to be an apostolic minister but could find no legitimate authorization for this role. See his discussion in *Roger Williams: The Church and the State*, esp. pp. 43–53. Ola Winslow argues that Williams felt that political restrictions limited his chances for a successful career and also suggests that he was temperamentally unsuited to the task: "There is little in his mature life to suggest that the lure of scholarship with its patient, lonely discoveries was the world toward which his heart inclined" (*Master Roger Williams*, 73).
19. *Bloudy Tenent*, 123.
20. *Yet More Bloody*, 209.
21. *Hireling*, 161.
22. Ibid., 176.
23. *Bloudy Tenent*, 225.
24. Many scholars have commented on the tension between Williams's desire to reform institutions and his unwillingness to join them. Edwin Gaustad, for example, observes that Williams "was out to do nothing less than alter the institutional structure of the Western world" (*Liberty of Conscience*, 75), but also points out that "on the basis of his theological convictions, [Williams] was not interested in exchanging one imperfect entity for another" (98). Perry Miller makes a similar observation (*Roger Williams: His Contributions*, 246). Ola Winslow details the many times that Williams was either excluded or excluded himself from institutional affiliation. She suggests, for example, that an experience early in Williams's career may have been emblematic if not formative. In 1623, James placed new restrictions on preaching and preachers, and—in Winslow's words—Williams "must have felt almost as though the door before him were closing even as it was first opened" (*Master Roger Williams*, 67). However, she views his refusal to take over for John Wilson as teacher at Boston in 1630 as an instance where Williams "shut the door in his own face . . . he had said no to the best pulpit offer he would ever have" (97). Interestingly, whereas other scholars see Williams as an idealist and purist, Winslow also sees him as "something of an opportunist as to the where and what of his life . . . his life shows no central unity of place or profession, but of an idea alone" (94).

    My own view of Williams rests on the assumption that idealism and careerism are not necessarily mutually exclusive; that is, Williams's idealism was so intensely strong that he would never find the perfect church. And yet, as I suggest in this chapter, he was also something of a pragmatist, at least when it came to civil and earthly matters; he clearly wanted to be around power even if he remained unwilling to assume power himself. Gaustad nicely captures this tension: "Williams spent much of his time criticizing civil magistrates and trying to circumscribe their activities. The rest of the time he spent assisting such magistrates or becoming one himself" (*Liberty of Conscience*, 122).

25. On various states of exile, Edward Said writes "While it is an actual condition, exile is also . . . a metaphorical condition." *The World, the Text, the Critic* (Cambridge, Mass.: Harvard UP, 1983), 52. The full citation from Revelation 11:3 reads: "And I will give power unto my two witnesses, and they shall prophesy a thousand two hundred and threescore days, clothed in sackcloth."

26. Other references to the witnesses of Revelation include the following: "Precious Pearles and Jewels, and farre more precious Truth are found in muddy shells and places. The rich Mines of golden Truth lye hid under barren hills, and in obscure holes and corners" and "The Most High and Glorious God hath chosen the poore of the World: and the *Witness of Truth* (*Rev. 11*) are cloathed in sackcloth, not in Silke or Satin, Cloth of Gold, or Tissue" (*Bloudy Tenent*, 180).

27. Stephen Greenblatt describes the general role of the martyr as follows: "Like any individual or group confronting a hostile institution that possesses vastly superior force, [the persecuted] has recourse to the weapon of the powerless: the seizure of symbolic initiative. He may be crushed, but his martyrdom will only confirm his construction of reality, for the very success of the dominant institution is exposed as a sign not of its rightness, but of the power of Antichrist." *Renaissance Self-Fashioning: From More to Shakespeare* (Chicago: U Chicago P, 1980), 78–79. A number of scholars have commented specifically on Williams's role as exiled witness. For example, Jesper Rosenmeier comments that Williams believed that "until the glorious return of Christ all that a Christian could do was to bear witness. Only an apostle had eyes clear enough to see when and where Christ would descend, and Williams could nowhere see an apostle at work" ("Teacher and the Witness," 417–18). Similarly, Anne Myles comments: "When disobedience proceeds not from misapprehension of God's truth but from an opposing conviction about what truth is, punishment can have no verifying effect; in fact, it only serves to convince the dissenter that truth must lie elsewhere" ("Arguments in Milk," 157).

28. Williams to Winthrop, 24 October 1636, in Glenn LaFantasie, ed. *The Correspondence of Roger Williams* (Hanover, N.H.: The Rhode Island Historical Society, 1988), 1:66. Of Williams's banishment and the letter to Winthrop, Rosenmeier writes: "It was an exhilarating sense of finally having found the opportunity to be a witness of persecution, seeking Christ with a soul pure and isolated from the corruptions of the world" ("Teacher and the Witness," 418).

29. *Fox*, 96 .

30. Ibid., 125–26.

31. *Yet More Bloody*, 295. This exclusion of "discoursing and disputing" from the definition of persecution warrants some attention, especially in light of the fact that certain kinds of verbal behavior were legally actionable in seventeenth century New England. For example, court records indicate many cases of individuals being sued for slander or defamation: men usually sued because attacks on

their trustworthiness (e.g., being called a liar or a thief or a cheat) could be politically and financially detrimental; women sued against attacks on their sexuality (e.g., being called an adulteress, harlot, or whore). Although Williams uses exactly these "slanders" in his book against the Quakers (he calls Quaker women "wanton whores" because they are allowed to speak at services, and he accuses Foxe of lying because he makes unfounded promises of salvation to his followers), as far as I know, he was never sued for slander or defamation because such discourse was protected under the sanction of religious dispute. Mary Beth Norton provides some useful information about the basis for defamation or slander suits: "English ecclesiastical and secular courts had traditionally discouraged slander suits. In England, the only actionable words were those that accused the target of violations which could, if true, lead to prosecution by the appropriate authorities. Common law courts in particular applied strict rules of procedure to defamation cases, requiring most complainants to prove specific damages." In Rhode Island of 1647, for example, actionable defamations included calling someone a traitor, felon, thief, bankrupt, cheater, whore, or whoremaster. *Founding Mothers and Fathers: Gendered Power and the Forming of American Society* (New York: Alfred A. Knopf, 1996), 258–59. For an examination of Williams's legalism, see Christopher Felker, "Roger Williams's Use of Legal Discourse: Testing Authority in Early New England," *New England Quarterly* (December 1990): 624–48.

32. *Yet More Bloody*, 55–56.
33. *Hireling*, 185.
34. *Bloudy Tenent*, 166.
35. Ola Winslow states that, to Williams, "toleration is an insult to the human spirit. It is a permissive act, implying superiority in those who confer it. He admitted no such superiority" (*Master Roger Williams*, 201). I agree with Winslow's description of the nature of toleration, and with her claim that Williams did not *admit* superiority. But as I'm suggesting here, he did implicitly *assume* a superior position at times, if only by virtue of his language.
36. *Bloudy Tenent*, 122, 124.
37. Ibid., 181.
38. Ibid., 244–45.
39. *Yet More Bloody*, 32.
40. Williams to Major John Mason and Governor Thomas Prence, 22 June 1670, in *Correspondence*, 2:611. In his answer to Williams's letter, Cotton remarks on Williams's desire to be seen as a martyr: "He banished himselfe from the Society of all the Churches in this Countrey" (53) and "And for him to withdraw himselfe from the society of all the Churches for their persecution of him, before he had suffered from them any thing but conference, and conviction, is to make them sufferers for well-doing, and to choose suffering that he might have cause to complaine of sufferings" (54).
41. For analysis of Cotton's and Williams's views on millenialism, see Rosenmeier, "Teacher and the Witness," and especially Bercovitch, "Typology."
42. *Yet More Bloody*, 342, 350.
43. *Bloudy Tenent*, 136–37.
44. Ibid., 148.

45. For further exploration of Williams's pragmatism, see John T. Noonan, "Principled or Pragmatic Foundations for the Freedom of Conscience?" *Journal of Law and Religion* (1987): 203–12.
46. *Bloudy Tenent*, 231.
47. Williams further argues that the true church does not need the protection of the state since it is already better protected by God. "But the Truth is, this mingling of the church and the world together, and their orders and societies together, doth plainly discover, that such churches were never called out from the world, and that this is only a secret policy of flesh and blood, to get protection from the world, and so to keep (with some little stilling of conscience) from the Cross or Gallowes of Jesus Christ" (*Yet More Bloudy*, 74–75).
48. *Bloudy Tenent*, 388.
49. Ibid., 142.

Chapter 4. The Case of Anne Hutchinson

1. "The Examination of Mrs. Anne Hutchinson at the Court at Newtown" (313–14) (hereafter cited as "Civil Trial"). Unless otherwise indicated, texts from the Antinomian Controversy are from David Hall, ed., *The Antinomian Controversy, 1636–1638: A Documentary History* (Durham, N.C.: Duke UP, 1990).
2. Michael Walzer suggests that Puritan interpretations of the Fifth Commandment demanded political allegiance more than natural affections: "Puritan ministers continued to believe, as Christians had believed for centuries, that the fifth commandment was an injunction to political obedience. . . . But Puritans were unlikely to revere a purely natural relationship and it was the divine commandment rather than its familial content that they respected. Hence Pricke [Robert Pricke, *The Doctrine of Superiority and Subjection Contained in the Fifth Commandment* (London, 1609)] dealt with the duties and office rather than the love of political fathers." *The Revolution of Saints: A Study in the Origins of Radical Politics* (Cambridge, Mass.: Harvard UP, 1965), 186. But even if Hutchinson was to obey rather than love these fathers, it still does not resolve the question about *which* fathers to obey.
3. "A Report of the Trial of Mrs. Anne Hutchinson before the Church in Boston," 383 (hereafter cited as "Church trial").
4. Andrew Delbanco sees the Antinomian Controversy in part as an attempt to challenge Cotton's preeminence. Thus, when ministers such as Thomas Shepard, Thomas Hooker, and Peter Bulkeley "brought Anne Hutchinson under attack in the late 1630s, it was something like assaulting the prime minister by calling a vote on an issue to which he was committed," *Puritan Ordeal* (Cambridge, Mass.: Harvard UP, 1989), 119. Janice Knight also sees the crisis, in part, as a competition between factions: "The drama of the moment made manifest and to some extent produced differences that had been only half sensed; now the participants realized the divide between them." *Orthodoxies in Massachusetts: Rereading American Puritanism* (Cambridge, Mass.: Harvard UP, 1994), 31. Along the same lines, Anne Kibbey sees the trials as a galvanizing moment for Cotton: "He did not so much alter his ideas during the crisis as find out

what he had assumed for some time." *The Interpretation of Material Shapes in Puritanism: A Study of Rhetoric, Prejudice and Violence* (New York: Cambridge UP, 1986), 115.

5. "Church Trial," 372. Cotton ran into similar trouble in England when he was temporarily suspected of inciting vandalism done to St. Botolph's church. See Larzer Ziff, *The Career of John Cotton: Puritanism and the American Experience* (Princeton, N.J.: Princeton UP, 1962), 51–53.

6. This sense that Cotton remains responsible for Hutchinson's mistakes is very consistent with an age where, as David Leverenz notes, "Rebellious children meant sinful parents." *The Language of Puritan Feeling: An Exploration in Literature, Psychology, and Social History* (New Brunswick, N.J.: Rutgers UP, 1980), 71. Indeed, this moment in the trial is emblematic of the kind of paternal affiliation I described in chapter 1, where the fathers, real and figurative, are held accountable for the actions of all those affiliated with them. Thus, Mary Beth Norton notes that "wives were convicted of lascivious conduct with other men, but husbands nevertheless had to pay costs or post bond for their spouse's future good behavior." *Founding Mothers and Fathers: Gendered Power and the Forming of American Society* (New York: Alfred A. Knopf, 1996), 86. Along these lines, Winthrop lays blame for Hutchinson's transgression not only on Cotton but also on her husband. He describes Hutchinson as "a man of a very mild temper and weak parts, and wholly guided by his wife" (John Winthrop, *Journal: History of New England: 1630–1646*. James Kendall Hosmer, ed., *Original Narratives of Early American History*, 2 vols. [New York: Barnes and Noble, 1908], 1: 295; quoted in Edmund Morgan, *Visible Saints: The History of a Puritan Idea* [Ithaca, N.Y.: Cornell UP, 1963], 44).

7. *Brief Exposition with Practical Observations Upon the whole Book of Ecclesiastes* (London, 1654) 158–59 (hereafter cited as *Exposition upon Ecclesiastes*).

8. From a certain perspective, assumptions about gender roles in seventeenth-century England and New England seem to have been fairly stable. These roles were thought to be naturally or divinely sanctioned and, as such, unopen to question or change. Basic ideas about female roles rested on an assumed paradox of women's virtue: a woman's weakness is her strength. Thus, women were thought to make good Christians because they did not—or should not—have the capacity for prideful, reasoned dissent but instead exhibited all of the passive virtues: humility, chastity, suffering, etc. For a further analysis, see Ian Maclean, *The Renaissance Notion of Woman: A Study in the Fortunes of Scholasticism and Medical Science in European Intellectual Life* (New York: Cambridge UP, 1980), esp. 20–21, 51–52. For a useful overview of early modern gender roles, see Linda Woodbridge, *Women in the English Renaissance: Literature and the Nature of Womankind, 1540–1620* (Chicago: U Illinois P, 1984).

9. For general information about *Hic-Mulier* and *Haec-Vir*, see Woodbridge, *Women in the English Renaissance*, 144–49. Lyle Koehler also discusses Puritan punishments for cross-dressing and censures for men with long hair and women with short hair. See *A Search for Power: The "Weaker Sex" in Seventeenth-Century New England* (Chicago: U Illinois P, 1980), esp. 42–43. Koehler further describes the Puritan's concern for women who displayed a "lack of femininity"

and men who displayed a "lack of masculinity" (231), a phenomenon very much consistent with the one I am describing here.

10. *Haec-Vir, or the Womanish-Man: Being an Answere to the late Booke intitled Hic-Mulier. Exprest in a briefe Dialogue between Haec-Vir the Womanish-Man, and Hic-Mulier, the Man-Woman* (London 1620), B4v.
11. Ibid., C2r.
12. Ibid., C2v–C3r.
13. A number of historians have noted that while gender roles in the early modern period were clearly and rigidly defined in theory, they were almost always confused and transgressed in practice. In his examination of patterns of premarital sex and teen pregnancy, for example, Roger Thompson has discovered that the facts of court records patently defy the ideal of the all-controlling patriarchal family. He writes: "The conventional wisdom about patriarchal power and suppressed dependents emerges somewhat dented. . . . The supposedly all-powerful patriarchs seem to have been left with the far from glorious task of picking up the pieces caused by their children's autonomous initiatives." *Sex in Middlesex: Popular Mores in a Massachusetts County, 1649–1699* (Amherst: U Massachusetts P, 1986), 53. Linda Woodbridge has suggested that the urbanization evident before the English civil war led to a blurring of gender roles and the consequent charges of effeminacy against men and sexual licentiousness against women (*Women in the English Renaissance*, 172–79).

    A number of scholars have argued that the Protestant Reformation itself was a factor in reconfiguring stereotypical gender roles. For example, early political defeats at court drove reformers underground and into private homes, where they held spiritual exercises, conventicles, and prophesyings (not unlike those held in the Hutchinson home). See Patrick Collinson, *The Elizabethan Puritan Movement* (London: Jonathan Cape, 1967). Puritan emphasis on personal piety, marriage, and the family may have also helped to redefine gender roles. See Edmund Morgan, *The Puritan Family*, and Lawrence Stone, *The Family, Sex, and Marriage in England, 1500–1600*. Additionally, Puritan emphasis on spiritual conversion may have also had an effect on conception of gender roles. Some believed that during conversion "imperfect" woman becomes "perfected" in man. Others believed, as Carla Freccero has pointed out, that the converted soul was essentially an androgyne, the spiritualized union of ideal male and female, a return to "primeval wholeness," Adam completed and perfected by Eve. See Freccero, "The Other and the Same: The Image of the Hermaphrodite in Rabelais" in Margaret Ferguson, Maureen Quilligan, and Nancy Vickers, eds., *Rewriting the Renaissance: The Discourses of Sexual Difference in Early Modern Europe* (Chicago: Chicago UP, 1986), 149.
14. Nathaniel Shurtleff, ed., *Records of the Governor and Company of the Massachusetts Bay*, vol. 1 (Boston, 1853), 3 September 1634 (hereafter cited as Shurtleff, *Records*).
15. The idea of a gendered rhetoric has a long history. For example, in *Institutio Oratoria*, a rhetoric familiar to many Puritan preachers, Quintilian writes that "a translucent and iridescent style merely serves to emasculate the subject which it arrays with such pomp or words. . . . It is with a more virile spirit that we

should pursue eloquence, who, if only her whole body be sound, will never think it her duty to polish her nails and tire her hair" (*Institutio Oratoria*, bk. 8, preface, 19–22). In her very useful book, Patricia Parker also points out that from classical antiquity up through the English Renaissance, rhetoric was represented as feminine because women and language were thought to share many features: they were both seductive, difficult to control, transgressive, and both could lead to effeminacy in men. See *Literary Fat Ladies: Rhetoric, Gender, Property* (New York: Methuen, 1987), esp. 104–6. These assumptions about rhetoric and gender clearly inform Hutchinson's trials. For example, Thomas Shepard claims that "seeinge the Flewentness of her Tonge and her Willingness to open herselfe and to divulge her Opinions and to sowe her seed in us that are but highway side and Strayngers to her and therefore would doe much more to her owne Jaolosie and to them that are mor nearly like to her, for I account her a verye dayngerous Woman to sowe her corrupt opinions to the infection of many and therefore the more neede you have to looke to her" ("Church Trial," 353). Shepard depicts Hutchinson as a literary fat lady by condemning both her rhetorical and sexual wantonness. He also echoes the *Hic-Mulier/Haec-Vir* debates by implying that Hutchinson assumes the masculine role of sowing seed.

In a provocative essay, "In a Radicallly Different Voice," *Early American Literature* 25 (1990), Lad Tobin has expanded this link between gender and rhetoric into an interpretation of Hutchinson's trials. Invoking recent rhetorical theory, Tobin delineates gender-based differences in rhetorical styles, and laments our failure to "read Hutchinson's fundamental ideas and speech as feminist or the ministers' responses as misogynist" (254). While I agree with Tobin's premises, I generally disagree with his conclusions on two grounds: (1) that, given the problematic nature of the trial transcripts, we cannot comfortably assume access to Hutchinson's ideas and speeches, and (2) that she was arguing for something like a modern idea of feminist individualism.

16. *A Practicall Commentary, or An Exposition with Observations, Reasons, and Uses upon the First Epistle Generall of John*, 2nd ed. (London, 1658), 47.
17. *Haec-Vir*, C3v.
18. It is important to remember that Hutchinson's trials were not the only court cases between 1636 and 1638 and that Hutchinson was not the only woman brought to trial in those years either. Other cases run from the somewhat famous (Hibbens, Hawkins) to the mundane and routine. Further, not only women were brought before the courts during the Antinomian Controversy. In fact, the final tally of those who were somehow dealt with by the court because of the controversy was approximately seventy-six men and one or two women. Many of these men were singled out because they signed a petition supporting Wheelwright. The punishments they received were similar to those given to Hutchinson: the men were banished, disenfranchised, dismissed from their posts on the court, and/or disarmed, although many sentences were later commuted upon repentance. For an account of the details of the controversy, see Emery Battis, *Saints and Sectaries: Anne Hutchinson and the Antinomian Controversy in the Massachusetts Bay Colony* (Chapel Hill: U North Carolina P, 1962).
19. All citations are from Shurtleff, *Records*, vol. 1. Wake, 1 December 1640; Vaughan, 30 January 1639/40; Luxford, 3 December 1639.

20. Shurtleff, *Records*, 3 March 1634, 5 August 1634.
21. Norton, *Founding Mothers and Fathers*, 329. Norton also writes: "Men were accused of 'not provideing for' or 'neglecting' their families, of permitting 'disorderly carriages' in their households, and of 'not ordering and disposeing of [their] children as may bee for theire good education' (51).
22. "Church Trial," 372.
23. The statute appears in Shurtleff, *Records*, 18 October 1631: "It is ordered that if any man shall have carnall copulation with another mans wife, they both shalbe punished by death. This was confirmed the first month, 1637 or 1638 (12 March)." The court later revoked this statute.
24. In *Monstrous Imagination* (Cambridge, Mass.: Harvard UP, 1993), Marie-Hélène Huet writes: "The mother's imagination [is] moved by an illegitimate desire—that is, a desire not directed toward her husband" and "Since the monstrous mother erases the image of the real father, the monster can be seen as the most illegitimate of offspring" (33).
25. The notion that Hutchinson actively sought to become her own authority serves as the basis for feminist readings of the Antinomian Controversy by scholars such as Lad Tobin, Lyle Koehler, Ann Kibbey, Amy Schrager Lang, and by Ivy Schweitzer in *The Work of Self-Representation: Lyric Poetry in Colonial New England* (Chapel Hill: U North Carolina P, 1991). Koehler, for example, argues that "the specter of male overlordship is so apparent in institutional, intellectual, economic and family life throughout the seventeenth century that it leaves little room to doubt women's difficulty in achieving, much less exerting, a sense of their own assertive independence" (*Search for Power*, 52). Lang also suggests that Hutchinson desired independence from the Puritan patriarchy: "Anne Hutchinson raised fears of a female autonomy that would disrupt the system of analogies to which the Puritan fathers turned in justifying their authority"; *Prophetic Woman: Anne Hutchinson and the Problem of Dissent in the Literature of New England* (Berkeley: U California P, 1987), 42. I would complicate these readings, in general, by asserting that the concept of individual autonomy was not quite as stable as such interpretations might suggest. On the issue of gender, my own reading comes closest to that of Amanda Porterfield, who posits a much more complicated relationship between Hutchinson and the Puritan elders in *Female Piety in Puritan New England: The Emergence of Religious Humanism* (New York: Oxford UP, 1992).
26. A wide range of interpretations have commented on the idea that certain kinds of piety place all believers, male and female, in the structural position of women. For the argument that the position of colonist itself equates with the position of women, see Patricia Caldwell, "Why Our First Poet Was a Woman: Bradstreet and the Birth of an American Poetic Voice," *Prospects: An Annual of American Cultural Studies* 13 (1988): 28. Lyle Koehler notes that in antinomianism especially "both men and women were relegated, vis-à-vis God, to the status that women occupied in Puritan society vis-à-vis men: that is, to the status of malleable inferiors in the hands of a higher being" (*Search for Power*, 221). Walter Hughes has delineated the homoerotic implications of having men assume the submissive role traditionally assigned to women. See his essay "'Meat Out of the Eater': Panic and Desire in American Puritan Poetry," in Joseph A. Boone and

Michael Cadden, eds., *Engendering Men: The Question of Male Feminist Criticism* (New York: Routledge, 1990). Other kinds of gender critics have argued that the male use of feminine imagery or imaginative assumption of female roles is an appropriation and devaluation of actual women. For example, Margaret Olofson Thickstun writes: "When the realities of women's experience are spiritualized to create metaphors for male spirituality, the actual earthly activities of childbirth and mothering become devalued." *Fictions of the Feminine: Puritan Doctrine and the Representation of Women* (Ithaca, N.Y.: Cornell UP, 1988), 20. Additionally, other scholars have suggested that the dynamic of patriarchal power and submission made antinomianism especially appealing to women. See, for example, Delbanco, *Puritan Ordeal*, 139ff, and Amanda Porterfield, who argues that "Puritan women were devoted to a patriarchal and authoritarian deity not only because that deity represented their belief that society should be organized around patriarchal authority, but also because they found that patriarchal and authoritarian deity attractive and because they were able to use that devotion to alter and control their social relationships" (*Female Piety*, 86–87).

27. John Donne, "A Sermon Preached to the King, at Whitehall, the First Sunday in Lent," in Neil Rhodes, ed., *John Donne: Selected Prose* (New York: Penguin, 1987), 270.

28. For a very nuanced reading of the theological debates at the core of the Antinomian Controversy, see Jesper Rosenmeier, "New England's Perfection: The Image of Adam and the Image of Christ in the Antinomian Crisis, 1634 to 1638," *William and Mary Quarterly*, 3rd ser., 27 (1970): 435–59. For further discussion of the relationships between agency and covenant theology, see Norman Pettit, *The Heart Prepared: Grace and Conversion in Puritan Spiritual Life* (New Haven, Conn.: Yale UP, 1966); Norman Fiering, *Moral Philosophy at Seventeenth-Century Harvard: A Discipline in Transition* (Chapel Hill: U North Carolina P, 1981); Charles Cohen; Janice Knight; and especially William Stoever, *"A Faire and Easy Way to Heaven": Covenant Theology and Antinomianism in Early Massachusetts* (Middletown, Conn.: Wesleyan UP, 1978). In part, Stoever frames the problem of agency as a question of responsibility for salvation. Does God, for example, "respect and work through the inherent capacities of human beings, empowering human faculties to perform holy actions" or does he "act directly upon human beings, overruling their natural capacities and transforming them apart from or in spite of any activity of their own?" (10). For the most part, those who opposed Hutchinson (variously called preparationists, legalists, intellectual fathers) held the former position, that "Grace . . . is received mediately, through a chain of second causes (causes other than God, the First Cause), which forms the 'middle term' between God's intent and man's condition" (63).

Janice Knight generally shares the view that preparationists placed greater relative emphasis on human action than antinomians did. She writes, for example, that "these preparationists hoped to preserve the freeness of grace while carving out a place for human agency" (*Orthodoxies in Massachusetts*, 129). As I suggest throughout this chapter, such observations about human agency force us to revise our notion that it was the antinomians, and not the preparationists, who advocated the autonomy of individual action.

29. "Mr. Cotton's Rejoynder," 141.
30. Cotton spells out this logic in his letter to Bulkeley, 39.
31. Here again, Stoever provides a clear description of Cotton's view of the relationship between covenant theology and human activity/passivity:

> Active faith could not be for Cotton a proper instrument for the receiving of Christ in union or a proper condition of entry into the covenant of grace. Indeed, "justifying faith" is not properly the faith that justifies but is, rather, the faith that reveals to us that we are justified. It is related to justification not as antecedent cause but as something following from it. In effectual calling, the Spirit works faith in the soul to receive Christ passively into union. Thereupon the soul enjoys communion with Christ, receiving faith to believe in him and other spiritual graces. Faith is thus the first of the graces of sanctification and the root of all the others. ("*A Faire and Easy Way*," 43–44)

Stoever further argues that "even after regeneration, we are still not really active agents; Christ acts through us: acted upon, we act" (45). Knight presents a similar argument. Here, for example, she quotes Richard Sibbes, an English theologian who was a major influence on Cotton: "We do all subordinately; we move as we are moved; we see as we are enlightened; we hear as we are made to hear; we are wise as far as he makes us wise. We do, but it is he that makes us do" (*Orthodoxies in Massachusetts*, 111–12).

Charles Cohen makes a compelling case for the psychological appeal of this view of grace and human agency: "Renouncing self-confidence effectuates a psychological salvation, release from the impulse to achieve perfection. . . . A person who trusts in God admits weakness and gains strength, asks less of oneself and accomplishes more."*God's Caress: The Psychology of Puritan Religious Experience* (New York: Oxford UP, 1986), 72.
32. *Commentary upon John*, 306.
33. Janice Knight has also noted Cotton's tendency to use passive verb constructions in his sermons (*Orthodoxies in Massachusetts*, 113).
34. *The New Covenant* (London, 1636), 16–17.
35. Cotton to Bulkeley, 37.
36. A case could be made that the Protestant Reformation did, in fact, allow—if not encourage—women to develop a sense of their own interpretive authority as thinkers and writers. Indeed, a number of studies have examined the role of women prophets during the English civil war. See, for sample, Hilda Smith, *Reason's Disciples: Seventeenth-Century English Feminists* (Chicago: U Illinois P, 1982); Phyllis Mack, "Women as Prophets during the English Civil War," *Feminist Studies* 8 (spring 1982); and Keith Thomas, "Women and the Civil War Sects," *Past and Present*, no.13, April 1958. It was often the case, however, that women were permitted to write not because of a recognition of their individuality but rather because it was assumed that their "feminine virtues"—passivity, receptivity, weakness—made them more receptive to divine prohecies.
37. An argument could be made that it was right around the historical period during which the trials took place that the idea of individual creative genius began to

emerge as a recognizable category. Indeed, Nancy Armstrong and Leonard Tennenhouse have asserted that it is Milton's *Paradise Lost* that "redefines truth as something that is produced by and within the individual rather than a message delivered from above." *The Imaginary Puritan: Literature, Intellectual Labor, and the Origins of Personal Life* (Berkeley: U California P, 1992), 110. While I am unsure that this moment can be located in one specific text or year, Armstrong and Tennenhouse's comment provides an important historical reminder that truth was primarily thought of as something discovered, not created.

38. For a discussion of the links between the rhetoric of violence and actual violence during the Antinomian Controversy, see Kibbey, *The Interpretation of Material Shapes in Puritanism*, esp. chapter 5.

39. A third possibility could be argued here: that Hutchinson is searching for a specifically female subjectivity. That is, it may be possible, as I'm suggesting here, that the elders want Hutchinson to think of herself as a modern individual subject only because that is the best means for controlling her (see, for example, Armstrong and Tennehouse, *Imaginary Puritan*, 42). As feminist critics such as Mary Nyquist and Catherine Belsey have argued, if women were permitted any sense of subjectivity at all, it was almost always some version of male subjectivity. See Nyquist, "The Genesis of Gendered Subjectivity in the Divorce Tracts and in Paradise Lost" in Mary Nyquist and Margaret Ferguson, eds., *Remembering Milton: Essays in the Texts and Traditions* (New York: Methuen, 1988), esp. 119–20; and Belsey, *The Subject of Tragedy: Identity and Difference in Renaissance Drama* (New York: Methuen, 1985), esp. 149–50, 181. Based on these assumptions, a case could be made that Hutchinson rejects this version of male subjectivity, not in the name of a radical denial of self, as I'm arguing here, but in the name of a distinctively female identity. While I find the possibility of such an argument intriguing, I am not sure how it could be made in Hutchinson's case, where, in the absence of any writing directly attributable to her, we must rely more on historical and theological context. Put differently, if Hutchinson was advocating some idea of female autonomy or subjectivity, I am not sure we would be able to describe or reconstruct it based on the evidence at hand.

40. My sense that each side of the controversy was essentially speaking a different language—or more precisely, had very different assumptions about how language works—derives from the interpretations of two scholars. In his analysis of what was really in dispute during the trials, Andrew Delbanco has suggested that "at her trial Hutchinson spoke about true and false voices, continually aware that she and her accusers were not only fighting an ideological battle but were *speaking* differently" (*Puritan Ordeal*, 135). Similarly, Janice Knight acknowledges that the "differences were as much matters of tone and sensibility as of doctrine" (*Orthodoxies in Massachusetts*, 32). The most compelling analysis of this difference in language can be found in Patricia Caldwell's essay "The Antinomian Language Controversy," *Harvard Theological Review* (July–October, 1976), where she argues that, unlike most of the ministers and magistrates, Hutchinson does not believe that inward judgment can ever be perfectly translated into outward expression (358). As always, Cotton stands somewhere in the middle: he desires to achieve a unity of inward judgment and outward

expression through the mediation of a converted rhetoric, but he fears that this will never happen.

41. "Civil Trial," 336.
42. In *Female Piety in Puritan New England*, Amanda Porterfield pursues a similar line of argument: "Thus for Anne Hutchinson, religious radicalism did not represent a consistent or self-conscious bid either for her intellectual authority as a theologian or for the intellectual authority or social equality of women" (102).
43. There is a historical basis for this sense that congregants could search for the best possible ministers, formally or informally. While still in England, for example, Cotton developed a devoted following—"a congregation within the congregation"—specifically because of his preaching and doctrinal practices. See Ziff, *Career of John Cotton*, esp. 48–50 (quote is from p. 49). The New England Congregationalists more or less institutionalized the right of a congregation to select its own minister. For a history of this process, see David Hall, *The Faithful Shepherd: A History of the New England Ministry in the Seventeenth Century* (New York: Norton, 1974).
44. "Church Trial," 337–38. Such devotion to a minister is not only defined by gender or status (e.g., a female congregant following a male minister). Many ministers were influenced by their colleagues' decision to migrate. Here, for example, Thomas Shepard sounds almost exactly like Hutchinson: "I saw the Lord departing from England when Mr. Hooker and Mr. Cotton were gone, and I saw the hearts of most of the godly set and bent that way, and I did think I should feel many miseries if I stayed behind" (from *God's Plot*, quoted in Porterfield, *Female Piety*, 55).
45. See Porterfield, *Female Piety*, 90.
46. "Church Trial," 381. Cotton addresses this point elsewhere in the civil trial: "I told her I was very sorry that she put comparisons between my ministry and theirs, for she had said more than I could myself, and rather I had that she put us in fellowship with them and not have made that discrepancy. She said, she found the difference" (334).
47. My argument here that Hutchinson desires stronger and purer patriachal figures owes a debt to two compelling accounts of the dynamics of Puritan piety. In her analysis of the Antinomian trials, Amanda Porterfield asserts that "Hutchinson herself is best understood in terms of this attempt to indulge in individual religious expression within the context of submission to patriarchal authority" (*Female Piety*, 105). David Leverenz has argued that Puritan believers wanted this authority to be as strong and pure as possible, so that it could fulfill "a dream of the pure father" (*Language of Puritan Feeling*, 41). Thus, he sees the Puritan attraction to patriarchy as "a cry for better authority, for fathers and ministers with uncompromising fidelity to the greater father's Word" (45). Much as I am arguing here, Leverenz suggests that it is the "perception of father's weaknesses" (41) and the sense of "watching one's father fail in the wider world" (265) as much as a sense of oppression or abuse that fuels Puritan anxiety over patriarchy. As he persuasively writes, "A call for pure and loving patriarchy became more intense as its absence became more evident" (103).
48. For general discussions of these births, see Emery Battis and Anne Schutte, "'Such Monstrous Births': A Neglected Aspect of the Antinomian Contro-

versy," *Renaissance Quarterly* 38 (1985): 85–106. Much of my analysis of the question of "monstrous births" derives from Marie-Hélène Huet's fascinating book, *Monstrous Imagination*. For general information on the history of child-bearing, see Catherine M. Scholten, *Childbearing in American Society: 1650–1850* (New York: New York UP, 1985). Much of the seemingly strange reaction to Hutchinson may partly be accounted for by the simple fact that she was pregnant. Pregnant women were thought to be atoning for the "curse of Eve," paying the price for initial female transgression (12). They were also thought to be "unstable, hysterical and fearful" (19–21). Further, pregnancy was seen as the fulfillment of women's divine mission to be fruitful and multiply, and since it often eventuated in death, it was used as an occasion to remind women to be pious.

49. John Winthrop, *A Short Story of the Rise, reigne, and ruine of the Antinomians, Familists and Libertines* 214–15 (hereafter cited as *Short Story*).
50. A description of the exhumation can be found in *Short Story*, 282. Quotation is from *Short Story*, 214–15.
51. *Short Story*, 214. Weld also remarks that Hutchinson "hatched" a "litter" of monsters (202).
52. Norton, *Founding Mothers and Fathers*, 195.
53. Huet writes that "monstrous progeny resulted from the disorder of the maternal imagination. Instead of reproducing the father's image, as nature commands, the monstrous child bore witness to the violent desires that moved the mother at the time of conception or during pregnancy. The resulting offspring carried the marks of her whims and fancy rather than the recognizable features of its legitimate genitor. The monster thus erased paternity and proclaimed the dangerous power of the female imagination" (*Monstrous Imagination*, 1).

Chapter 5. Institutions and Nostalgia

1. For a discussion of how the Puritans view all of church history as a declension from the first church and how reformation functions as an act of recovery or recuperation from that declension, see Theodore Dwight Bozeman, *To Live Ancient Lives: The Primitivist Dimension in Puritanism* (Chapel Hill: U North Carolina P, 1988). For example, Bozeman writes: "Puritans perceived the historical career of the Christian church as one of progressive decline. Despite its splendid beginnings, the church had fallen prey after apostolic times to ecclesiastical managers and thinkers who forsook the vision of biblical finality" (17) and "To move forward was to strive without rest for reconnection with the paradigmatic events and utterances of ancient and unspoiled times" (11). Nancy Armstrong and Leonard Tennenhouse have noted a similar phenomenon in Puritanism in general and Milton in particular. They suggest that "in looking forward to the new world that was supposed to emerge with the coming of Christ, the author [Milton] has his own eyes cast only backward. The 'forward' movement of the narrative must be understood as an attempt to 'return.' The desire on the part of North American English men and women to return to an originary speech community required reproduction at once of that community and of the lack

that cannot be filled by written words" (44). *The Imaginary Puritan: Literature, Intellectual Labor, and the Origins of Personal Life* (Berkeley: U California P, 1992).

2. Susan Stewart, *On Longing: Narratives of the Miniature, the Gigantic, the Souvenir, the Collection* (Durham, N.C.: Duke UP, 1993), 23.
3. About first institutions, Williams writes: "The Church of Christ is a congregation of Saints, a flock of sheep, humble, meek, patient, contented, with whom it is monstrous and impossible, to couple cruel and persecuting Lyons, subtle and hypocritical Foxes, contentious biting dogs or greedy and rooting swine, so visibly declared and apparent." *The Bloody Tenent, Yet More Bloody: by Mr Cottons endevour to wash it white in the Blood of the Lambe* (London, 1652), 143.
4. *George Fox Digg'd out of his Burrowes* (Boston, 1676), 103.
5. *The Hireling Ministry None of Christs* (London, 1652), 160.
6. For discussions of apocalyptic thought in Puritanism, see James Maclear, "New England and the Fifth Monarchy: The Quest for the Millennium in Early American Puritanism," *William and Mary Quarterly* 32 (3rd ser, 1975): 223–60; James Holstun, *A Rational Millennium: Puritan Utopias of Seventeenth-Century England and America* (New York: Oxford UP, 1987), David Hall, *Worlds of Wonder, Days of Judgment: Popular Religious Beliefs in Early New England* (Cambridge, Mass.: Harvard UP, 1990); and the essays collected in C. A. Patrides and Joseph Wittreich, eds., *The Apocalypse in English Renaissance Thought and Literature: Patterns, Antecedents and Repercussions* (Ithaca, N.Y.: Cornell UP, 1984), especially the following: Bernard Carp, "The Political Dimension of Apocalyptic Thought"; Bernard McGinn, "Early Apocalypticism: The Ongoing Debate"; Michael Murrin, "Revelation and Two Seventeenth Century Commentators"; and Stephen Stein, "Transatlantic Extensions: Apocalyptic in Early New England."
7. For analyses of the differences between the two versions of Cotton's sermons on Canticles, see Prudence Steiner, "A Garden of Spices in New England: John Cotton's and Edward Taylor's Use of the Song of Songs," in Morton Bloomfield, ed., *Allegory, Myth, and Symbol*, Harvard English Studies 9 (Cambridge, Mass.: Harvard UP, 1981), and Jeffrey Hammond, "The Bride in Redemptive Time: John Cotton and the Canticles Controversy," *The New England Quarterly* 56 (1983): 78–102. Steiner notes only that the New England version is "longer, dryer, and more systematized than the first." Hammond contextualizes the sermons in the historical debates over the proper exegesis of Canticles. Of the differences between the two versions, he notes only that the first is more intimate since it deals with an individual's relationship to Christ, whereas the second is more public since it narrates church history. I would suggest that Hammond inherits this difference from Anthony Tuckney's preface to the 1655 edition, which was perhaps an attempt on the part of Cotton's cousin and contemporary to get people to buy both books. I would argue, instead, that Cotton's ideas about converting institutions and individuals render a precise distinction between public and private difficult if not impossible. A number of other scholars have mentioned, in passing, some differences between the two versions of the Canticles sermons. See, for example, Jesper Rosenmeier, "The Teacher and the Witness: John Cotton and Roger Williams," *William and Mary Quarterly* 25 (1968), esp. 424–26; Mason Lowance, *The Language of Canaan: Metaphor and Symbol in New England* (Cambridge, Mass.: Harvard UP, 1980); Everett Emer-

son, *John Cotton* (New York: Twayne, 1965); and Larzer Ziff, *The Career of John Cotton: Puritanism and the American Experience* (Princeton, N.J.: Princeton UP, 1962).

8. *A Brief Exposition upon the Whole Book of Canticles* (London, 1648), 126 (hereafter cited as *Canticles*, England).
9. "Mr. Cotton's Rejoinder," 85, in David Hall, ed., *The Antinomian Controversy, 1636–1638: A Documentary History* (Durham, N.C.: Duke UP, 1990) (hereafter cited as "Rejoinder").
10. Ibid., 95–96.
11. Ibid., 96.
12. *Canticles*, England, 161.
13. *A Brief Exposition with Practical Observations Upon the Whole Book of Canticles* (London, 1655), 161 (hereafter cited as *Canticles*, New England).
14. Ibid., 28.
15. *An Exposition Upon the Thirteenth Chapter of the Revelation* (London, 1655), 192 (hereafter cited as *Exposition upon Revelation*).
16. John Winthrop, *A Short Story of the Rise, reign, and ruine of the Antinomians, Familists & Libertines*, in David Hall, ed., *The Antinomian Controversy, 1636–1638: A Documentary History* (Durham, N.C.: Duke UP, 1990), 243.
17. "Rejoinder," 142.
18. *A Treatise of the Covenant of Grace, As it is dispensed to the Elect Seed, effectually unto Salvation* (London, 1650), 177.
19. *The Powring Out of the Seven Vials* (London, 1642), 235.
20. *Canticles*, England, 229–30.
21. *Canticles*, New England, 213.
22. *A Reply to Mr. Williams his Examination; And Answer of the Letters sent to him by John Cotton* (London, 1647), 155 (hereafter cited as *Reply*).
23. Ibid., 36. Cotton also writes: "For, take away (as Mr. Williams doth) all Instituted worship of God, as Churches, Pastors, Teachers, Elders, Deacons, Members, publick Ministery of the Word, Covenant, Seales of the Covenant, (Baptisme, and the Lords Supper) the Censures of the Church, and the like, what is then left of all the Institutions, and Ordinances of God, which the Lord established in the second Commandment, against Institutions, Images, and Inventions of men in his worship?" (23)
24. Ibid., 131.
25. Ibid.
26. Ibid., 223. Cotton also writes: "If any through hypocrisie are wanting here in, the hidden hypocrisie of some will not prejudice the sinceritie and faithfulnesse of others, nor the Church estate of all" (300).
27. In England, Cotton seems to have put this theory into practice by creating a "congregation within a congregation." That is, without ever declaring official separation from the Church of England, Cotton gathered a relatively small group of congregants who practiced reformed religion. See Ziff, *Career of John Cotton*, 48–50.
28. *Reply*, 177.

29. *Exposition upon Revelation*, 197.
30. *Brief Exposition with Practical Observations Upon the whole Book of Ecclesiastes* (London, 1654), 252; 132 (hereafter cited as *Exposition upon Ecclesiastes*).
31. Bozeman, in *To Live Ancient Lives*, provides a useful explanation of the difference between "the past" (actual historical time) and "the Past" (transcendent time):

> Here indeed was an interest in the church's historical experience, but one not to be confused with the modern devotion to historicity. The given objective was, not study of an institution in time, subject to causality and change, but demonstration of linkage to the time of times. Strictly speaking, the subject matter of this history was not temporal at all. The true church of the present was not a historical product and in that sense to be understood in terms of its history. Analogy and correspondence were the appropriate analytical categories, not causality and intrinsic development, for the church was true only so far as it incorporated the timeless doctrine and forms of Scripture. . . . Primitive antiquity must stand forth as the unmoved center from which that narrative was comprehended and as the absolute historical good whose alternating loss and retrieval structures the flow of events. (246)

32. *Exposition upon Ecclesiastes*, 129–30.
33. Ibid., 130.
34. "A Sermon Delivered at Salem, 1636," 59. All quotations from Cotton's congregational writings are from Larzer Ziff, ed., *John Cotton on the Churches of New England* (Cambridge, Mass.: Harvard UP, 1968).
35. *The Way of the Congregational Churches Cleared* (London, 1648), 312 (hereafter cited as *Way Cleared*).
36. Robert Baillie, *A Dissuasive from the Errours of the Time* (London, 1645), 56.
37. Samuel Gorton, *Simplicities Defense against Seven-Headed Policy* (London, 1646), 64.
38. *Way Cleared*, 308.

Index

UNIVERSITY PRESS OF NEW ENGLAND publishes books under its own imprint and is the publisher for Brandeis University Press, Dartmouth College, Middlebury College Press, University of New Hampshire, Tufts University, and Wesleyan University Press.

ABOUT THE AUTHOR

Michael Kaufmann is associate professor of English at Temple University.

LIBRARY OF CONGRESS CATALOGING-IN-PUBLICATION DATA
Kaufmann, Michael W., 1964–
Institutional individualism : conversion, exile, and nostalgia in Puritan New England / Michael W. Kaufmann.
p. cm.
Includes bibliographical references (p.) and index.
ISBN 0-8195-6352-8 (alk. paper). — ISBN 0-8195-6350-1 (pbk. : alk. paper)
1. Puritans—New England—History—17th century. 2. New England—History—Colonial period, ca. 1600–1775. 3. Individualism—New England—History—17th century. 4. Institutionalism (Religion)—History—17th century. I. Title.
F7.K38 1998
974'.02—dc21 98-19291